GHOST LIGHT

RANDOM HOUSE / NEW YORK

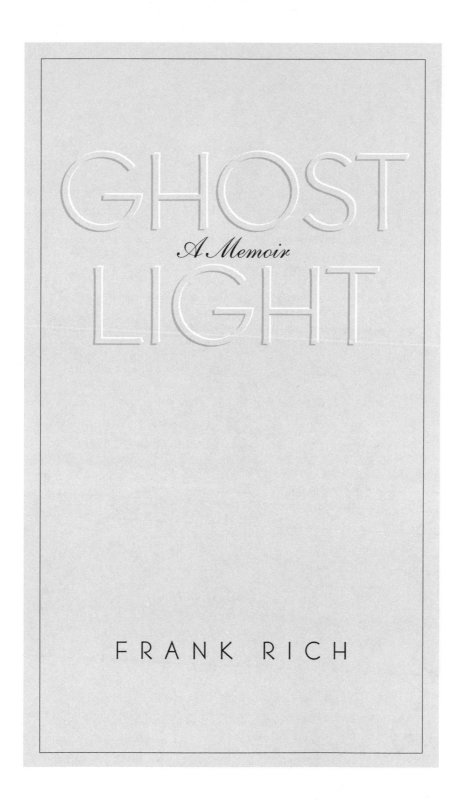

GHOST
LIGHT

A Memoir

FRANK RICH

RANDOM HOUSE and colophon are registered trademarks of Random House, Inc.

Owing to limitations of space, acknowledgments of permission to quote
from previously published materials will be found on page 317.

Library of Congress Cataloging-in-Publication Data
Rich, Frank.
Ghost light : a memoir / Frank Rich.
p.   cm.
ISBN 0-679-45299-0
1. Rich, Frank.   2. Theater critics—United States—Biography.   I. Title.
PN1708.R53 A3 2000   792'.092—dc21   [B]   00-029070

Random House website address: www.atrandom.com
Printed in the United States of America on acid-free paper
24689753
First Edition

Book design by J. K. Lambert

This book was written with deep love and

gratitude for the family I found—

ALEX

NATHANIEL

SIMON

—and in loving memory of the one I lost—

H. A. F.

J. H. F.

C. C.

GHOST LIGHT: Especially in the professional theater, a single light left burning in center stage when the theater is empty. The source of the term is a superstition that a ghost will move in if the theater is left completely dark.

—*An International Dictionary of Theater Language*

The spotlight, I now realize, was a product of my imagination. My mother was not on a stage but on the floor of National Airport, perched on a stack of suitcases. She, her two children, and the baggage had been deposited there a couple of hours earlier by a helpful Chevy Chase neighbor with a station wagon. It was Christmas, and we were supposed to be on a plane to Miami Beach.

Looking back on that scene, I always see Mom in the middle distance, as if she were illuminated by a spot from above and framed by a proscenium: the uncertain flicker in her shy eyes, the thick wave of her brown hair, the dark wool coat unbuttoned to reveal her gray cashmere sweater crowned with a small pearl pin. The light picked her out dramatically from the blurry dark background, isolating her from us and all the other heavily bundled holiday travelers making their way through the terminal.

At the counter, a man in a uniform had turned Mom away—though we had tickets, the plane was already full. Mom didn't know what to do. Recently separated from her husband, she was, at thirty, a single woman again, and in those days single women, let alone single mothers with children, were not expected to make their own way in airports. Mom's parents were out of reach—in Florida, awaiting our arrival. I was seven, Polly was five; we were a pair mismatched in more than age: a short, fair boy with expectant blue eyes and a yet-to-be-corrected overbite, and a dark, round girl whose overcast expression kept its secrets. Neither of us had ever been to an airport or on an airplane before.

So I stood a few feet away and watched Mom, who was more often prone to laughter, sitting in her spotlight, in tears. Her head slightly bowed, her makeup smeared, she looked so lonely, as if she had been dumped on a street corner like an abandoned child. She waited—for what? The moment stretched as if it would never end. Were this a play, it would be the Act One curtain, and the audience could look forward to a resolution of Mom's predicament, happy or tragic, in Act Two.

Real life, I would learn, is never so tidy. On this particular night I was not just a spectator but an actor in the drama. The problem was, I didn't know my role. I had no idea if it was up to me to get us on the plane. Father knows best, and if Father is no longer around, isn't the only son, the elder child, supposed to step in as understudy? At least I might be expected to stop Mom's crying somehow. But I just stood there, frozen, and watched, as if I were in a theater, hoping that someone, some grown-up man, surely my father, would somehow materialize and come to the rescue.

Only years later—long after our Christmas trip to Miami Beach had been packed away with the rest of my childhood memories—would I realize that a man who was not my father had in fact come to our rescue, albeit clandestinely, by phone, on that winter night. I didn't yet know that drama happens in the shadows of the wings as well as in a spotlight center stage, in life as in the theater. I assumed that it was Mom's tears—ratified by mine and Polly's—that brought us our provisional happy ending. We were on a plane an hour later.

Once in Miami, we had all the fun Mom had promised. One night we went to a movie theater that, ablaze in blinking lights, rose before us in the tropical dark like a palace. There we saw a movie about a man who wins a bet that he can travel around the world in eighty days. In the lobby, Mom took a dollar out of her purse and bought me a large program full of pictures of the actors. She suggested that I start a collection of these programs, much as she had done when she was my age. I said I would, though at that moment I had no idea just how large and precious my collection would become, or that I would haul it around with me from home to home as Mom had hers, long after the pages had yellowed and the faces on them had begun to fade.

PART

1

CHAPTER 1

To be an American kid in the fifties was to live in a sparkling, hopeful world where ignorance really was bliss. Parents spoke in euphemistic private codes rather than say anything that might mar the tableaux of contentment they tirelessly constructed for wide young eyes.

We lived in Somerset, where the streets were called Dorset and Warwick and Uppingham and Trent—their very names a farcical affront to reality. The English did not dwell in our bonny Somerset, and neither did their local heirs, the Protestants, who had their own, restricted neighborhoods barely miles away. Somerset, a subdivision built just across the District line in Maryland but not far enough from a city turning black to be among the most desirable of suburbs, was mainly the province of Jews. The houses were not baronial estates but mostly small and new, inhabited by men who had come back from the war to build careers and families and to tend continually to their front lawns and backyards, also small but, as a point of honor, impeccably green. Inside the houses was a riot of wallpaper, some of it depicting scenes more in keeping with the neighborhood's cosmopolitan aspirations. April in Paris? The Weinsteins' dining room was a fanciful rendering of a Parisian boulevard sketched in broad lines and pastels, the kiosks and flower stalls circled by a profusion of dancing pink and black poodles. Even this scene had a recognizable air of American domesticity; it was the cartoon Paree we'd glimpsed in Looney Tunes.

Our universe was as buoyant and tightly sealed as a balloon. After we walked down the hill from the redbrick Somerset Elementary School each weekday at three, we played tag and ball in the street without fear that a stranger or stray car might intrude, secure in the knowledge that our mothers were only one loud shout away and that the worst that could happen to us would be to fall off a bike after the training wheels were removed. The only temptation to danger was provided by a forest that hadn't yet been cleared for new houses; it was a handy laboratory for our earliest experiments with matches, one of which led to the arrival of a fire engine and a rare outbreak of mass parental recrimination in a neighborhood whose kids were not the kind to get into trouble.

The best hope for a daring adventure worthy of our Bobbsey Twins books was the occasional foray into what we took to be a haunted house — any house that had just been built or had just changed hands, and whose new tenants had yet to move in. It was easy to identify these haunted houses: The realtors marked them with red-and-white metal signs planted in the center of their lawns. And it was easy to enter them and commandeer their unfurnished rooms for games of hide-and-seek, all the creepier for the absence of lights and for the reverberant effect on our screams of the bare floors and walls, especially in that fast-dimming twilight just before dinner. We told ourselves there must be ghosts in residence in these houses, that spirits haunted the shadows of the vacant dens and bedrooms and rec rooms with their acrid fragrance of fresh paint.

When darkness fell, we retreated reluctantly from the horseplay in our front yards, each according to his assigned bedtime, until the whole neighborhood was tucked in for the night. But muffled behind the venetian blinds of each house there might still be a flicker of light, a visual echo of the fireflies we collected in Mason jars in our backyards each summer, now emanating from the magical hearth of television.

Sitting before the TV sets in our living rooms—they hadn't invaded bedrooms yet—we watched our neighborhood in a faithful black-and-white replication: the same driveways jutting like tongues from garage to street, the same lawns awaiting the next weekend mowing, the same father with his genial grin and firm but calming voice, the same perpetually amused, slightly distracted, occasionally flustered, but resolutely uncomplaining mother poking around in the kitchen preparing the next meal, the same mischievous but fundamentally good brothers and sisters committing only the most innocuous infractions of their parents' painstakingly codified rules. Sometimes it was hard to figure out where Somerset ended and the TV neighborhoods, with their similarly pastoral place-names, began. If there was a man in the moon—the opening credits of one of our favorite TV comedies, *The Honeymooners,* promised us one—what would he make of these look-alike families in their look-alike homes staring each night at other look-alike families in their own look-alike homes on small cathode-ray tubes burning through the inky shadows of our living rooms?

Contentment and prosperity smiled back at us from everywhere we looked then, as shiny as our reflections in the voluptuous curves of our parents' bright new cars.

———

Not unlike Lucy and Desi, Mom and Dad had moved from their small newlyweds' apartment in the city to their first house right after I was born. They had landed in Somerset from culturally conflicting ports of origin. Mom, a grandchild of Russian immigrant families, had been born in Brooklyn—in Manhattan Beach, at the end of Coney Island, in a house just a block from the shore where crates of bootleg liquor were dropped by boat to make their way to New York during Prohibition. But the Depression ended this beach idyll when Mom was seven, sending her father, Nat, and mother, Lil, into the provincial swamp of Washington, D.C. There Nat took what remained of his savings and bought his way into a paper-goods wholesaler of Dixie cups and big brown envelopes and paper clips and glistening mass-produced miracles like Scotch tape. In Washington, the Aaronsons had to settle for raising Mom and her sister in an apartment—on Connecticut Avenue, on the city side of the District line.

By contrast, Dad and his parents, Herbert and Rose, were true Washingtonians. Dad was fonder of telling stories about how his ancestors had fought only dozens of miles away in the Civil War than he was of recounting his own adventures as an Air Force commander in the China-Burma-India theater in World War II. The Riches were German Jews who would have found Brooklyn as foreign as Madagascar. It would have been hard to guess that the Riches were Jewish, since they spoke no Hebrew, ate pork chops, and, in further defiance of their nominal religion's practice, named their firstborn sons after their living fathers: I was Frank, Jr., as Dad's older brother was Herbert, Jr. When Grandma Rose, at our Wednesday-night family dinners at her and Grandpa Herbert's apartment, wanted to identify anyone as Jewish, she lowered her usual booming decibel level—she had been near deaf since Dad was a boy—and spoke cryptically, sotto voce, of "one of us" or "a member of our tribe." I always wondered from whom she was keeping our Jewishness a secret. The only outsider within earshot was Irene, the black maid who had worked for Grandma Rose since before the Depression and who seemed to be more cognizant of Jewish holidays and rituals than her employers were. As my Rich grandparents refused to acknowledge their Jewishness, so they never spoke of anti-Semites or pogroms or Nazis. Each spring, Grandpa would drive his Packard to tour the splendid front lawns in the suburban enclave of Kenwood, where Grandma, having only potted plants and no yard to tend, would cluck over the newly blooming azaleas and cherry blossoms she longed for, never acknowledging the neighborhood's notorious antipathy to Jewish residents, no matter how lofty their provenance.

Dad grew up in a more affluent Washington than Mom's, in a house off Sixteenth Street, the prosperous Jewish district near downtown. His childhood home was only a short trolley ride from the store his great-grandfather had started near Ford's Theatre four years after Lincoln was shot. B. Rich & Sons had been the store's original name, but a bitter fight over which siblings would run it had led to the permanent banishment of some of those Riches from both the business and the family just before I was born. Grandpa, Mom later confided in me, had gone so far as to curse his own mother, his antagonist in the Rich family civil war, even as she was being lowered into her grave. Now the store was known officially as Rich's Shoes—simply Rich's to its customers. Grandpa Herbert had vanquished all dissidents—including Herbert, Jr., who had exiled himself to New York—and now ruled by absolute fiat, with my father, the only son left in the fold, as his unambiguously subordinate heir.

When Dad came back from the war he had asserted his independence by taking a job three blocks away at Hecht's, a department store with a competing shoe department. Though the Korean Conflict put him briefly back in uniform, with an office job at the Pentagon, he had by then rejoined his father at the old store on F Street. The only time I ever heard Dad angry was when he was on the phone with Grandpa at night, arguing about the marked-down price of one shoe or another in a sale. For Polly and me, the store was a treasure chest: Rich's gave its youngest customers comic books and crayons in brightly colored cardboard tubes that looked like rocket ships, and Dad brought home as many as he could carry.

Mom didn't give a damn about shoes. She never mentioned them and seemed to prefer not to wear them, tossing them off with abandon to savor the feel of grass or wall-to-wall carpeting under her bare feet, much as she had loved to walk in the sand of her Brooklyn beach in childhood. While Dad was at the store, her domain was Somerset. Her job was the house, and she had her own employee, as did almost every white middle-class housewife in Washington at the time—a black maid to help vacuum, clean, and cook.

Not that Mom was averse to cooking. Some afternoons, she baked coffee cake, fragrant with powdered cinnamon, and concocted a thick, meaty spaghetti sauce on top of the stove. But these domestic vignettes were special, not regular, occurrences. Mom and Dad had been plunked down in the perfect setting and equipped with all the props for carrying out the family life we watched on television, but they dropped in and out of the role of parents at whim, like novice actors improvising from a script still in rough draft.

It couldn't have been easy for Mom to bring off her half of the illusion. She was virtually a child herself. When she married Dad in the spring of 1946 at the Mayflower Hotel downtown, she was only nineteen—the unknown quantity in an across-the-tracks marriage into a family whose status dictated modest note of the wedding in the Washington papers. She was comely, but shy and insecure—a second child after her sister, Frances, vivacious Frances, who had known my father while in high school, before Mom did.

Yet Mom didn't have to act at loving her children. During the war, she had majored in education at the University of Maryland, in College Park, just beyond the Washington suburbs. For her, loving kids and teaching them were one and the same. With only the gentlest nudges, which felt more like caresses than instruction as we sat side by side on Mom and Dad's bed poring over a book, she had Polly and me reading before we were in school.

When I was a little older, Mom started taking me on what she called Adventures, another kind of education. Mom and her mom were both big on Adventures. Grandma Lil liked to "get lost"—meaning we would speed off in her Chevy Impala convertible with the top down, taking turn after turn down dusty country roads in deepest Rockville until Grandma would declare herself lost—so lost she could never find her way back, so lost she didn't know what to do—and would search for the nearest gas station that could offer directions. We laughed all the way home, and no one laughed more than Lil, with her gassy Brooklyn smoker's cackle.

Mom's idea of an Adventure was the opposite of Lil's. Instead of galloping into the country, we'd head for town. This, too, was a trip into the unknown. The city was still to me an unimaginable foreign land full of the sounds and lights and tumult I associated with the exotic concept of traffic—of which there was none in Somerset. Washington was where we usually went under the cover of darkness, twice a week no matter what, to have dinner with my grandparents—one night Mom's parents, one night Dad's. On the way home after those dinners Polly and I always fell asleep in the backseat of the car, lulled by the streetlamps we counted by tilting back our heads and looking up through the rear window. Seen only through yawns, the city remained as elusive as a dream.

Far from aspiring to get lost in her Adventures, Mom seemed to be trying to find something. Her favorite Adventure inevitably took us to a dusty old brick mansion, a museum that resembled a miniature castle—the Phillips was its name—where we looked at paintings of circus jugglers and ballerinas and men playing baseball in a stadium at night; there were collages made of newspapers and old blue jeans and tickets with foreign writing on them. If there were other people sharing our Adventure, I never noticed them: Mom and I seemed to have the place to ourselves.

Sometimes before going to the Phillips we had lunch in a nearby restaurant that looked more like the basement of a house than like the gleaming

Hot Shoppes that usually meant "eating out." The tables and lights were low, and the sandwiches were the same kind they had in Denmark, wherever that was; the ingredients were arranged like the gallery's collages on single slices of thin dark bread cut into triangular shapes. After lunch and the Phillips, we might stop by a store where I would be outfitted with paints and pastels and pads and colored paper to make pictures and collages of my own. Mom took a sensuous delight in amassing supplies that could be used for painting or drawing or writing; the drawers of her desk at home brimmed with pads in all shapes and sizes and colors, and notebooks and pencils and pens, only some of them from Grandpa's warehouse.

For a while, Mom took art classes sponsored by the Jewish ladies' club where she and Lil had lunch each Wednesday. She came home just before dinner breathless with enthusiasm for her teachers and armed with large frenzied canvases still smelling pleasantly of fresh oil paint, thick with color and splashes and raw brushstrokes in yellow and carmine and orange. The pictures sat unframed but expectant against the wall in her bedroom until she eventually decided that she would never be a good painter, and why bother, who was she kidding? Her initial ardor and gaiety trailed off into a dazed forgetfulness, an unexplained and seemingly unprompted concession of defeat, until finally she stopped talking about her paintings and her classes altogether.

Then she would return to her principal and expected activity, "doing errands," which usually meant driving beyond Somerset's stone-pillared gateway and then returning home with a station wagon overflowing with bulky Giant grocery bags. In this, she was no different from any other mother in Somerset. Buying and consuming the bounty of the new supermarket—the red-and-white cans of Campbell's soup, the balloon-decorated Wonder bread and the Peter Pan peanut butter, the cellophane-wrapped chocolate Hostess cupcakes with their squishy white fillings—was the neighborhood's most pervasive ritual. It, too, was duplicated, brand by brand, meal by meal, station wagon by station wagon, on TV each night. But on TV, the moms didn't strain under the weight of all those heavy brown bags as Mom did, or get harried and anxious because they discovered once home that they'd forgotten to buy the most essential item on their shopping list. ⌐NAIR

Dad was never around to help at home and wasn't expected to be. Gone

all week at the store or the office, the fathers of Somerset reappeared magically on weekends—though in Dad's case, only half the weekend: Rich's
biggest day was Saturday, demanding his full attention at Grandpa's side.

Decades later, I tried to remember a time when Mom and Dad and
Polly and I were together on one of those Sundays when Dad was at home.
I tried to reassemble one of those TV tableaux, those Brownie snapshots,
of the four of us in our first house on Warwick Place or in the larger house
we moved into on Trent Street, around the corner—all sharing the same
moment in the same place, enjoying a meal or a story or laughter. But it
was easier to remember life outdoors with my gang—or the family life of
the Nelsons and Ricardos and Kramdens beamed into our living room
from afar—than to compose that family portrait. Mom and Dad were out
a lot, confident that Polly and I were in the safe hands of the baby-sitter,
the maid, the tight-knit neighborhood in which we knew every family on
our block and most of the blocks leading to the boundary where tranquil
Somerset gave way to the busier Chevy Chase artery of Wisconsin Avenue.

On Sundays, in truth, we were not often a foursome. Whether at home
or out, we were usually a part of large family dinners and parties, larded
with grandparents and aunts and uncles and cousins, often held for what
Dad called a Big Birthday or a Big Anniversary. (Big round numbers were
as important for family occasions as they were at the store.) Failing that,
we'd trek en masse to Woodmont, the Jewish country club in Rockville
that ensured large weekly crowds by charging its members for a daunting
Sunday-night buffet whether or not they actually showed up to stuff themselves with fat pimiento-stuffed olives, chopped chicken liver, roast beef,
and yellow seven-layer cake with thick chocolate frosting.

The only surviving home movies of Mom, Dad, Polly, and me gathered
together in Somerset all by ourselves show us on Christmas morning, as
Polly and I sit self-consciously under a modest, wilting tree—a mortally
embarrassed Jewish Christmas tree, no doubt—to unwrap our toys. And
even there Mom and Dad can't be seen together, because it's Dad who's
behind the camera, watching from a distance, recording everything except
his own phantom presence.

—

If Mom and Dad shared anything besides Sunday-night festivities, our home in Somerset, and their children, it was a love of music. In college before the war, Dad had discovered he could get jazz records free if he wrote letters explaining that he was the school paper's music critic. He built a large collection of 78s, too big for the apartment in which he and Mom lived as newlyweds; he had to store the stacks in his new father-in-law's paper-goods warehouse, but after they were ruined in a flood, he decided it would be too costly to replace them. In Somerset, Dad developed the habit of talking reverentially about Benny Goodman without actually listening to him, as if the Platonic ideal of jazz was as warming as the music itself.

Mom's life had been transformed by *South Pacific*. In the warm Washington spring of 1949, its music was like a hurricane, she told me, that swept down from New York remaking everything in its path, including Mom, who was then only weeks away from giving birth to me. *South Pacific* was the first record—records—I ever saw. Each song was on a side of a large disk of heavy black vinyl, each disk in its own brown-paper pocket in an album whose leaf-green cover images evoked tropical trees and the love between an unidentified woman and man.

Mom was still listening to *South Pacific* over and over, she liked to recall, when it was time to go to the hospital and have her first baby on a warm, sunny June day. When she played some of the songs for me a few years later, I didn't quite understand what they were about, but the longing in one song captivated me, even if I couldn't yet know what longing was. "Mos' people live on a lonely island, lost in de middle of a foggy sea," the woman on the record sang in a tremulous voice in a strange accent as the song began. Then her voice gathered strength as she described the dreamlike beckoning of a more beautiful island, the kind of enchanted setting I recognized from fairy tales:

> *Bali Ha'i*
> *May call you,*
> *Any night, any day.*
> *In your heart*
> *You'll hear it call you*
> *"Come away, come away."*

Mom longed to see *South Pacific*, which she explained had been in a theater in New York. Dad wanted to see it, too; it was a show about the war he had fought, in his own Pacific theater. But with a store and errands to run, Mom and Dad never made it there and now it was too late. *South Pacific* wasn't in New York anymore. I took this all in, not knowing exactly what a show, or New York, was, except that they were both magical in my parents' eyes, or at least Mom's, and both well out of reach of Somerset.

———

It was on a night in 1954, I have figured out in retrospect, that I saw Mom and Dad share their own moment of what the songs they liked to listen to called love. It was around the time that I had started to get sick with some regularity, not with the dread polio that was Somerset's most feared intruder but with the eternal litany of minor childhood ailments—an upset stomach, sore throat, pinkeye, stuffy nose—requiring foul-tasting pink or brackish red medicine. On this particular night, Polly and I were being watched over by an elderly baby-sitter we didn't like when my parents returned from a night out. As soon as they came through the door they started talking both at once, finishing each other's sentences with an animation I had never before witnessed. They had gone to see a special movie, they said; a terrific movie, they said. Dad handed me a record on which I, too, could hear the songs they had heard in the movie theater that night.

The record was larger and more elaborately packaged than any I'd seen, in a box with gold lettering on its spine reading *A Star Is Born* and a photograph of a woman's face on its cover. The woman, Mom explained, was the same actress who, as a girl, had been Dorothy in one of her favorite movies from childhood, *The Wizard of Oz*. The box was all tied up in ribbon, like a present. Dad announced that the record inside would require a new "hi-fi"—for "high-fidelity"—record player that he was going to buy at a store downtown the next day.

But for now, Mom decreed, it was time to go to bed.

But when would I be able to hear the record?

Soon, said Dad, but I would have to be instructed carefully in how to work the new machine, which would be very expensive and fragile. I'd have to learn how to handle the new records, which the advertisements said were "unbreakable," unlike our easily shattered 78s.

The record sat in its box for a week, until Dad found just the record player he wanted. One night he came through the front door carrying a big cardboard carton, which he deposited on the living-room floor and then unpacked. Once the record player was ready, he took the record out of its own box and began an elaborate ritual that required fastidious care of the disk, of the envelope that contained it within its box, and of the record player itself, which had an arm that made a busy clicking sound as it miraculously performed the task of moving the needle to the beginning of the record. After this process was complete and the music actually began, Dad stood a few feet away and concentrated intensely for a few seconds, as if to savor the moment, then pronounced himself satisfied with the sound, which *did* seem different from the old 78s. It was as if the singers were right there, Dad said, visiting you in your own home.

Some of the songs themselves, though, belied their festive packaging. They sounded sad, not like fun, to my five-year-old ears. Another told a story like those I heard at bedtime. Though even in this song, what the words were saying was an abstraction, a jumble of phrases that didn't immediately arrange themselves into thoughts whose meaning I could parse. The woman's tone, however, struck me as familiar: young and strong, with just the slightest undertow of distress. "I was born in a trunk," she sang—*born in a trunk?*—"in the Princess Theatre in Pocatello, Idaho"—*Poca-tello?*

I asked Mom and Dad if they would take me to this movie, but they said no. It was too "grown-up." It was not until I had myself grown up, when the house in Somerset was if anything a more distant memory than the record they brought home that night, a record I still have, that I saw *A Star Is Born* on my own in a small theater for old movies in a city far from Washington. It tells of a woman who is born only figuratively in a trunk. She grows up wanting to be onstage and eventually becomes a singer and an actress. No matter what terrible things happen in her life, she keeps performing—even after her alcoholic husband kills himself. The movie ends with the woman, by now a famous Hollywood star, sadder but wiser, onstage one last time to bask in the embrace of an audience's applause.

—

The new record was the first of many to march into the household on what seemed like—though surely wasn't—a daily basis. Dad was more in evidence, as if he were propelled home from work on the wings of all this music. On those rare nights when he returned from downtown before Polly and I went to bed, he often had a large flat brown paper bag under his arm from which he would pull a new record with a flourish. I was delegated to put on the record, which I did carefully according to the procedure devised by Dad, who decided he trusted me with this task. When the second side of the record was over, more often than not I started side 1 again immediately—always making certain first to wipe the disk's surface with a soft cloth, a Rich's shoe-shining cloth. And when the record was done again, and if it still wasn't bedtime yet, I immediately repeated the whole process one more time.

The first record I listened to without letup was one I had pestered Dad to buy: *Davy Crockett,* which contained countless variations on the theme song of the Disney frontier hero who had provoked every boy in Somerset to wear a "coonskin" Davy Crockett cap equipped with a furry tail. Davy Crockett was the latest ambassador from the newly opened, faraway amusement park called Disneyland that we had been able to see on a TV show of the same name.

Walt Disney had insinuated himself into our afternoons as well by enlisting us in a televised club of Mouseketeers that convened every day, enticing us with cartoons and songs and cliff-hanging adventures in which the Hardy Boys, much like Somerset's boys, survived narrow escapes in haunted houses. These goodies were doled out by a grown man in Mickey Mouse ears named Jimmie, who acted as if he were the Mouseketeers' father, and ours, while our own fathers were busy at work.

We were all dying to see Disneyland, where there was a neighborhood called Frontierland in which we could act out Davy Crockett's Western adventures in a far more realistic setting than that afforded by our tamed green grid of Eastern suburbia. But California was a paradise so far away that only millionaires could visit it.

The *Davy Crockett* record, played by every child day and night in every

Somerset home, soon became a casualty of its ubiquity. On our turntable it was usurped by a record that Dad brought home for him and Mom one night. It had a red cover with a cartoon showing a row of men's faces staring down at a woman dressed only in a man's striped pajama top. Its unlikely title was *The Pajama Game*. Pajamas I understood—and games, certainly—but what *The Pajama Game* had to do with either was puzzling. What grabbed me the moment Dad put on the record was the blast of sound at its very start. It pulsed through me as it did through the house, like an electric jolt.

The sound was just music, not really a song at all. It began with an impressive rumble of drums, which was then followed by a blare of trumpets announcing something (but what?), and then by another part of the band, softer and slower, playing a tune that was so catchy—almost caressing, really—that I found myself wanting to sing along with it even though I didn't know if there were words or what the words might be. The melody was soon picked up by more instruments and then still more as the sound swelled. I felt I was being raised higher and higher by the force of the music, as if I were bouncing in the waves at Rehoboth Beach. But no sooner had I reached that crest than the melody, to my surprise, was cut off, sending me back into low tide: Another part of the band started playing another tune, no less beguiling but more casual, low and conversational, as if the musicians were tossing off an extended joke through their instruments.

Then came another melody: loud again, exultant, with the horns shouting triumphantly, only to fall away and be answered by violins that were less merry, that sounded as if they were about to weep, though quietly. And then another new melody arrived and another—with tune leapfrogging over tune in a rush too rapid to keep up with, until the last tune was reached and the trumpets interrupted, again announcing something exciting, this time with a flourish outmatching the one at the record's start.

After a pause—you had to have one to catch your breath—came a progression of songs sung by men and women, singly and in pairs, and sometimes by large groups of people. I soon realized that some of the tunes were those I'd heard at the beginning of the record. The first was actually called "The Pajama Game," though its words gave no clue as to what a pajama game was. Somehow it didn't matter. I quickly took to playing the record over and over, happy to be matching the words to the music played by the orchestra at its beginning, never questioning or much wondering what the words meant. It was as if the record were a world of its own, with its own mysterious logic, that I could enter and enjoy without being able to explain where it was taking me—other than that it was someplace pleasurable that I'd never been to before.

By the next day Mom was caught up in *The Pajama Game* too. As I listened to the record yet again in the living room after school, she floated in from the kitchen during the overture—as she had by now explained to me this wordless introductory music was called—swaying to the jubilant tune that the whole band played and singing the lyrics that belonged to it: *"I'm not at all in love, not at all in love, not I!"* As the violins restated the phrase in a more somber key, she laughed at herself and left the room, only to pop in and out again as *The Pajama Game* played over and over. The music, our shared affection for it, became a private language of the afternoon, a whole vocabulary of joy.

What was *The Pajama Game*? Mom explained that like *South Pacific* it was a Broadway show—"a musical comedy," as words on the record's red jacket put it. On the back of the jacket was a description of the show's story—for Broadway musicals, like books, had stories—and Mom read it to me. It seemed dull next to the songs themselves, which were more than a story: In the singers' voices, in the confident swagger of the band, there was a promise of bolder happenings than a story in a book or on TV. I tried to picture a "show" as best as I could but had few pieces with which to assemble the puzzle.

The idea of New York was also hard to imagine. Mom had mainly told me about the Brooklyn of her childhood, particularly Coney Island, where there was a Fantasyland kind of park that was supposed to be the faraway country of India and where she had once taken an elephant ride. But she hadn't told me about Broadway before.

She hadn't seen it herself, she said, until she was eleven and living in Washington. Nat and Lil took her there on a trip, and she still had the scrapbook she'd kept. On one page there was a sugar packet from a restaurant; it didn't look any different from any other white sugar packet, but

Mom stroked it lovingly as she showed it to me—this was a restaurant that was very busy, full of crowds and open all night, she explained, because New York was a city with many more people than Washington. On another page, there was a program for a Broadway show with a ticket stub glued to its cover, and on the facing page another program, for what Mom said was the biggest movie theater in the whole world, Radio City Music Hall, with a notation in hesitant, penciled script: "Was there the first night. Spilt milk on it at the Automat." Mom explained that the Automat was a restaurant where you put nickels into machines, and real food, not just candy bars, popped out. She might as well have been describing Tomorrowland in Walt Disney's California.

When I asked if we could ever go to New York, Mom said, Of course, one day. But the closest we came was when television brought New York and one of its musical comedies to us a few weeks later. The whole neighborhood came to a standstill on a chilly March Monday night to watch singers and dancers from Broadway act out a story we already knew from a Disney cartoon movie, *Peter Pan*. The actor playing Peter Pan was Mary Martin, a name I knew because she was the woman on the leafy green cover of Mom's beloved *South Pacific*. In *Peter Pan*, she didn't look like what she was, a woman old enough to be one of our mothers. There wasn't a child in Somerset, me included, who disputed the proposition that she was a teenage boy.

We didn't question the illusion of flying, either. Watching *Peter Pan* a second time when it was on TV again a few years later, I could spot the wires every time Mary Martin moved near a window. But at age five, I couldn't see the strings; Peter's defiance of gravity was as much an article of faith as the arrival of Santa Claus and the Tooth Fairy. Think lovely thoughts, and up you go!

The night after *Peter Pan*, Mom had to instruct our baby-sitter to make sure Polly and I didn't get carried away by our own ambitions to take flight. Since coming home from school, we'd spent the entire afternoon leaping from the chairs and sofa in the living room—all the while making crowing noises, as Peter had the night before.

Peter Pan didn't look like the mysterious New York show I had been fantasizing about while listening to *The Pajama Game*. It looked like other shows on TV. But when I was bedridden with the measles not long there-after, Dad brought home the record of *Peter Pan*. As a special consolation for my regimen of hot soup and cold calamine lotion, Mom moved the record player right to my bedside. I started listening to the new record and didn't stop for the entire week of my quarantine, quickly discovering that, of course, *Peter Pan* was a show! It had an overture, just like that of *The Pa-jama Game*, in which the horns promised excitement beyond measure, then deferred to the rest of the band for some quieter, more melancholy tunes, then returned for a final fanfare that had to leave anyone listening in a state of almost unbearable anticipation.

As was not the case with *The Pajama Game*, though, this time I knew what the songs were about. Yet alone in my room day after day, isolated by my measles, I found that the songs became untethered from their story. The more I listened to "I Won't Grow Up," the more I found myself at odds with its credo. Far from not wanting to grow up, I wanted to grow up as fast as possible. Only then, I sensed, would I get to that "place where dreams are born and time is never planned," as Peter defined Never Never Land. To me, Never Never Land sounded like Mom's descriptions of New York. In another song, the Lost Boys cheered the arrival of their substitute mother, Wendy. "She'll be waiting at the door, we won't be lonely any-more!" they sang, and to their voice I added my own, over and over, in the privacy of my sickroom. Why? I had a home. I had a mother. I was not a Lost Boy.

Nearly a year later, after months of campaigning by me and Mom, Dad announced that he was going to take the family to see an actual Broadway musical—not on a movie screen, not in New York, but downtown, where *Damn Yankees* was visiting.

It could not have been a better choice. As I knew from the record, *Damn Yankees* was a show set in, of all places, Washington itself. Its sub-ject was of keen interest to me and my friends in Somerset: the Senators, our perennially ill-fated major-league baseball team, who played in a green stadium we had visited a couple of times as a special treat, for boys-only birthday parties. In *Damn Yankees*, the Senators got to live out a fan-tasy as far-fetched as a trip to Disneyland: They snatched the pennant away from the Yankees of Mantle and Bauer, New York titans as towering as the skyscrapers and Coney Island roller coasters in Mom's descriptions.

On the day of the show, I jittered about in the backseat during the interminable ride downtown, fearful that we would be late. In fact, we got to the National Theatre early enough for Mom and Dad to take Polly and me down the aisle to a railing where Dad picked each of us up in turn to peer down at the musicians in the pit. So that's where they kept the orchestra! Then we went back to our seats and waited for what seemed an eternity. When the lights in the theater finally went dim, a spotlight picked out a conductor I had to strain my neck to see. The musicians started playing—making a sound even louder than that on our record player, a sound more encompassing than any music I'd yet heard—and I found it hard to stay still; I bounced ever so slightly to the beat. Though I knew the music by heart, its spontaneous presence in the theater gave it a power larger than mere music. When, just as the band reached the overture's final few notes, the lights in the theater went out entirely, leaving only the gold curtain before us illuminated, I could at last understand why every overture, just like the first one I'd heard, for The Pajama Game, sounded as if it was announcing a spectacular event.

That event was the raising of the curtain, of course, but as the overture ended and the entire audience was suspended in the pause that followed, the same pause I knew from the record, there was still another surprise: The lights shining on the curtain dimmed, too, plunging the theater into complete darkness. Then, just when the suspense became overwhelming, the whole audience holding its breath, the curtain did rise, ascending heavenward so fast (where did it go?) and revealing such an explosive cacophony of light and costumes and people singing and dancing that it was more than I could absorb. The whole whirligig of sights and sounds and bodies rushing forward seemed to be aimed directly at me. And there was no letup. Each moment that followed passed too quickly, each shock of delight slid instantaneously, cruelly, into memory—a pileup of double-edged sensation in which exhilaration turned instantly inside out into a kind of sorrow.

If only there was a way to hold each moment, to freeze it in time and put it in my pocket and preserve it forever, before it was hopelessly lost!

When the show was over, the curtain falling for good, the lights coming back on, the theater emptying, I wanted to relive the whole afternoon immediately. I wanted to relive the afternoon not just once, really, but again and again, in slow motion and fast, to learn how each piece of the whole big Tinkertoy worked. I wanted to study and master the trick by which a roomful of furniture representing a house could in an instant be replaced by the infield at Griffith Stadium. I wanted to figure out how the young woman who fell in love with the ballplayer turned into a bent, beak-nosed crone—"the ugliest woman in Providence, Rhode Island," they called her—when the villainous Devil decided to punish her in the second act. This metamorphosis was a genuine surprise I hadn't figured out in advance from the record, and it filled me with wonder more than fear.

As we went to retrieve our car from the parking garage and drive back to Somerset, afternoon was giving way to evening. The waning sunlight seemed unnaturally bright and, strangely enough, artificial, after the warm indoor glow of the stage. Once home, I found myself drawn to the dark. With the lights off in the living room as Mom prepared dinner in the kitchen, as Dad called the store to check on business and Polly drifted into her bedroom to play with her dolls, I sat alone before the record player and listened to *Damn Yankees* again, reconstructing in my head as best I could the sights I had seen onstage. Once more I felt the sensation I had noticed that afternoon—that my pleasure was inextricably bound up with pain, that I was happier than I had ever been but, for reasons I couldn't explain, unhappier, too.

In bed that night I had a sensation I associated with Christmas Eve, when my mind would be overrun by all the anticipatory prospects of the presents that might turn up the next morning. Like then, I felt my life was on the brink of glorious change even as I worried I might never fall asleep.

Exactly ten months after that, as the next Christmas Eve was about to arrive, Mom gathered Polly and me and our suitcases to go to the airport where we would at last take flight—to Miami Beach—just like Peter Pan.

CHAPTER 2

had never heard of divorce until my parents' marriage was ended by one, and even then the word was said only in an embarrassed whisper, after the fact, as a desperate, retroactive attempt to contain within two flat syllables an unpredictable series of earthquakes that had already upended the world as I'd known it.

On the day some weeks after *Damn Yankees* that Mom told Polly and me that Dad was leaving home, the term used was not "divorce" but "separation." It was certainly nothing we should worry about, we were reassured. "Separation" was a temporary condition in which Dad "would move away for a little while." Mom and Dad still love each other. Mom and Dad still love their children very much. It's just that sometimes parents have trouble getting along and that leads to . . . "separation."

With so little information, there was no way for me to know what was happening. I didn't even know what questions to ask. There was no "separation" in Somerset, there was not so much as a *rumor* of separation that could be used as a yardstick to measure my own experience. Even among our surrogate families on television, the concept of separation, let alone divorce, was never mentioned. If Mom and Dad had not been getting along, they certainly hadn't fought the way Polly and I did, goading each other and roughhousing the way all brothers and sisters in Somerset battled. Nor had they yelled like the Kramdens—who always made up after their fights, no matter how boisterous, with a big hug and a kiss. I had never heard my parents raise their voices at all, except to order us for the third time to heed our bedtimes or remove our toys from the living-room rug. Then again, I'd never seen any big, sloppy hugs and kisses, either.

No one could or would add to the sketchy details offered by Mom, who herself seemed uncertain of what the future held. The turmoil this amorphous "separation" whipped up became as much a fixture in my life as the books I devoured, as the routine of school and neighborhood games. It was a constant ache in the pit of my stomach that I found I could aggravate into dizzying pain just by massaging it with my thoughts.

The adults around me joined together in an unacknowledged conspiracy to maintain the illusion that nothing out of the ordinary was happening. Grandma Lil spoke testily to Mom in muffled conversations just past the nearest doorway but was in a constant buzz around Polly and me, joshing and laughing lest a pause invite us to ask questions she didn't want to answer. We never seemed to be alone with her anymore; our afternoon Adventures getting lost in her Chevy with the top down were relegated to the past. Grandma Rose and Grandpa Herbert settled for speaking in remote, clipped cadences when we arrived for the first time at dinner as a family of three, not four—as if someone had died but the cause of death was too gruesome to be described before sensitive ears. Grandma's own weak hearing now seemed to conk out altogether, and Grandpa's fixation on the irresponsibility of Rich's suppliers, who eternally delivered their shoes later than promised, and Rich's customers, who were slower still to pay for them, grew even more dyspeptic.

Mom's announcement of the separation was followed by Dad's relocation to another house—just across Wisconsin Avenue, only a five-minute drive at most, but not in Somerset. Dad was now definitively exiled from the only neighborhood we had ever known. I wasn't certain whether to feel sorrier for myself or for him. His new house looked like a Somerset house, with its redbrick façade and green shutters. But Dad wasn't living alone there. He was a guest, he explained, in a stranger's home, and he now inhabited a single, narrow room. He took us there only once, for a few minutes one afternoon. His brush, comb, and toothbrush were lined up on top of a chest of drawers beside his bed, solitary testaments to the immutable identity he had carried with him to his alien new surroundings.

In the blur of events that ensued—blurry because they happened so quickly, blurry because I couldn't cobble together the narrative they told until long after they were over—fear became my constant companion. Fear, I learned, is not prompted only by villains like Captain Hook, or the swarthy robbers who always imperiled the Hardy Boys, or the Devil who changed young Lola into an ugly old witch in *Damn Yankees*. Real fear is fear of the unknown, and it contains no traces of comedy. It's that haunted-house terror where you can't tell who or what is in the next room, when you don't know what's hiding around the corner—what I felt when left to guess what might happen next to Polly and me. Not all the bedtime stories in the world, not all the Adventures I might go on with Mom, could weaken its tight grip. I felt as if I were falling from a great height, a long and unending fall, with only my parents' vague promise of a safe landing as a buffer against smashing into the pavement.

How much this promise was worth we couldn't assess. Mom and Dad seemed scared, too. Dad, a compact man, short for his age as I was, looked like a kid in his room at his strange new home, a forlorn kid who'd been told to go to bed without dinner but had been given no explanation as to what he had done to merit the punishment. Mom was distracted, her attention never fully fixed on wherever she was or whatever she was doing. All it took was the accidental dropping of a plate or the mildest misbehavior by Polly or me—all common occurrences now—to send her into an outburst of frustrated anger or, defeated, into her bedroom, where she would collapse on her bed and in time drift into a nap. She was sick a lot. The sickness made her tired all the time, despite the doctor's giving her tiny turquoise pills the same shade as her bedspread.

Her behavior made me determined not to misbehave. If my parents' separation was to stop, it was up to me to do my part to speed a happy ending. If I was perfect, that would be an incentive for them to resume their roles in the perfect household as well. I would be so good that Dad would have no choice but to return home. How could he not return home to the best son in Somerset? I spent hours working on a project for Miss McHenry's second-grade class that I knew he'd like: building a perfect cardboard replica of the new Rich's that had just opened in Chevy Chase's first shopping center.

—

But sometimes rage took charge of me despite my strenuous efforts to contain it, dashing my hopes of becoming the perfect boy who would make my home whole again. The anger would seize me like a fever, prompted by nothing more than the smallest momentary frustration—the misplacing of a toy or a book. It would pour out of me with a violence I found terrifying. The anger was bigger than I was—surfacing in a shrieking fit of tears that would escalate into violent hiccups and then into a flood of convulsions that only complete exhaustion could slow. By that point, Mom would come in and sit on my bed to try to calm me down. There's nothing wrong with "having a good cry," she'd say; as I knew, she often had them herself. But I'd reject her soothing words and embrace, pulling away from her and refusing to talk.

Once she'd left my room, I would up the ante. Blindly, tearfully, I would pull the drawers out of my bureau, dumping all my clothes into a heap. Then I'd turn to my shelves and sweep every book and toy I could reach onto the floor with as loud a clatter as the thick wall-to-wall carpeting would permit. I didn't care what I destroyed. I wanted to punish Mom, myself, the house, anyone or anything handy. When my tantrum was over, I still wouldn't be sated. I'd cry some more and then some more, howling with all my might, tacitly begging Mom to come in and comfort me again. Sometimes she would. More often she'd disappear into her own room, slamming the door behind her, and wait for me to knock and seek her forgiveness. Soon enough I'd go to her, exhausted and whipped in my tear-drenched shirt, because the closed door to her bedroom induced a fear that not even my anger could compete against: What if I lost my one remaining parent?

In her room, Mom would hug me, healing me for a while. Then I'd retreat to my bed, closing my eyes so I could escape the ruins I had made—the ruins not only of my room but of my hopes of Dad's return. If I was lucky, I would have exhausted myself to the point where I could fall asleep.

Late one afternoon when Mom wasn't home, even this routine could not do justice to the anger I felt. As my sobs subsided in the hollow chamber of my bedroom, I got a second wind of rage—all the scarier because it was a rage without tears, too strong to be expressed even by smashing up my bedroom. Since the house couldn't contain my fury, I fled outside, pressing with a manic stride toward the entrance to Somerset and then, more timidly, past that crucial threshold where our mothers had told us a thousand times safety ended and danger began.

I was determined to leave my home forever, but once I was beside Wisconsin Avenue, with traffic zooming past, it occurred to me I had no destination in mind and, even if I had had one, no clue how to get anywhere. What I did have was a vague notion of starting my life over again someplace new—maybe at Lil and Nat's, where I could shake off this bad feeling and be free of both my parents for good. Or better still, maybe the very act of running away could accomplish what my failed attempts to be a good boy had not. Maybe Mom and Dad, who were by now surely fearing I was dead, would band together to find me. Once united in this desperate search, they would realize how much they loved each other and how foolish a mistake their separation had been. Dad would have no choice but to move back home immediately.

These dreams churned in sync with the hard-breathing V-8 engines of the passing cars and pushed me forward toward the District line. But a slight second-grader wandering through the grass beside a busy thoroughfare in the early rush-hour gloom was a conspicuous sight. Within minutes, a police car pulled up alongside me, and soon I was back home.

Going home didn't feel like going home anymore. Mom hugged me hard, but she didn't look as if she had been worrying about whether I'd return, and she didn't, as I had fantasized, announce the imminent end of the separation. She didn't mention Dad at all. I knew that the anger that had spirited me to Wisconsin Avenue would soon visit me again, an unpredictable visitor I loathed with all my being but could not shake.

One night not long after that, Polly and I came up with a plan to build a new house of our own. We dragged from the garage to my bedroom a

huge brown Rich's carton—more than large enough to contain us, our favorite toys, and some clothes, should we need them. Using our arsenal of
art supplies, we decorated the box's walls, inside and out, with drawings of
flowers and color photographs we cut out of *Life* magazine. We patrolled
our small plot of domesticity with Dad's olive-green Air Force flashlight.

We found that we could busy ourselves in this cozy home-within-our-
home for hours at a time, enjoying the security of a self-contained, self-
invented universe that no one could alter or take away from us. And since no
one else talked about the separation, Polly and I didn't either. For now we
were happy just rearranging our possessions inside the box and simulating
the making of meals, using odds and ends from Polly's dollhouse acces-
sories and a few cans we took from a kitchen cupboard. Mom good-
naturedly visited us in our box sometimes, enthusiastically admiring our
handiwork, but gradually Polly and I ran short of new activities to fill up
the hours. Though we soon returned to our real beds, we didn't dismantle
the box; it remained, intact, in my bedroom, a shrine to our short-lived
sanctuary and to an intimacy that, like our home-within-our-home, we
would never again reconstruct.

—

Some evenings, as Mom was preparing dinner, I played the records Dad
had left behind. It was different to listen to them in Dad's absence; I was
glad—if guiltily so—that he hadn't taken them with him, and yet I felt that
the records, like me, had been maimed in some way, orphaned. The label
on the back of each one—for The Disc Shop, the store where he'd bought
them—testified to his ghostly absence. His Broadway record collection,
like his jazz record collection, was lost to him, at least for now. So was the
record player, whose safekeeping, so important to Dad, had fallen into my
less-experienced hands.

Was Dad lost, too? No, of course not. I saw him every Wednesday night
for dinner at Grandma and Grandpa's, and every Sunday afternoon after
my weekly incarceration at the downtown Jewish Community Center's religious school, where we were aggressively taught how to induce guilt in
relatives so that they would contribute quarters to help plant trees in Israel.
On those lazy Sundays, Dad took Polly and me bowling or, if it was sunny,

to Woodmont, where I would swim with unfamiliar boys with deep tans and loud voices who snapped their towels in the locker room and made ostentatious display of the colored chits their moneyed parents gave them to trade in at the poolside snack bar for cheeseburgers and lemonade.

No, Dad wasn't lost. He was the one who had left, voluntarily, without telling us why.

The last record Dad had brought home before the separation was *The Most Happy Fella*. Its songs were composed, he'd explained, by the same man who had written two other records we listened to all the time, *Guys and Dolls* and *Hans Christian Andersen*. But *The Most Happy Fella* was different—it was a special boxed set of *three* records that contained the entire Broadway musical, including the dialogue. There were three overtures—one for each act—and tucked into the box with the records was a large program filled with photographs of all the actors as they'd appeared when singing the songs on Broadway.

In the aftermath of the separation, *The Most Happy Fella* was my most dependable immersion into the theater. It alone could fill the hours between school and dinner. As I listened to it, I'd stare at the program—I could half-guess which photograph went with which song—and try to imagine what lay beyond the edges of the pictures. With a pencil, I labeled each photo Act 1, Act 2, or Act 3, according to my guess about the scene being depicted, and I'd prop the appropriate page against the hi-fi when that part of the show turned up on the record. Thanks to our trip to *Damn Yankees*, I could fill in many more details of what it might be like to actually be at *The Most Happy Fella:* the dimming lights and the rising curtain, the full-throated sound of the orchestra in the pit, the smoky intermissions, and the pounding rain of the applause at the curtain calls.

The show's story was quite clear, thanks to all the dialogue on the recording. The hero was an older man who loved a beautiful young woman but had a fight with her after they were married, prompting her to leave him. Then they kissed and fell back in love again. As the show ended, the husband was, once again, the most happy fella.

The Most Happy Fella didn't always sound happy. In the three overtures, the horns sounded not exuberant but agitated, rumbling like distant thunder. Soon the whole orchestra picked up their morose theme, until the living room filled with the swelling lamentation. I was intrigued by this aching music—unlike any I'd heard before—but the song I really liked best was brighter and more in tune with *The Pajama Game*. It came in Act 2, when the hero, Tony, and the woman he loved, Rosabella, met for the first time after their fight and began to make up. They played a game, pretending that they'd never met in the first place, and started their romance over from scratch, like children, with an exchange of simple introductions: "How do you do? Pleased to know you!" Soon they were back in love again, as if nothing bad had ever happened.

It all seemed so easy. Couldn't Mom and Dad do the same? But what is love?, I wondered. Mom never stopped telling us that she loved us, and I never doubted that she meant it. Yet love had never made me feel any better except when men and women I'd never met, whose faces and lives I could only dimly picture, sang about it on a record.

There was fresh evidence that Dad might not be moving back as quickly as I wished when we went to Miami. When he didn't show up at the airport to help get us on the plane, I was certain he had forgotten us altogether. I felt another fever rise within me—not anger, but light-headedness. My head felt hot; in December, I broke out in a summer Washington fever. How could Dad have moved away and left me in charge of our family without providing any instructions? I don't know what would have happened if Mom hadn't eventually stood up, wiped her eyes, gone to a phone booth, and then returned, much more like her calm self, to take us to another set of stairs that led, at last, to a plane.

Mom assured me later that I had only imagined the worst; Dad missed us very much, she said, and we would see him as soon as we got back to Washington. But in Miami, his name was hardly ever mentioned unless Polly or I spoke about him—not by Mom, not by Lil and Nat, not by any of the other relatives who passed through the garden apartment my grandparents had taken for the winter. As the days grew into weeks, I found myself living a life in which Dad played no part.

Once we were back home, Mom dropped another clue that she didn't expect Dad back soon. She said she was in love with a man on TV. She said it as a joke—that much I could tell. But it was a kind of joke that, coming from her, was new to me.

The man she loved was a contestant on one of the quiz shows that promised to make millionaires of anyone clever enough to answer impossibly hard questions. The contestant, Charles Van Doren, was a teacher, and Mom revered teachers. She showed me a book on her shelf that was written by another Van Doren—Charles's father—who was "a brilliant professor at a university in New York."

On the quiz show, Charles Van Doren had to give his answers while locked in a glass booth. The level of tension, as demonstrated by his expression of fervent concentration and the loud ticking of a clock, was terrifying. We didn't dare move until he had disposed of all five or six answers to the long, multipart questions. I rooted along with Mom, secure in the knowledge that the man she "loved" was not about to turn up in Somerset anytime too soon; I knew, as Mom acknowledged from the start, that there was no way she could actually meet him.

Charles Van Doren was so brilliant that he stayed on the show for months, and Polly and I joined Mom for her rendezvous with him every week. I grew fond of him. He was polite, he was shy, he was smart. I grew attached to Charles Van Doren, and on the night he finally lost and was banished from the show forever (albeit with riches beyond measure), I was shocked: A light had been extinguished in our living room. I studied Mom carefully to gauge her response—worrying how she might feel, worrying that she might sink into her bed and cry—but she didn't seem to mind that much. She was "philosophical," she explained. "No one is perfect. No one can be a genius every day."

Maybe, I thought, she wasn't in love with Charles Van Doren after all. Maybe she was just in love with his genius for knowing the answer to any question; it was another reason to work harder, harder than I ever had before, in school.

Despite my Herculean efforts in Miss McHenry's classroom, none of my achievements seemed to change Dad's mind about having left home. If anything, he seemed farther and farther away. He didn't attend Parents' Day, and when I sat next to him on the couch and read to him from whatever schoolbook I was immersed in, he told me how proud he was, just as Mom did, but I could tell that he was only pretending to listen. Then he'd make a fast exit, leaving Somerset in his new station wagon, full of shoe cartons urgently awaiting transfer from the new Chevy Chase store to F Street, or vice versa.

When the school year came to an end, I was bereft, having lost Somerset Elementary as the second home I had come to depend on. I spent the days playing with my friends on Trent Street. This was one of those Washington summers when not even our huge standing Westinghouse fan, as large as the grown-ups who had to wheel it into place, could dispel the torpor; only the afternoon arrival of the white Good Humor truck, with its nickel Popsicles, and the occasional communal drive to Gifford's ice cream parlor in Bethesda, with our heads sticking out the windows, offered a temporary reprieve. Prickly heat on our necks and thighs, which Mom treated with smelly powder, was a nightly curse.

To keep myself busy, I started a newspaper, pounding on Mom's gray portable typewriter as hard as I could to make as many carbon copies as possible of my neighborhood bulletins: "Latest hurricane: Audry. The Frietags new baby is named Sara Ellen. The Plaers have 3 cars. The Mettgers have a new pool. Patty has 4 puppies."

Polly and I had named our little black mongrel Patty because we liked to pat her. We gave her puppies to other families in the neighborhood, but we didn't have much time to mourn their departure. As it turned out, we were moving, too.

Mom told us that sometimes parents who are separated find that they still can't make up, and when that happens, they get divorced. She and Dad were divorced, she announced one Saturday—it was all done—and we were going to have a new home. Dad was moving to an apartment in another part of Maryland, Rockville, and we would be moving to an apartment, too, in still another part of Maryland called Silver Spring. We'd have to make new friends and we'd be farther away from Dad than we were now, but we would see him the same as always, on Wednesdays and Sundays.

I shuffled these few details like cards, feverishly rearranging them, trying to find a pattern that would make sense. But some cards were missing from this deck—of that I was certain—and without them, I couldn't begin to put the future in order.

The future arrived anyway, soon enough. Our house was overrun with brown boxes like the shoe cartons from Dad's store. Mom said that I should set aside any toys or other special things that I wanted to keep with me while moving, so they wouldn't be packed away. As I surveyed my room, I realized that my special things were few: the frail beginnings of a baseball-card collection Dad had once said he'd help me with, my big yellow box of forty-eight crayons, and the books I read most, the four volumes of Winnie-the-Pooh stories and poems by A. A. Milne.

When moving day arrived, Mom drove Polly and me to a neighborhood with a pretty name: Rosemary Hills. It had a sign at its entrance, just as Somerset did. But there were no hills I could see and no front yards, just a few streets of stout redbrick buildings surrounded by shrubbery and connected by concrete walkways that shimmered in the hot August sun.

As we walked into our new home for the first time, Mom explained that Polly and I would now be sharing a bedroom. In our new room, there was a bunk bed—I invoked my seniority to put dibs on the top bunk—and a small desk for me. I sat at the desk for a while silently, as if to catch my breath, and then started unpacking. I put my crayon box squarely in one corner of the desktop, and my baseball cards in a drawer, and then I took some new pads that Mom had given me, and some pencils and notebooks that we'd bought at Murphy's five-and-ten for the new school year, and arranged them neatly in another drawer. It was as tidy as I remembered Dad's desk looking in his office at the F Street store.

Before long, we saw Dad's new home, too. It was in a tall apartment building that, unlike ours, had an elevator. Dad had almost no furniture, but he did have a new kind of record player: a tape recorder, which played large reels filled with yards of brown tape. This new machine was too complicated, Dad said, for me or Polly to handle; only he could make it work. He put a reel on top of the tape recorder, threading the loose end of the tape into an empty reel beside it, and then pressed a button to make the reels spin. Then we heard two nameless, voiceless people playing Ping-Pong: The ball bounced between speakers on either side of the room while we sat on the couch in awed silence.

The sharp ricocheting of the ball, back and forth, in the spare white room sounded like a portent. This is the future, Dad said, offering a rare grin. This is the new, modern world of Stereo.

—

Mom: I see her still, climbing the stairs to our apartment, an armful of bags or books pressing down her spirits. Her hair was parted on the side and held in place by bobby pins. The fabric of her blouse strained against her breasts.

We were asking for more than she could give us. In Rosemary Hills we knew no one, not one kid, not one parent. Polly, just entering the first grade, and I, going into third, were days away from having to negotiate a school full of strangers, and Mom was too. She had taken a job teaching the fourth grade at an elementary school in a neighborhood a half hour away. There was lots of preparation to be done before school started, she said, and we would have to be patient when she sat at her desk in the living room late at night, planning her lessons.

As if to make amends for our new circumstances, she surprised us by announcing one Saturday morning that she was going to take us into Washington to a theater where they performed Broadway shows outside— if it didn't rain. It was a show she had seen in Washington the year after the war ended, the year she married Dad. It was one I knew from its record— but not well enough, it turned out. I thought it was mainly about the fun of going to an amusement park: It was named *Carousel*, like the slow-gaited merry-go-round Polly and I always rode at Glen Echo.

The idea of seeing a show at night was itself thrilling—we'd be up way past bedtime. Still, I was disappointed, as we took our seats, that the sun had not yet set. With no darkness and no ceiling and no curtain, the theater didn't seem like a theater—any more than our fatherless family seemed like a family.

There was no overture, either. The first music in the show was for a dance in which the actors onstage swirled as if riding a carousel.

The merry carousel dance was a false clue to the sad story that followed: A pretty woman fell in love with a handsome man—a "barker" who worked at the amusement park. They married, and they fought a lot. The husband hit his wife. She became pregnant. The man died trying to rob a rich factory owner to get money to take care of the baby who was expected any minute.

Time passed, years and years passed as quickly as the waves of melody played by the orchestra, and the baby grew into a teenage girl. But she had no friends to play with, and all the other kids in her high school made fun of her for having a father who had deserted his family.

Just when the girl became so miserable and angry that she started sobbing in paroxysms of choking that frightened me with their familiarity, her dead father returned through a miracle. God had sent him down from heaven—and I could look up and see heaven now, for the stars had come out above the Carter Barron Amphitheatre—to visit his child. But no sooner did he meet his daughter for the first time than he lost his temper and hit her and ran away before she could even figure out that he was her father. Though a happy ending followed, her father never came back for good.

Long after we had returned to Silver Spring, I found myself thinking about the girl's anger and tears when her schoolmates mocked her for not having a dad. I listened to the record carefully, again and again, trying to find that part of *Carousel*, trying to recapture it as it had been onstage, so I could relive every word and feeling. But whatever I was searching for couldn't be found on the record.

I had to depend on memory instead, and what I most remembered was the girl's plan of escape. There was a show coming through her town the next week, she had told her father before he ran away. And in this show, she continued, there was a man—an "advance man"—who had promised to rescue her, to take her with him. The man said he would help her become an actress, and after that she would never need a home again, because she would travel with all the other actors in the show, all over the country, forever.

CHAPTER 3

What I remember about our first year at Rosemary Hills is mainly the dark: tossing on my top bunk at night, unable to sleep, too anxious to do anything except worry about what might happen next. I didn't need nightmares to experience the sensation of falling through a floor I had thought was secure, barreling into a deep pit whose bottom I struggled in vain to see. I now felt these terrors while wide awake.

I focused on the thin slit beneath the door, a sliver of light from the television set in the living room. In our new apartment, the rooms were not separated by hallways; you could always tell what was happening just beyond the next door or wall if you listened closely enough.

In the living room sat a baby-sitter, an opaque figure new to us like everyone else in this new neighborhood. In silence, she watched the TV shows that came on past our bedtimes.

From my bunk, as Polly slept, I listened intently, straining with every ounce of my being to hear whatever might reach me through that illuminated slit under the closed door. On one of the shows, *Bachelor Father*, a man was raising a child alone—but she was a niece he'd taken in. Didn't anyone get divorced on television? Or at least separated?

In bed those nights, I channeled all my fear into the single turn of a switch: If the TV was extinguished, I decided, part of me would be too. In a foreign place, with a stranger in the next room and a sleeping little sister in the bed below, I dreaded being cast into complete darkness, because then I would be completely alone. As I lay there worrying if I would ever fall asleep, trying not to worry because worrying only added to my agitation and made sleep all the more elusive, the TV was my lifeline to a world where no one ever had to go to sleep at all.

Even if I couldn't hear the words the people were saying on TV, I was sustained by the sound of the other, faceless inhabitants of that world—the audience. No matter how faint the words of the actors, the merry chorus of the crowd always reached my top bunk. Where was that big, welcoming audience? In a theater, of that I was certain. On Broadway? These people were always on tap, night and day, weekdays and weekends, to laugh, to applaud, to love. I basked in their warmth as I turned, and turned again, wondering where Mom was, when she would get home, if she would come home before I fell asleep.

Many times Mom would return before I could drift off. I'd hear the front door open, and then her perfunctory words dismissing the baby-sitter before she came into our bedroom to check up on us. I would let her know I was awake. I had convinced myself it was her fault.

"Mom?"

"Yes, Frank," she would say with a smile. She'd stand close by the bunk bed, her head right next to mine. "Now, what are you doing still up?"

"I can't get to sleep."

"You're not trying hard enough."

"I can't try any harder. I missed you."

Then she would lean over and kiss me.

"I'm here," she'd say, in a voice both weary and gentle.

———

One Friday night, Mom decided to take Polly and me to see the movie of *Damn Yankees*. I had been begging to see it since I first spotted the advertisement on the movie page of our newspaper, but I had given up hope. The movie theater was downtown, and downtown was farther away than ever. Fridays, returning home from school a couple of hours after Polly and I did, Mom was usually too tired to take us anywhere. But on this Friday night, Mom was radiant. The plan, she told us with a smile anticipating our own, was to go to the Hot Shoppe on Connecticut Avenue, where we could order Mighty Mos, our favorite kind of double cheeseburger, and french fries through a walkie-talkie like the one at a drive-in movie, and eat on trays in our car in the parking lot. Then we'd drive to the Ambassador movie theater, which Mom especially liked to go to because it had a creepy history she liked to tell us about. Back when Mom first moved to Washington, the Ambassador was still remembered by its old name, the Knickerbocker, as the theater whose roof caved in when a snowstorm struck in the 1920s, killing more than a hundred people. Now the Ambassador was well into its second life, hugging the corner of Eighteenth Street and Columbia Road, its curved façade looming like the prow of a ship.

I couldn't believe my good fortune. I was not only about to revisit the first Broadway show I ever saw but to be transported back to an afternoon of our abandoned Somerset life that now, two years later, seemed almost as distant as Broadway itself.

Mom told me not to expect a repeat of that matinee. "They always change Broadway shows when they make them as movies," she said, laughing. "It's what my mother calls *meshuggah*—they always make them worse."

I thought that was hilarious and couldn't possibly be true.

In this case, it wasn't. True, seeing a movie wasn't the same as seeing a play on a stage. I missed having the actors in the theater with me, so close that we shared the same air, so responsive that I thought they were reacting directly to me each time I laughed or clapped. But the movie riveted me just the same. To identify the real Griffith Stadium on-screen, with its familiar National Bohemian beer scoreboard, instead of the make-believe Griffith Stadium I'd seen in the stage *Damn Yankees*, was to be validated in my conviction that I might someday revisit the heart of a bustling city beyond Somerset and Silver Spring.

The biggest surprise in the *Damn Yankees* movie was my discovery of parts of the story that I simply hadn't noticed, for all my intense concentration on every inch of the stage, on that long-ago afternoon with Mom and Dad. I hadn't realized before how sad the wife was when her husband disappeared, taking off without warning or explanation after the Devil transformed him into Joe Hardy, the young slugger who would win the pennant for the Senators. The wife wasn't just sad; she was heartsick with longing for her runaway husband. The husband, too, was overwhelmed with regret, even though he and his wife had quarreled all the time about his spending six months out of every year caring only about the Washington Senators and not about her.

Why hadn't I understood his song before? Why hadn't I understood what the husband was saying when he wrote his farewell note and left it in the living room? The song was on the record, after all; I had listened to it a thousand times:

> Goodbye old girl, my old girl.
> When you awaken, I'll be gone. . . .
> And though your Joe has to go,
> He may come back to you again. . . .
> Our love will keep, old girl,
> Till then.

Nor had I noticed the twist in the story a little later when Joe Hardy goes back to his old house and rents a room there — without telling his wife that he is really her husband in disguise. In the movie of Damn Yankees, the house was in Chevy Chase — it looked just like the house where Dad had his rented room before he moved to his new apartment. Only now his wife was there, too — so near to him and yet so far away, as another song put it.

They were back living together — and not quite. They were in Somerset — almost!

When, at the end of the movie, Joe Hardy turned back into his old self and returned to his wife, this time forever, it was the happiest ending I had ever seen; I all but forgot about the happy ending that had excited me so much the first time, the Senators' victory over the damn Yankees.

No baseball pennant could be better than this. The husband had kept the promise in his goodbye note — Our love will keep, old girl, till then — and was back safe and sound in Chevy Chase, no damage done.

There was another song I hadn't understood the first time I saw *Damn Yankees*. It was sung by the Devil's beautiful assistant when she first meets Joe Hardy in the Senators' locker room. The words had always struck me as nonsensical: *Whatever Lola wants, Lola gets*.

Sitting between Polly and Mom in the dark plush seats at the movie, I hardly paid attention to the words; I couldn't take my eyes off Lola herself. She kept taking off her clothes as she sang, until she was in her underwear. It was black and very tight and sheer, with a pattern of holes that permitted Lola's white skin to peek through. As she crawled on the floor in her tights and some kind of lacy brassiere, the contour of her breasts and her bare shoulders pushed toward Joe, who sat open-mouthed on a bench. All those curves were rolling toward me, too, and I watched no less open-mouthed. I couldn't stop staring at her neck, her arms, her breasts, except when I stole a look at her legs as, eventually, they entwined themselves around Joe Hardy. Her legs were not nude, but the black sheen of her stockings was easily as powerful a lure as her skin.

At the end of the song, which I knew by heart, I was barely listening to the insistent, drum-punctuated words: *Give in . . . give in . . . give in.* Did Lola do this onstage two years ago? How could I have missed it? As the song ended, Lola was lying arched on her back across Joe's lap, her arms extended as far as they could reach, her breasts practically poking into the ballplayer's face, her nipples almost visible through the black lace. If he reached down and touched her—which he did not—what would happen then?

That night in my bunk, I asked myself that question again and again, once more trying to imagine grown-up happenings that were beyond my field of vision, once more reshuffling the incomplete set of cards I had been dealt as I tried, and tried, to fall asleep.

———

In school, I had new friends, particularly Kenny Ettleman. Kenny and I taught ourselves one of the Senators' songs from *Damn Yankees*—*You gotta have heart!*—for the third-grade talent show. I worked hard to prove myself to the new teacher. Cub Scouts filled up the afternoons. Since Rosemary Hills didn't have the front lawns and backyards of Somerset, we flipped baseball cards in its paved culs-de-sac. Towering above us was the largest apartment building we'd ever seen, still in construction just beyond the neighborhood's border. It was too large and unapproachable to be a haunted house.

Rosemary Hills didn't look like the setting of TV's *Father Knows Best*, where there were no apartment buildings and the front lawns were, if anything, larger and more immaculate than those I'd known in Somerset. I hated *Father Knows Best* and didn't care who knew it. The show was boring, I announced, and the Anderson kids were stupid little goody-goodies. What I wouldn't admit—even to myself—was that each episode of the show that everyone loved was an acute reminder that I was different, in a family unlike any other family I knew in life or on television.

Our family was now defined by that two-syllable word, almost a second name, that was uttered—in my presence, at least   only in the whisper that Grandma Rose used when talking about being Jewish or having cancer: *divorce*. When my new friends asked where my father was, I would try out the word for size, trying to mutter it myself, and then discover that half of them had no idea what I was talking about and the other half had only recently learned it—no doubt from their parents, who had instructed them in advance about my aberrational household, much as they might warn them not to play with a classmate who'd come down with chicken pox. Others whispered a synonym for divorce—*broken home*—that enhanced the medical analogy, though clearly a broken home was more lasting and crippling than a broken arm or leg.

—

The hardest nights in Rosemary Hills were those when Mom used baby-sitters who didn't watch TV at all. The silence of the room beyond our room became like a weight pressing upon me, suffocating me, shortening my breath, making me sweat, accelerating my panic at being unable to sleep. No ordinary night-light plugged into the wall could dispel the darkness. I would try to counteract it—as Mom had told me to, taking a cue from Peter Pan—by thinking lovely thoughts. The only lovely ones I could find involved Lola: her red hair, her white shoulders, her breasts, her legs. In my fantasy, I took off more of her clothes than she had in her song, though my mind remained sketchy about the details; there was a point past which I couldn't budge, no matter how hard I tried to will myself forward.

To fill in what was missing, I looked at pictures, scouring *Life* and *Look* for visual information. My most successful catch was from an unexpected source—my Boy Scouts magazine, *Boys' Life*. One issue showed a photo of a movie star, Doris Day, playing a Scout troop mom wearing a shirt with its top button undone and tied in a knot at the bottom, revealing the flesh both above and below her breasts. In my mind this image joined a small, improvised cavalcade that included the photograph of Lola in black tights on the cover of the *Damn Yankees* record and another Broadway record jacket, *Silk Stockings*, with its own picture of a pretty woman's legs. With time, I gathered enough clues from every conceivable source to concoct an attenuated unveiling of Lola's obscured anatomy. On those wide-awake nights, I rocked myself to sleep with my undressed Lola—if, that is, I could be certain that Polly was already asleep below me, insensate to the sound of creaking bedsprings. Lola became the company I was so hungry to find in the dark, if only just long enough to guide me into the oblivion I craved.

Dad continued to see us on Wednesday nights for dinner with his parents and on most Sunday afternoons. I was glad we didn't have to spend the night at his new apartment—not that that was a prospect, since there was no room or beds for us there anyway. As much trouble as I had getting to sleep in Rosemary Hills, I knew it would be worse in the less familiar setting of Dad's place. There Polly and I often sat around the living room after Sunday lunch like anxious guests waiting for the clock to run out on the afternoon, so that we could meet Grandma and Grandpa for dinner, whether at the Woodmont country club or in the palatial restaurant of the ancient Kennedy-Warren apartment house, with its high ceilings and obscure murals, near the zoo. In self-defense, I developed the habit of always having a book with me, wherever I went, should I be trapped in a place where there was nothing to do, like Dad's, or, worse, no way to go to sleep. I would take along the book—my latest Hardy Boys, or a Landmark biography of a famous American from the school library—to meals, whether at home or out, and at night I'd place it under my pillow. The bricklike presence was itself a comfort.

Some weekends we didn't see Dad at all. Business was more hectic than ever, now that there was more than one store to fill with shoes, and Dad explained that he had to spend more time in New York, where he bought the shoes that he then sold in Washington.

Every time he came back, I asked the same question: Did you see any Broadway shows in New York? No, Dad would say. There was just too much work to do.

———

"Well, it's not Disneyland," said Mom with a raised voice, an uneasy smile, and a guttural laugh like Grandma Lil's; her tentatively sarcastic tone was her way of letting us know that she expected we'd be let down by what was about to happen but that we must keep a sense of humor anyway. It was a sweltering Saturday in July, and we were on our way to a place called Storybook Kingdom, the best substitute Washington could muster for Walt's unreachable mecca. Storybook Kingdom was actually in Virginia—which might as well have been Alaska. Virginia, even suburban Virginia, was an alien territory to Maryland suburbanites. We knew it only from that perennially tedious trip to Mount Vernon that dogged every grade-school child in the Washington area like a local curse.

We were barely in the car when I started complaining. Storybook Kingdom—it sounded suspiciously babyish to my elevated third-grade tastes. The midsummer sun was punishment enough in a life without air-conditioning; we were damp with perspiration well before we left the apartment. Why would I want to go to some kiddies' park to meet Rumpelstiltskin and Humpty Dumpty and Goldilocks? Why not a movie at the "ice cool" Silver or Avalon, or the rides at Glen Echo? Mom ignored us. She was light-spirited, almost giddy, especially for a Saturday, the day when a week's fatigue usually set in. The drive was long, and Polly and I got crankier and crankier. When we finally pulled into the parking lot, I wasn't assuaged by the first sight: a tall but crude Jack and his Beanstalk, carved out of wood like a totem pole, Jack's features painted as primitively as the illustrations in a nursery-school picture book cast off long ago.

Once we reluctantly emerged from the car to scrutinize Jack, we were confronted by another figure, nearly as large. A huge man stood in the lot only a few feet from where we parked, as if he'd been lying in wait for us. He was wearing a florid madras shirt and baggy shorts. His eyes seemed to pop out at us from behind boxy, black-rimmed eyeglasses. His grin was broad enough to reveal a wide expanse of teeth framed by thin, visibly moist lips. Behind him, a boy and girl were halfheartedly chasing each other in the heat, playing tag on the blindingly sun-baked concrete, ignoring him and us.

The man walked toward Mom. She greeted him with a "Hello!" whose peppiness sounded slightly forced, while Polly and I stood there resigned to the inevitable tedium of the afternoon yet surprised by this unannounced intrusion.

"Frank and Polly," Mom said, "this is my friend Joel."

"Hello, *Frank!* Hello, *Polly!*" Joel cried in the cheerleading cadences of an announcer on a TV show. Then he swiveled abruptly toward the kids behind him, calling in a deeper but not unfriendly voice: "Susan! Johnny! Come here!" The boy and the girl moved haltingly toward us, as Polly and I did toward them, and we were all introduced.

"Sue and John are twins," Joel said, still speaking loudly, as if he were addressing a whole parking lot of listeners. But they looked nothing alike: The boy was big and blockish, like his father, while the girl was thin, with light-brown hair matted by the heat.

Joel rapidly established that Sue and John were one year younger than me and one year older than Polly, and he told us that they went to a school we'd never heard of, in Washington itself—the city I had never thought of as a place where kids might actually live.

Joel seemed pleasant; so did the twins. But the sun glared. The air felt heavy.

As we walked toward the entrance to Storybook Kingdom—adults swiftly ahead, we four kids falling behind—I saw Joel reach into a bag he was carrying, a small blue plastic suitcase with the name of an airline on it. He pulled out a messy wad of green paper that looked almost but not quite like money. On closer inspection, I realized that the paper was another form of valuable currency: S&H Green Stamps. Mom often busied us pasting these stamps into thick books, the way you would a real stamp collection, so that we could exchange them at a store called a redemption center for products we didn't need and couldn't even fit into our cramped, yardless home, but that tempted us anyway.

Joel turned to the four of us. "No use in paying for what you can get free! Do you know what Green Stamps are?" We nodded. "I have enough here to get tickets for all six of us!" he continued enthusiastically. But I could see that there was a problem: Joel had not pasted the stamps into the books, the way we did so neatly and laboriously with Mom, and he now expected the man at the gate to accept the stamps as is, thousands of them in sheets of various sizes that would have to be counted up—or pasted into books on the spot. I knew from experience that this could take hours.

As we waited at some distance, it was impossible to make out the exchange between Joel and the man guarding Storybook Kingdom, but it was clearly animated. Joel's bombastic tone traveled, even though the specific words did not. Mom kept her back to the scene we were witnessing: Joel waving the stamps right in the gatekeeper's face, practically brushing them against the man's nose. All the while she asked the twins questions about their teachers, their favorite subjects, and their favorite books, as if she were calling on them in her fourth-grade class. Sue did most of the answering. John didn't seem shy, exactly, but he tilted his head back at a cocky angle and squinted his eyes, as though surveying Mom and the rest of us from afar. With a slightly out-of-focus smile that stopped just short of being a jack-o'-lantern grin, his expression suggested that he was in on some secret joke—with a punch line that might be guessed, but only by someone as wise as he.

The sun was scorching, and I wondered if we'd ever enter Storybook Kingdom. Then Joel charged toward us, his large arms flapping, his madras shirt stained with islands of sweat, his open airline bag swinging from his shoulder, green sheets still in his hand, and his grin back at full intensity.

"The midgets are trying to cut me off at the knees!" he shouted in an excited voice tinged with a childlike delight. "But I beat them!"

He swept us into the park, bragging about how he had outwitted the ticket man and broken his silly rules. Not that I cared. This was already a lost afternoon. I didn't want to play with kids I didn't know or want to know. There was no fun in the sparsely populated Storybook Kingdom—just parched patches of lawn and clumps of trees alternating with garish statues of fairy-book characters like those outside its gates.

At a refreshment stand, we begged for lemonade, ice cream, and hot dogs. Joel enthusiastically took our orders—we could have whatever we wanted. The only hitch was the size of our drinks: Did we want small, medium, or large?

"Have large!" he declared magnanimously, as if he would be insulted if we settled for less. But once we chose large, he thought better of it and his voice dropped an octave: "Are you sure you can drink that much? If you can't, don't order it."

Then: What did we want on our hot dogs? Mustard, ketchup, relish? Why not all three?

And ice cream, too! What flavor? Two scoops, or one? Why not one of each flavor?

By the time we finished ordering and eating, we were too pooped to do anything else. But Mom and Joel prodded us to try out the adjoining playground, and the four of us dutifully hauled our bloated, sweaty selves onto the slides and swings. As we did, Mom receded with Joel into the background, talking with the easy familiarity she had with all her friends, not the shyness with which she typically retreated from strangers. She and Joel stood very close to each other, Mom barely coming up to his broad shoulders. I could tell she was having a good time, but I didn't see why we had to be subjected to Storybook Kingdom as part of the bargain. I couldn't wait to go home.

Finally, just as John started climbing the jungle gym as high as he could, Mom and Joel signaled that my wish of departure was at last coming true. As the five of us stood there watching and waiting for John to reach the top rung, Joel raised his voice again, even louder than usual.

"*John! Now!*"

"I'm almost at the top!" John yelled from his lofty perch.

"*NOW!*"

John seemed to ignore Joel and climbed the final rungs before starting his descent. In seconds, he had leapt back to earth and was coming toward us—but his father had already moved to intercept him. As they met, Joel grabbed the boy's shoulders and lifted him a few inches.

"*When I say NOW, I mean NOW!*" Joel yelled in a raw, seething tone nothing like his previous vocal outbursts. Then he threw John down as quickly as he had picked him up, almost propelling him into the concrete with the violence of the gesture.

I looked at John, expecting him to burst into tears, as I surely would have under the circumstances, but he registered no expression whatsoever. He brushed the dirt off his pants, then walked to join Sue, Polly, and me — all the while maintaining the same half-grin he'd had from the moment we arrived. Joel and Mom, walking together with their backs to us, had started toward Storybook Kingdom's exit without further exhortation. With John in tow, we scrambled to follow, only to find Joel back to his jocular loud self in the parking lot.

"Goodbye, *Polly!* Goodbye, *Frank!*" he said, bowing toward us in an exaggeration of courtliness, as he, John, and Sue got into their station wagon and we got into ours.

—

Except for Mom's innocuous query — "Aren't Sue and John nice?" — buried in a steady stream of chat as we drove home, the afternoon was little mentioned thereafter. In a few days, Storybook Kingdom was forgotten. My own focus turned to the news that I would be spending August at Inverness, a day camp for boys. I would be picked up by a bus making a special stop at Rosemary Hills — a bus full of boys from other neighborhoods, with their own Cub Scout troops and alliances. I dreaded the prospect of having to ingratiate myself with another set of kids only months after I had worked up the courage to fit into a new elementary school. And I didn't like the idea of a camp without girls: I liked girls, from Lola in my nighttime assignations to Mona Malumut at my new school, and thought about them more and more.

I also knew that I was on my way to becoming the worst athlete in the history of American boyhood. I loved baseball but had mastered none of the skills necessary to play the game. Maybe this was another consequence of divorce: I was bad at baseball because I had lost the paternal half of my upbringing. Despite being as short as I was, Dad had been a good athlete in high school, but divorce meant that he didn't have time to teach me how to throw, hit, or catch; in the brief time we had together, he concentrated on teaching me to swim—an activity that, unlike baseball, could be pursued at Woodmont on Sunday, our only afternoon together.

Fearful of being humiliated in front of new peers, I begged Mom to change her mind about camp. I was glad, I told her, to stay at home in Rosemary Hills and do nothing until school started again.

"You have to try it," she insisted, assuming her classroom mode. "You can't have an opinion about something you haven't experienced."

Oh yes I could, and as it happened, the reality of camp exceeded my fears. Within two days at Inverness I found myself the runt of an enormous litter, conspicuously chosen last for every team (or next to last if I was vying with the camp stutterer), picked so tardily that half the players were on the field and had forgotten I existed by the time I was dumped into the squad forced to adopt me. I tried to hide from the humiliation, showing up late whenever possible to each new activity. In the outfield, I deftly escaped any balls that might be hit my way by deferring to any other fielder nearby—or by feigning an absentmindedness otherwise alien to my being, hoping this might protect me from responsibility for all activity within a ten-yard diameter. I prayed for rain (and for even more biblical natural disasters), which would mean movies indoors, however mind-numbingly "educational" they might be.

None of these strategies worked; my every move provoked groans and ridicule from the few who noticed. No less futile were my efforts to find at least one other boy in my group who was as athletically retarded as I was and might be a commiserating brother in rejection. I simply had no equal in spastic misthrows and bobbled catches; with everyone looking at me, my body felt like an ugly, unwieldy mass. Only in swimming and riflery did I escape utter embarrassment; I had a surprising native talent, baffling to a Jewish family whose idea of a lethal weapon was a Swingline stapler, for hitting bull's-eyes with a BB gun. As far as I could tell, this was my sole visible heritage from Dad's Civil War ancestors.

Even lunch hour was mortifying. Every day, Mom packed me an elaborate lunch box, each sandwich and brownie and piece of fruit wrapped in wax paper *and* foil to ward off the germs and other predators of the untamed wilds of Montgomery County. Because of the heat, she did not, mercifully, send along the mixture of raw hamburger and Lawry's Seasoned Salt—her irresistible "steak tartare"—that made my friends look askance in the school cafeteria. But I couldn't win. Other boys regarded the large array of paper goods generated by my lunch (all from Grandpa's warehouse, no doubt) as bizarre eccentricity—another mark of divorce, I figured. Often I ate alone, at the vacant corner of a long wooden picnic table inhabited at the other end by boys talking festively about team ambitions in which I could play no part.

I further isolated myself from the Inverness norm by becoming the star of woodworking period—a dubious distinction, though one that had the virtue of filling time. I spent an hour each day meticulously carving, sanding, and shellacking a piece of wood I had fashioned into a cutting board meant to look like Wilbur, the pig in *Charlotte's Web*. While most of the other boys were content to sit around and do nothing during woodworking except make faces behind the back of the bored counselor saddled with arts and crafts, I labored on, perfecting a skill that even I could tell would be of scant future use in suburban Maryland.

Back in the apartment each night, I begged Mom to let that day be the last at camp. Each night she refused. In time, I tuned out the whole experience—and was anesthetized further by the compounding exhaustion of my insomnia. Now I almost never fell asleep at bedtime, and the later sunsets of summer only increased my nightly panic. By the time darkness descended, I was drenched with the intermingled sweats of heat and anxiety. I was terrified by my inability to calm my mind, which teemed with unruly thoughts of camp, parents, and that persistent, novel urge I hadn't yet learned to call sex.

When the single-digit countdown of Inverness's final few days arrived, so did a giddiness that ascended into ecstasy after Mom announced a trip that would fill the pause between the end of camp and the start of fourth grade just after Labor Day. On the last weekend of August, she, Polly, and I would go by car for a three-night vacation that would conclude with our first visit to New York—a trip to culminate in seeing a Broadway show on Broadway itself.

As Mom recited the itinerary, I couldn't remember when I had felt such unequivocal joy. I wondered if I had *ever* been so happy. Every hour at Inverness was now a milestone on the way to the experience I craved above all others. On the last day of camp, I was so buoyant that my hurt and anger about the weeks there were forgotten, at least for an afternoon. The trip to New York and the prospect of a Broadway show were secrets that made me, for once, more powerful than all of my tormentors. While I could never be normal—while I would always be seen as an inferior species of child in a mutant breed of family—for the first time I entertained the fantasy that I might extract some glittering consolation prize for being different and alone.

CHAPTER 4

Jubilant as I felt, I still could not get to sleep the night before our departure. Over and over in my head I replayed the songs from the record of the Broadway show Mom said we were going to see, trying not merely to imagine the actors onstage but to anticipate the ritual of going to a theater in New York. I knew that our Broadway visit was not until the third and last night of the trip—only three days away, and yet, to me, still an eternity.

As the hours passed, as my mind refused to stop playing and then replaying the familiar tunes of *Bells Are Ringing*, I started, once again, to panic. But this time the source of my unrest was not the usual mixture of fear, loneliness, and self-pity. I had hit a bleaker bottom. Though my fondest wish was coming true—or my second fondest wish, after an end to my parents' divorce—it was not the miraculous tonic I'd always assumed it would be. Far from ending my nightly terrors, the trip to Broadway was, if anything, exacerbating them.

I climbed down from bed, reeling from my thoughts, and walked into Mom's darkened room.

"I'm trying, Mom," I wailed in her direction, "but I just can't get to sleep!"

"What?" she said, turning on her bedside light, suddenly wide awake, her manner unusually firm. "Try harder!"

"I can't!"

Mom was unyielding: "If you don't get into bed right now, I'm canceling the trip!" I knew that the threat was empty—Mom was never big on punishment, which she looked down upon as a brutish alternative to reasoning calmly with children—and I thought she might laugh, as she sometimes did after such a meaningless warning. But when she didn't, I cried, and was soon heaving with sobs, unable to see beyond this moment, let alone all the way to New York. I told Mom that if she canceled the trip, I would run away forever. I would run away to Dad's house, and if I couldn't find it, I wouldn't care where I ended up. I would die. I would kill myself, I said, shocked at the vehemence of my own empty threat.

"I'm going to give you one more chance," Mom said, modulating her tone again, getting up to walk me back to bed. "You have to start by calming down. Think of New York and how wonderful it will be."

Up in my bunk, the warring impulses of anticipation and fear did not recede. It was dawn before I passed out, only to be awakened soon thereafter for the ride north.

—

The Pennsylvania Dutch country was our first destination. As we sped along the highway through the bleached August sunlight, Mom told us stories from history when she wasn't consulting her AAA route map. She explained that we were going to a community where the people wore exotic costumes, practiced a strict religion, and didn't like to have their pictures taken. "They're different from us," she said, speaking in her teacher's voice, "and we must respect them. They may know something we don't."

Near Lancaster, Pennsylvania, we had lunch at a restaurant where we saw what Mom was talking about. The women who served us wore long, dark dresses and spoke in friendly but cheerless cadences that were foreign to our ears. We sat at a "family table" with other families, each of whom, to my chagrin, had two parents, rendering our single-parent family all the more brazenly anomalous.

We visited a nearby farm and a small town until night approached, then checked into a hotel in an area I immediately recognized, with glee, as a "downtown," complete with a movie theater that Mom said she'd take us to.

The flashing marquee lights beckoned as romantically as any on F Street in Washington. Like the Capitol, Palace, and Columbia at home, it welcomed us that night with the familiar name Loew's. As we entered the vacant lobby, Mom said, "I always liked sitting in the balcony at the movies when I was your age" — and we followed her upstairs, our feet sinking into the thick patterned carpet on the wide, shadowy staircase. The small popcorn stand, adrift on the landing identified as the "loge," was deserted. The chill of air-conditioning, a luxury we experienced only in movie theaters and stores, added to the cathedral-like aura of mystery and wonder.

Inside the auditorium, where the lights were already as dim as my nightlight at home, a black-and-white newsreel was going through its busy paces. We took seats in the balcony's front row, a bit to the right, so that as I swiveled to my left I took in a broad panorama that included the vast gilded ceiling as well as the eye-stretching CinemaScope screen. Leaning forward, I gaped at the plush sea of seats, most of them empty, stretching out in the velvet darkness below me.

When the movie itself started, it was of a type I'd never seen — a horror movie, Mom had explained. It was, she reassured us, *supposed* to be scary. It told the story of a man who kept shrinking and shrinking until he was in jeopardy of being crushed by every other living thing in the universe.

Polly seemed unaffected by this tale, but I wasn't. As the man became smaller and smaller on the gargantuan screen, my worry about his fate brought back that suffocating sensation I recognized from my daily fear of the unknown.

After the movie, as we walked back to the hotel, I clutched Mom as tightly as I could, hiding in her skirt. She tried to make light of *The Incredible Shrinking Man*, patiently explaining how they made the man shrink with camera tricks and how easy it was to see that the movie was a fake. Though I understood that, I could still feel fear galloping out of control inside me.

In our hotel room, I asked Mom if she could keep the light on when we went to sleep.

"Of course," she said cheerily.

"Will you stay awake until I fall asleep?"

"Of course."

Polly was already dozing—or, as she liked to put it, "just taking a nap." I climbed inside the cool white sheets of my bed, the first hotel bed I'd been in.

"Would you like to hear a story?" Mom asked, perching beside me. My mood changed at once. I loved it when my parents told stories, but I hadn't heard one since their separation. The stories Dad had spun in Somerset, of college and jazz and the war, were a frayed and distant memory.

"A story about our family?" I asked.

Mom thought a second, maybe to avoid the potential traps of a trick question, then went on: "Did you know that long before you were born, before *I* was born, your grandfather was in the circus?"

"Pop-Pop Nat?"

Mom nodded. "Back when his family was very, very poor, and he had six brothers and sisters. They didn't have enough money to buy food."

"Really?" Starvation, I thought, was something that happened only to characters in books or on TV.

"They were really poor. Pop-Pop's father died when he was six. His mom was a peddler—she sold things on the street—and couldn't speak English. Pop-Pop and two of his brothers had to move into an orphanage to save their mother money. He lived there six years. Remember Uncle Izzy in Miami? He was one of the brothers. One day, Pop-Pop couldn't stand it anymore. He ran away and joined the circus."

"How old was he?"

"Fourteen. He'd played the cornet in the orphanage band. He got a job in the Ringling Brothers circus and went up and down the country in a train with all the circus performers, from New York to Florida and then all the way up to Maine and Canada, playing with the circus band in every town."

"Pop-Pop never told me that."

"My father doesn't like to talk about himself."

"Then what?"

"After two years, he had saved enough money to return home and help his mother get his two brothers out of the orphanage."

"And then?"

"A few years later, he married my mother, and then Frances and I were born."

"That's when you lived in New York, right?"

"Yes, Pop-Pop lived in New York the whole time. He was born in New York—not Brooklyn, but Manhattan."

"What's Manhattan?" I remembered the word, though not its meaning, from a record Dad had once played by his favorite singer, Ella Fitzgerald.

"Manhattan is where we're going."

"That's where Broadway is?"

"Yes."

I still didn't understand. "Why didn't Pop-Pop stay in the circus?" I asked. I could not imagine wanting to come home from a show once you were lucky enough to be part of one. The thought of a young Pop-Pop running away blurred with that of the girl who couldn't wait to run away with an "advance man" in *Carousel*.

"Sometimes I wondered, too," Mom said. "What would be more fun than working in a circus? But he was very young, you have to remember, and he always said that it was time for him to grow up."

"Mom, I'm still scared by the Shrinking Man."

"It was the only movie in Lancaster—what did I know?" she said, making a joke of it. "I didn't know what it was going to be about. So sue me. It was only a movie."

Only a movie? To me there was no such thing as *only* a movie. A movie was a concentrated form of life, as far as I was concerned, not a pale facsimile that could be easily dismissed. Movies, books, TV shows, the few plays I'd seen, the pictures Mom and I had stood before at the museum—once they entered my mind they became part of its permanent furniture, never to be packed up in boxes and moved out.

"Honey, try to relax," Mom said in a quieter voice. She stroked my back through the cotton of my summer pajamas, leaning over and kissing me on the cheek. The window was open and I could feel a breeze. With the light still showering down on my closed eyelids from a smoky glass fixture, I fell into a dreamless sleep.

New York, I learned two mornings later, could be reached only through an underwater tunnel of a length I'd never imagined, let alone seen. The mesmerizing monotony of the tunnel's walls was soon relieved—and my anticipation spiked even more—by a painted demarcation line midway through denoting the end of New Jersey and the beginning of New York. Once the tunnel disgorged us into the city, my eyes were scarcely big enough to take in the imperially tall buildings; in Washington, no building except the Washington Monument could be more than a dozen stories high, or it might sink into the swamp. And I wasn't prepared, either, for the ceaseless clogged stream of chrome and color and noise that was New York traffic. On the sidewalks, hordes of people walked with a speed and animation also unknown in Washington, where crowds were rare and the leisurely cadences Southern. Nor had I ever seen so many shops and restaurants and department stores, all outfitted with elegant signs in different typefaces and colors. I wanted Mom to take us on an Adventure through every one of them.

"There's not a lot of time," Mom said as we reached our hotel, another tall building with an elevator proclaiming more than thirty floors. From the window in our room more than halfway up we could hear the far-off din of bleating car horns; the room itself, with its starchy beds, dark carpet, and blank walls, was alien territory, with a formality I recognized from the apartments characters lived in when they lived in New York on TV. The hotel had the same name, Warwick, as the street we first lived on in Somerset.

Mom seemed right at home in New York; the uncertainty of the Florida trip never resurfaced in her face. Though she didn't really know her way around the city, nothing fazed her. She seemed possessed by a confidence that warded off her usual fretfulness. It never occurred to me that life had somehow changed for the better for Mom, if not for Polly and me, since the separation. Whatever the source of her new happiness, it was unfolding at some veiled periphery beyond my field of vision.

But I could feel her self-assurance now. Taking Polly and me by the hands, Mom walked us to Broadway with a purposeful stride so unlike her tentative driving on our rounds back home in Silver Spring. Now and then she stopped and told us to look skyward, where not even the blazing Au-

gust sun could dim the blinking spectrum of neon. One sign atop a building featured an imitation waterfall to advertise Pepsi-Cola; another blew
out smoke rings to advertise Camel cigarettes. On every corner was a billboard heralding a Broadway show with pictures and lettering I recognized
from my records at home: The drawing of God dangling a man and a
woman with strings like a puppet master meant *My Fair Lady*.

Mom took us into an alley that she said was famous: Shubert Alley. In a
row on one side was poster after poster advertising the countless plays on
Broadway, most of them unfamiliar to me, each more extravagant in its
promise than the last. At the end of the alley we walked into the lobby of a
theater—the Shubert Theatre—and Mom lined up in front of a window to
pick up our tickets for *Bells Are Ringing*.

From there it was to the Automat she'd told us so much about. Polly and
I each took a dollar to a woman sitting in what looked like a ticket booth
in the center of the enormous room; the woman gave us each twenty nickels. Then we took cafeteria trays like those in school and picked out our
lunch from behind glass doors that popped open with startling jolts after
we deposited our coins. Behind the windows and the food we could see an
army of men and women in white uniforms putting new food in each glass
cell as soon as it had been emptied by a customer. Was this not a theater,
with its own transparent front curtain, offstage cast, ever-changing scenery,
and appreciative audience? Broadway was a place, it seemed, where you
didn't have to go into a theater to see a show.

A nap was called for after that, but there was no way to sleep. Mom,
Polly, and I lay on our beds in the dark hotel room. I listened intently to
the noise from the streets below, taking comfort from the muted cacophony. It was a sound like the laughing audience on TV, assuring me that
there were people out there, thousands of happy people, as happy as they
could be because they were in New York, as happy as they could be because they could go to a show. I would, at long last, meet them in the theater tonight.

We had a reservation for dinner—you had to make a reservation by
phoning in advance because it was a "fancy" restaurant, Mom explained.
The place was called Dinty Moore's, and it was two blocks from the Shubert Theatre. When we stepped inside, the colors and sights that greeted

us were as exotic as everything else I'd seen in my few hours in the city. The warm glow of brass gleamed from every nook; a long wooden bar with bottles and gold spigots aligned behind it ran the length of a wall. Our table was covered with a crisp white cloth that was both soft and hard to the touch. The waiter wore a shiny black suit that reflected the glitter all around him, a white shirt as starchy as our tablecloth, and a bow tie. He asked us, Polly and me included, lots of questions; in my limited Washington experience, I had known only sullen, impersonal waitresses in aproned maids' uniforms.

Mom told us we could order anything we wanted but explained that there were certain dishes at Dinty Moore's that were special—like "chopped steak," which was a hamburger without a bun—because no one else made them as well.

Looking up to survey the diners around me, I was astonished to find a face from television: Jack Benny, whose show was usually on so late that I knew him mainly as one of those voices that kept me company by traveling through the slit under my bedroom door. Mom and Polly were surprised to see him, too. Mom encouraged me to go over and ask for his autograph, the way I had once done at Griffith Stadium when we arrived early for a game and were able to get the attention of our favorite home-run-hitting Senator, Roy Sievers, as he lolled around waiting for his turn at batting practice. Shy as I was with strangers, I slipped out of my seat, a piece of paper from Mom's purse in hand, and asked Mr. Benny for his autograph. Up close, he looked larger than he did on TV, and he smelled of perfume. He smiled, shook my hand, and asked me where I was from, then removed a ballpoint pen from his jacket pocket and wrote out his signature. Returning to our table, I felt elated. I liked having Jack Benny's autograph, but more than that I was amazed at my new ability to initiate a conversation with a stranger. A bravery I didn't have in Rosemary Hills or at Inverness I suddenly possessed in New York.

As we walked to the theater after dinner, I was even more mesmerized by the lights than I had been that afternoon. It wasn't quite dark; a burnt-orange light bathed the theaters all around me, imbuing them with a presence that was monumental even by Washington standards. Above each was a sign almost too high to read, with the name of the play and its stars spelled out in lightbulbs. Some of the letters were slightly crooked, as if to testify to the existence of the human hands that put them up there. Who had that job?

When we arrived at the Shubert Theatre, the lobby was bustling. It wasn't the same as *Damn Yankees* in Washington. This lobby was smaller; the crowd was stepping faster, pushing harder. Somehow we made our way, Polly and I both clutching Mom, and landed in our seats with the help of a small woman usher. It took forever for the lights to dim; finally a conductor appeared, his head picked out by a small spotlight just as I remembered, to start the overture.

The overture began with the sound of bells — phone bells — tinkling, and they had an alarm-clock immediacy that made the hi-fi sound of our *Bells Are Ringing* record at home seem meek. When the overture ended, again with the lights throughout the theater dimming to black, creating almost unbearable anticipation, the curtain rose to reveal the last thing I expected: another curtain! It was brighter and more colorful than the theater's curtain and was part of a TV commercial for the telephone answering service where the show's heroine worked as an operator.

I had never heard of an answering service except in *Bells Are Ringing*. It had to be the kind of company that existed only in New York, where people were out having fun all the time, too much fun to sit around at home, answering their phones. *Bells Are Ringing* was like another window on New York, of which we had seen so much and still so little. Its story took place all over the city — in a subway car packed with dancing and singing New Yorkers and in a fancy restaurant and on a beautiful street with houses that had no front yards but did have "penthouses." When the people in *Bells Are Ringing* weren't on the subway, they were zooming up skyscrapers in elevators or pushing through traffic in fast taxicabs. They were staying out all night at parties where everyone knew everyone else and everyone had seen every play on Broadway and knew all the actors.

But part of the *Bells Are Ringing* story was the same as *The Most Happy Fella* and *Damn Yankees*: A woman and a man fall in love, and it takes the whole musical for them to realize that they really love each other — just in time (as one song put it) to get married.

In this show, though, the woman was no Lola. She did not appear in her underwear. She was a slave to her job, with little time to herself. She loved children. She was funny, a little lonely, soft-spoken except when she got in a giggling mood, pretty but not pretty in a way that suited my nighttime rendezvous. Unlike Lola, this woman reminded me of Mom.

The actress who played this part drew me to her with her warmth and sense of humor, not with how she looked. She was Mom with most of the sadness washed out, Mom living back in New York, Mom with a happy ending. I knew her name, Judy Holliday, because she was one of Mom's favorite actresses; we'd gone together to see a funny movie called *The Solid Gold Cadillac* in which she outwitted all the grumpy men in a corporation and ended up becoming the new boss. Mom and Judy Holliday didn't look anything alike, really; for one thing, Mom wasn't blond. And even at her funniest, Mom didn't make me laugh so hard. Judy Holliday was funny whether she was dancing or talking or singing or just standing there.

At intermission, Polly and I went to look at the orchestra in its pit, but this time, older and bigger, we didn't have to be picked up to be able to spy on the musicians. I tried to imagine what it would be like to play in this orchestra, to work in a Broadway theater every night, to be at every performance of *Bells Are Ringing*. I couldn't think of a happier life.

Act 2 brought Mom's favorite song, the one she sang along with whenever I played the record at home. Judy Holliday sat on a couch at the very front of the stage, practically in our laps, to sing it now. The whole stage was dark except for a light picking out her face. I had never before thought about what the song was saying:

> *The party's over—*
> *It's time to call it a day—*

The party's over. Tomorrow we would be back in Washington. *Bells Are Ringing* was our last night away from home.

> *No matter how you pretend*
> *You knew it would end this way.*

At one point Judy Holliday didn't sing the words, but just hummed, with a voice of resignation, of exhaustion, like Mom's when she came home late from teaching. *La-da-da-da-dee-da, la-da-da-da-da.* Then the light on her started to fade, and all the other actors in the play, somewhere in the shadows behind her, finished the song.

> *Now you must wake up—*
> *All dreams must end. . . .*

And all too soon, the show had ended. After the curtain calls, we stayed in our seats to hear the orchestra play the songs again. Some grown-ups stared or pointed at us as they left—we were the only children in the theater, it seemed, on this Saturday night in late August. When the orchestra stopped playing, there was a deathly silence in the nearly empty but still bright auditorium. Then Mom, holding our hands tight, led us out, back into the glowing darkness of Shubert Alley. A few dozen people were standing there, right outside the theater, not yet leaving.

Mom pointed to a sign behind them: STAGE DOOR. She explained that the actors, including Judy Holliday, would soon be coming out that door, which opened onto the stage and the rooms where the actors changed into their costumes. Mom let us stay and watch; though Polly was sleepy, the thought of extending the night, the show, was all I wanted.

An old man with a crooked gait walked from the stage door in our direction. He said hello to Mom and, gesturing toward me and Polly, asked, "Would you and your children like to meet Miss Holliday?" After marveling at our ability to stay up so late, he said he would talk to Miss Holliday and come back for us.

In the minutes that followed, I couldn't focus on what the man had said, or what it might mean to go inside the stage door. More than the promised entry, I was enjoying the wait—just standing outside the theater late at night with Mom to protect me and with all of New York and its theaters around me. When the man emerged again and said that he was very, very sorry but Miss Holliday could not see anyone that night after all, I was disappointed but not crushed. I already had in my head more of her lonely eyes and hopeful voice, of the night's sights and music and laughter, of all of New York, than I could hold there.

For now, I was happy to stand in an alley next to a theater, to stand with the crowd that went to shows on Broadway. Looking up, looking up to the Shubert Theatre sign with its bulbs spelling out Judy Holliday's name, looking up as high as I could above all of New York's tall buildings, I felt that the night itself, which had terrorized me for so long, was just where I was meant to be.

CHAPTER 5

What I didn't realize that night in New York was that my life had jumped off its tracks yet again, without warning, to race down still another new, unexpected, and possibly perilous path.

I didn't realize that *Bells Are Ringing* would flip an important page, from which there was no turning back, in the calendar by which I measured time. As other kids might calibrate childhood by a progression of birthdays, report cards, athletic trophies, and family celebrations, I was now destined to trace my childhood almost exclusively through an accelerating progression of plays, good and bad, that would captivate and kidnap me in circumstances both mundane and dramatic, in different cities, in the company of a multitude of audiences. In Shubert Alley that night, I had unwittingly reached the threshold of an entire landscape of alleys that would lead to a world of theaters, each a house packed with strangers both generous and mean, shabby and grand. It was to be a life full of the transitory moments, double-edged with ecstasy and loss, that I had already come to think of as theater. And following the example of Mom and her scrapbook, I would try to memorialize this life as it passed, hoping to freeze time and hold each moment before it fled. I was fated to preserve the trash most other people throw away without a second thought: dog-eared programs, fast-yellowing newspaper photos, and rainbows of confetti-colored ticket stubs.

The other momentous development I had yet to discern that night in New York was the intrusion of the unseen hand of the puppeteer who was manipulating Mom, me, and Polly as surely as God was controlling the puppets of Henry Higgins and Eliza Doolittle on the *My Fair Lady* billboard hovering over Broadway. That hand belonged to Joel, who had planned this trip, tickets for the Shubert Theatre included—and who, I would learn long after I entered adulthood, had also masterminded the sudden rescue of our plane tickets to Miami at National Airport some twenty months before. He was the missing piece in the puzzle of Mom's unexpected confidence while in New York.

Joel, we learned from Mom upon return to Washington, was soon to become Mom's husband—which meant, she said with a smile dented by apprehension, "He'll be your stepfather."

Stepfather? We knew of a stepmother from "Cinderella," and it was scarcely an auspicious omen. Could a stepfather be any better?

We had met Joel only one other time after Storybook Kingdom, when he had taken us to dinner in the restaurant at his Washington apartment house. John and Susan had come, too, from their mother's house, for Joel and their mother were also divorced—the first other divorced family Polly and I had met. Every waitress in the place knew Joel and greeted him as "Dr. Fisher," chuckling along as he made a substitution in every order so that each of us could get exactly the dishes we wanted without it costing more. Mom laughed a lot that night, always looking in our direction as if to seek our approval and ask, Isn't this the funniest thing you've ever seen? Joel was more loud than funny, I thought, but Mom's eyes sparkled as they rarely had. If she was this happy, shouldn't we be happy, too? Her merriment did not diminish as Joel pounded geysers of ketchup over his entire plate, not always hitting the target. As he ate, he lobbed solicitous questions at Polly and me nonstop, paying no notice to the sauce and pieces of meat that dribbled out of his mouth, onto his lips and chin, and from that temporary holding ground onto his tie, jacket, and shirt. Mom didn't mind it either when Joel questioned every item on the bill, or when he suddenly erupted at our nice waitress once she brought over a menu to prove that Sue's chocolate ice cream really did cost thirty-five cents, not twenty-five.

The dinner, like the visit to Storybook Kingdom, seemed at the time like a passing curiosity. It never occurred to me that a man I'd met only twice could be anyone other than just one of Mom's grown-up friends—her one divorced friend, the one with children "your age," the one who told a lot of jokes that Mom alone seemed to find priceless. It never occurred to me or Polly that Joel might marry Mom—that anyone would—and become our stepfather.

Now, weeks after our trip to New York, when Mom did hand us this piece of information, that sinking sensation of falling from a great height returned as acutely as ever before. This feeling was, in a way, my childhood pet—more so than our dog, Patty, was—and now it snarled and bit. I felt myself turn red—a flush deeper than anger alone could have produced. Instead of sorting out the details of the new existence Mom had announced—and how could I, since I didn't know any of the details?—I saw only a heavy, cloudy blankness ahead of me. With an intuitive and precocious theatricality that belied my actual, limited experience of the theater, I decided once more that my life was over.

Dad was never coming back. The divorce was permanent. A strange man was moving into our home. Whatever little knowledge I had gleaned about the unmentionable subject of divorce by that point, I had never actually considered the possibility that a parent could get married again, to someone else. I had never heard of any such example, anywhere. Even TV's Bachelor Father never found a new wife. If at first the news of Mom's remarriage left me dumbstruck, it felled me once it sank in, sending me to my bunk bed scheming how I might escape.

Eventually, Mom came in to comfort me. As soon as I saw her, I boiled over into tears and turned away in anger.

She stroked my back, turned me toward her, and wiped the tears off my cheeks. She explained that nothing would really change, that I would like Joel as much as she did once I got to know him well, and that we'd all have a lot of fun.

Did Dad know what was happening?

Yes, of course.

I wondered why he hadn't said anything.

The first time I saw Dad after that and could verify Mom's version of the latest twist in our lives was the following Wednesday, our regular dinner date. As usual, we went to his parents' apartment. But I was already learning that nothing, not a dinner out, not the book I was reading, not the new year starting at school, not a Broadway record, could distract me from the weight of Mom's news. The confusion and shock didn't abate at all with the passing of hours or days or with any change of scene.

As the odor of mothballs fought the aroma of pot roast to a standoff, I found it hard to focus on what anyone was saying or doing—especially since everyone, Dad included, was working with grim determination and no little skill to act as if nothing had changed at all or ever would. Grandma Rose, once more stone deaf, did at least notice my dark mien; she looked downcast herself as she directed the maid, Irene, to dish out the vegetables. Not that Grandma said anything outright; she acknowledged the news only in her heavy eyelids and in the diminished volume and animation of her voice. After dinner she retreated into her mysterious private realm of creativity—the obsessive knitting of large, beautiful afghans of ornate design for which she would ultimately receive patronizing compliments from the friends and family members on whom she bestowed them after months of mute labor.

Grandpa Herbert was entirely unaffected, perhaps incognizant, of recent events; he plunged into his usual evening recitation of misplaced store receipts, overdue bills, and insufferable customer peccadilloes, and Dad kept up his side of that conversation, too. I kept fantasizing that Irene might break the silence on the only topic I cared about. Though almost as small as I was, she was someone I looked up to: She often seemed to be winking conspiratorially at the antics of "Mr. Herbert" or "Mr. Frank" or even me, "Mr. Frank Junior." But she had never married and had no family of her own, so maybe she didn't understand divorce, I decided. She said nothing now; her emotions, if any, had gone into hiding behind her thick horn-rimmed spectacles and exaggerated repertoire of bowing and scraping. Her voice, always loud to compensate for Grandma's poor hearing, ascended to a nearly screaming pitch as she ran through her usual litany of questions: "Who wants more creamed spinach? Where did that serving spoon go? Mrs. Rich, do you want me to serve the Sanka now?"

I wondered if I was crazy, and how it could be that grown-ups never seemed to notice events I regarded as cataclysmic. Was I imagining or exaggerating what had happened?

Once we were in the car and driving back to Rosemary Hills, Dad's real mood became clear. He was morose and hurt; I could tell from his downcast eyes, not unlike his mother's. I didn't know whether to pity him or be angry: If Dad hadn't moved out to begin with, Joel wouldn't now be taking his place.

Dad had little specific to say, though; he was locked away in gloom, as remote as if he were speaking from behind a pane of glass. It will all work out fine, he said, in the same even-toned, slightly put-upon voice with which he discussed business with Grandpa. He knew Joel, he said, letting the thought hang there, noncommittally, without further elaboration. Repeating what Mom had told us, he said that he would always be our father, and that that would never change, no matter what.

What he didn't say was that every other coordinate of my life and Polly's would change almost immediately. Within days, Mom told us that we would be moving once more—not so far that we would have to change schools again, she reassured us, but to a bigger apartment in Rosemary Hills. That weekend we went to see it—with Joel joining us. It was only a few blocks away, in another short redbrick building, but unlike our current home, it had two stories—the first home we'd ever had with two stories. Polly and I would still be sharing a room, but it was a bigger room. There was an even bigger bedroom for Mom and Joel, and another room for Joel's "home office"—not to be confused with Joel's "office office" downtown, where he was a lawyer.

A lawyer? I thought he was *Dr.* Fisher.

"I always say I'm Dr. Fisher when I'm going to a restaurant," Joel explained, with one of his very broad grins and the expansive tone of a mastermind letting a few privileged underlings in on the secret of an ingenious conspiracy. "It's something you need to know in life: Doctors are always treated like kings, even when they're schmucks."

Our sole knowledge of lawyers came from *Perry Mason*—a fact Joel seemed instinctively to grasp, since he then likened himself to that familiar TV courtroom advocate, who wowed us each week with his uncanny talent for getting his client off the hook in the final two minutes of each

episode. But as Mom elaborated later, Joel was a different kind of lawyer—
no murderers, no trials, but lots of free travel that would allow us to see the
entire world. Most of his clients were airlines that needed government approval for their routes. Another part of Joel's job was to help convince
Americans that the exotic-looking foreigners of his biggest client, Air India,
could pilot planes safely, a humanitarian mission that was sabotaged on a
dark day some months later when the photo of an Air India jet that had
crashed in the Himalayas turned up on the cover of *Life*.

In our tour of the new apartment, Joel was as loud and elaborate of gesture as during our two previous encounters—but he struck a new note of
possessiveness about Mom, Polly, and me. It was an unexpected sensation
to hear the intimacy with which Joel constantly invoked Mom's name—
"Helene, come here!" "Did you see this, Helene?"—and to hear him refer
to her when speaking to Polly and me as "your mother." Which made Joel
. . . *what?*

"You can call me anything you want to, but I suggest *Joel!*" he said.
" 'Stepfather' is a *goddamnawful* word, don't you agree?" He roared—his
deep laugh sounded like (and usually trailed off into) a hacking cough—
as if we were all enjoying some prank.

The wedding, it turned out, was just weeks away. It would not be a big
wedding like those we saw in the movies, Mom said—her way of telling
Polly and me that we would not be going to it. A judge would perform the
ceremony in a downtown office at eleven in the morning on a school day
in late November. The wedding would be very brief, like a business ap-
pointment, and so would the honeymoon, because we had to move right
away into the new apartment. Mom had hired a new, boisterous, nineteen-
year-old maid, Willie Mae, to look after Polly and me when she was gone.

My school days were long. When Mrs. Young, my new fourth-grade
teacher, offered a Spanish class after three o'clock dismissal to any students
who were interested, I signed up, not because Mom told me I should—she
said it was important to learn another language for when I traveled—but
because I wanted to spend as much time as I could with Mrs. Young. She
had what I recognized as a New York accent, and her eyes crinkled as if she
was always about to smile, even when she wasn't. Mom was never around
in the afternoons—she was still teaching and was occupied with errands
after that—so it didn't matter when I arrived home.

One afternoon, when Spanish was over, Mrs. Young asked if I would stay behind. It turned out that she knew somehow that Mom was getting married; as she straightened piles of paper on her desk, she asked me how I felt about it. She was the only person outside my family who knew anything about it, as far as I knew, and the first person to ask my opinion on her own, without prompting. I started to talk, sitting in a chair facing her. I'm worried, I said. Joel is a lawyer, I explained. I don't know him well. We're going to move soon. I don't know what's going to happen after that.

The more I talked, the more I tried to present what information I had as calmly and objectively as possible, the harder I had to try to keep from crying. I had never cried about any of this outside my own home, and I didn't want to start crying now. It was too humiliating, like peeing in your pants. It was not what an exemplary student was supposed to do, and I was nothing if not a good student, always ready with the right answer or a smart remark or a joke in class, still hoping that my academic success would be the glue to mend my parents' ruptured marriage. But as I talked about Mom marrying Joel, a drop fell out of one eye and ran down my cheek, and then another. I was ashamed. Mrs. Young said nothing but handed me a Kleenex from her desk.

She looked at me with her big brown eyes, her red lips frozen in mid-expression—not smiling or frowning but almost quivering (or so it struck me) at some boundary in between, as if she didn't want to reveal her own feelings, whatever they were, and was trying to figure out what attitude might be appropriate.

"There is nothing to worry about," she said finally. "Your mother loves you very much." Then Mrs. Young told me that I should feel free to hang around after school; there were always chores, like washing the black-boards, that I could help with. And, she said, it might be fun to use that time to do a project. I could write some more stories like we'd already been doing in class. I liked books, so why not write one?

It was hard to imagine I could write a story that long—a book as long as *Charlotte's Web*.

Mrs. Young said, Yes, of course you can.

I called the book *A World All My Own*. I decided I was writing it for Mrs. Young. I wrote it on lined composition paper in my new, large, and ungainly script, illustrating it with little pictures I drew in crayon. Each day I wrote a new chapter of five or six sentences.

My book told of a boy who lived all alone and was very happy in a world he created out of a big box. Around the cardboard box were some pretty flowers, drawn with all the brightest, most exotic colors in his Crayola set. Sometimes the boy would have Adventures, exciting Adventures, but they would always be in or near the box. There were no other characters.

Mrs. Young said she loved the book; I immediately wondered if that meant she loved me. She asked me to read it aloud to the class, and I tried to guess how my friends would react. To read my story to them would be like being an actor performing in a theater.

I loved Mrs. Young; that much was certain. At night, as I tried to fall asleep, I thought about her, though keeping her fully dressed, before I thought about Lola and the other woman with red hair and freckle-sprinkled breasts that Jeffrey Harwood had showed us from the stack of *Playboy* magazines he'd found in his father's closet. I wondered if Mrs. Young was missing me. I wondered who Mr. Young was, and whether he would love me as much as Mrs. Young did. I thought about running away from Rosemary Hills and finding the Youngs' house and begging to sleep there, if only I could sleep. But what if they had children of their own?

These thoughts grew and grew until the day of the wedding arrived. It was the day before Thanksgiving and, in a way, a day like any other. I went off to school and was sitting in class as usual. As the time of the wedding approached, I looked up from my book—it was silent-reading time in Mrs. Young's classroom—and stared at the big clock on the wall, trying to will it to slow down.

But I failed. I failed so miserably, I hated myself. The sight of the minute hand smacking the 12 was overpowering; the clock grew in size like an apparition out of *Alice in Wonderland*; the click, which usually you had to listen carefully to hear, boomed in my ears like Big Ben just before Peter flew in the Darlings' open window in *Peter Pan*.

Then it was one minute after 11, and Mom was married again, just like that, in a scene I couldn't quite picture in a downtown office I had never seen. I couldn't believe that I had been powerless to stop it, and that no one else in the room, no one else in the world, perhaps not even Mrs.

Young, either knew or cared. It was a short, pre-holiday school day, and at lunchtime, without my having a chance to talk to Mrs. Young, Polly and I were met by Grandma Lil, who took us to stay at her apartment. Mom and Joel were going on their weekend honeymoon to New York, where, Mom had told me that morning, they would see some Broadway shows — not just one, but two, maybe three. In one weekend? For one second — if only one — I'd forgotten about the wedding.

"Yes," Mom had said. "Joel loves the theater."

———

That, at least, was verifiable. When she and Joel returned, I was given *Playbills* from two shows so new that I hadn't heard of them. Two *Playbills* for each show, actually.

"Take mine, Frank," said Joel. "It never hurts to have an extra." I agreed. It didn't even bother me that his *Playbills*, unlike Mom's, were creased, covered with unidentifiable greasy stains, and torn at the corners as if a dog had been chewing on them.

We seemed to have two of everything now. Though not entirely un-packed, we had settled, more or less, into our new, spacious apartment. We had two TVs — one in the living room, one in Mom and Joel's bedroom — and two phone numbers. Only at my father's downtown store had I seen such an invention: A row of buttons beneath the dial lit up and blinked every time the phone rang, which was often. Joel did most of his business on the phone. He often did it in his and Mom's new king size bed, sprawled in a white undershirt and baggy boxer shorts while simultane-ously watching television, eating ice cream out of a carton, and rifling through the pages of a huge book that looked like a phone directory but ac-tually listed, in the tiniest print, the schedules of every airplane in the world.

Joel did not like it when the phone rang and it was not for him. His voice bellowed fearsomely through the apartment when he yelled, "He-lene, it's for you!" — as if Mom had done something wrong. But Mom didn't mind.

With Joel in the house, and with the TV on all the time in one room or the other or both, I no longer had to worry about being shut up in complete darkness when I went to bed. If Mom and Joel went out at night—as they did almost daily, even if Mom was exhausted from school—Willie Mae stayed with us, and she liked to watch TV, too. She also let us cheat on our bedtimes, winking and laughing and saying she'd get in trouble for doing so, though she never did. When I did finally go to bed, it was, for the first time I could remember, less of a struggle to fall asleep.

Only two weeks after the wedding, as Christmas vacation was about to begin, Mom and Joel told us that they were going away again—on a second honeymoon, this time far away, to London and Paris and Israel.

"There are Broadway shows in London, too," Joel said, having figured out that injecting the theater into a conversation was a surefire way to distract me.

I hoped that Polly and I would stay with Dad while Mom and Joel were away, but he was going away for much of the holidays himself, on a long business trip to New York. Instead, we'd stay at home with Willie Mae, who would sometimes be visited by her husband, Billy, a bearish, soft-spoken man who worked in a gas station downtown, or past downtown, or in whatever unspoken, unvisited, unmentioned Washington neighborhood it was that black people lived.

"I don't want you to go," I told Mom when we had a rare moment alone one afternoon.

She looked at me nervously, as if she was having second thoughts about the trip. But if she was, they didn't last long.

"You'll have a lot of fun with Polly and your friends," she said. "Willie's going to take you on some surprise Adventures while we're gone, and I'll write every day."

I wasn't convinced. We were sitting on the living-room couch. I got up and started toward the record player. Mom was grateful for the opportunity to change the subject.

"You know, Joel likes the same records we do," she said.

"Uh-huh," I responded, unconvinced.

I flipped through the records, looking for one to play. I gravitated toward an old set of 78s, *South Pacific*.

"He really does," she continued. "Be patient. You just have to get to know him. That takes a while."

"How can I get to know him if you and he are away all the time?" I countered, surprising myself with the speed and sarcasm of my rejoinder. It was the kind of wisecrack Joel himself might make.

"We're not away all the time. We're just going away for two weeks." As if she didn't know two weeks was an eternity.

The record player clicked, and a record dropped onto the turntable. The chords of "Bali H'ai" at the beginning of the overture filled the room, sounding scratchy and antique now on a hi-fi record player.

Mom stood up, half-closed her eyes, and tossed her head back, as if she were at the beach and the music was washing over her like waves. The overture jumped from tune to tune, and finally Mom sang along:

> Who can explain it?
> Who can tell you why? . . .

Just as suddenly she broke out of her reverie and looked at me. I was half in the music, half out. She walked over and kissed my cheek.

"You have to trust me," she said. "Joel loves me, and he loves you and Polly. You'll see."

The last night before their departure did not augur well, however. Joel decided that as a treat we would eat out at a Chinese restaurant he particularly liked on Connecticut Avenue. The restaurant was exotic to my eyes, decorated with faded Oriental screens and drooping green plants; the Chinese waiters didn't speak much English. Joel said it was almost like the real Orient, where he had been many times.

We sat at the table with high expectations. Joel explained with corny humor every dish on the menu, each with a gibberish name like "Moo Goo," but Polly and I were skeptical of any meal that did not include recognizable meat or tuna fish or peanut butter. Our father didn't take us to foreign restaurants, and we resented our new stepfather's insistence that we "must try everything." It was a culinary notion as alien as ordering "à la carte" (French for "too expensive," according to Grandma Lil) at Woodmont Country Club.

Midway through his recitation, Joel signaled the waiter that he wanted us all to be brought water. A few minutes later, as he finished translating the last dishes on the menu, he stood up and left the table, pouncing across the restaurant to where our waiter was standing.

"I asked for *water*," Joel yelled in a voice so loud that it carried through the entire place.

The waiter looked shell-shocked. "Yessir, yessir, yessir," he muttered as he scrambled to grab a tin pitcher.

Joel beat him back to the table and sat in his chair fuming, his eyes squinting behind his glasses and focused nowhere in particular as the waiter poured water for each of us.

Before the waiter could finish, Joel yelled again: "You can take our orders *now!*"

The waiter set down the pitcher and retrieved an order pad and pencil from a side pocket of his soiled white jacket.

"Frank, what are you going to have?" Joel asked me, his voice still angry and impatient, as if *I* were the one who had neglected to bring the water.

"I'm not sure."

"Well, *look*, will you?" His voice lost a little of its edge as he turned to Mom: "What about you, Helene?"

"I thought a shrimp dish would be good."

"*Which* shrimp dish, honey?" Joel asked, hurling the question as if it were an accusation.

"I don't know," Mom answered, chastened. "Whatever you recommend."

As Joel started to go through the shrimp dishes, telling Mom the ingredients and virtues of each, the waiter drifted a few steps away to deliver a check to another table where a diner was waving at him. When he came back, seconds later, Joel forgot all about shrimp and screamed at him again: "Where the hell were you? You are either taking our order or you're not!"

The waiter stammered and stared at the floor. His shoulders sagged, and he suddenly looked old and tired.

Joel slammed down his large black menu. "Come on, Helene, *we're leaving!*" he shouted, pushing out of his chair so violently that it tipped over and clattered to the floor. He left it there.

I couldn't bring myself to look at Mom or Polly or the other diners. I was too embarrassed. What if there was someone I knew at the restaurant? I felt the earth might open and I would fall in right then.

In the car on the way home, Mom was silent and never turned to look at us in the backseat. We were silent, too. Joel concentrated on his driving, which was faster than I had ever seen before. Somehow we made it back to Rosemary Hills without further discussion of what had happened.

After a dinner of hastily assembled peanut-butter-and-jelly sandwiches, I knew there was no hope of getting to sleep. In bed, I thought as hard as I could of Lola's striptease in *Damn Yankees*. It was no use. I had convinced myself that when Mom walked out the door to go on her trip with Joel, she was never coming back.

I was so anxious that I had to climb out of bed. Tentatively I headed toward Joel and Mom's bedroom. This was the first time Joel would hear of my sleeping problem. I feared he'd get angrier still.

When I reached their room, the reassuring flicker of the TV radiated through the open door. I stepped inside, not knowing what to expect.

Mom turned on a bedside lamp right away.

"I can't sleep, Mom," I said, with little of the drama I might invoke normally, so as not to infuriate Joel.

Mom was reassuring, and to my surprise, Joel chimed in with gentle-sounding concern as well, the fireworks at dinner apparently already forgotten. Every time I tried to predict his behavior, it seemed, I guessed wrong.

"Frank," Mom said, "I have something that will help you sleep."

"What?"

"A pill."

"A pill? How big a pill?"

"Very small."

"Really?"

She got up, went into the adjoining bathroom, and came back with a glass of water and a bottle full of little white pills the same size as pink children's aspirin. She handed me one, and I swallowed it.

"That will help," Joel chimed in pleasantly.

"But you can't do this every night," said Mom. "It's only for special occasions like tonight, when I know you're upset because we're going away tomorrow."

I kissed Mom good night, said good night to Joel, and went back to bed. Within minutes I was asleep.

—

With Mom and Joel gone for two weeks—and with Dad gone, too, for the first week of their trip—I fell into a state of suspended animation, occasionally interrupted by brief, person-to-person phone calls from Mom in which she, Polly, Willie Mae, and I would in rapid-fire succession announce that everything was fine as static and operators' voices competed with us on the line. Mom had left behind bags full of Christmas presents, each elaborately wrapped, and given Willie Mae the go-ahead to indulge us. Most nights, Billy slept at our house too, sharing Mom and Joel's bed with Willie Mae. As a special treat, Patty was allowed to sleep in our room with Polly and me.

To supplement the phone calls, we wrote Mom and Joel, using the many blue air letters they'd left behind along with the dense itinerary typed by Joel's secretary. They'd been gone only two days when I wrote with a new fountain pen in blue-black ink, Mom's favorite:

Saturday, Dec. 20, 1958, 2:02 p.m.

Dear Mommy,

Billy drove us to the Hecht Company today. I bought a Cub Scout fountain pen and pencil for $1.95 with my money and Willie Mae bought me a kit you build buildings with. Grandma coming over tonight. Everything is fine. I don't know whether or not to go to clarinet lessons and if I don't it won't make any difference to my lessons because nobody in my clarinet group at school is going either. Todays a clear day, in the 20's, pretty sunny. My nose got runny this morning and still is, but I had no temp. I miss you very much.

Love, Frank

P.S. Patty has to be locked up when Billy's here, and you know how Patty follows you around, and I say it's because she likes you. Patty now cries day and night because she misses you.

More Love, Frank

Polly, still in second grade, printed her part of the letter in pencil, next to crayon drawings she made of "Mommy and Joel":

Dear Mother

    I love you. I miss you very much and so does Patty.

Love, Polly

Mom wrote us, too. One day she was in Tel Aviv, then she was in Paris, writing on feathery stationery from a hotel called the Royal Monceau: "Nearby there's a forest—the French call it a 'bois'—where they filmed some of 'Gigi.' " And then, a day earlier than the itinerary said, Mom and Joel were home, barging through the front door in a clatter of noise and expectation. The noise was Joel yelling at Billy to be sure to bring in each of the four airline bags that were in the car along with the half-dozen suitcases. The expectation came when Mom opened her arms wide to embrace me and Polly in turn; she was bursting with delight, laughing and pink-cheeked, and so were we. As would become a ritual in the many trips to follow, Mom had one whole bag just full of presents for Polly and me— books and pads and art supplies like those she bought us at home, though in foreign brands that made them more exotic, more "artistic." Surely a box of pastels from Geneva was superior to any that could be found in Washington, was more special than any art supplies possessed by children whose parents were *not* divorced. For the first time, Mom was seeing the actual landscapes that were in the pictures at the Phillips, and I wondered if these were the same paints the great painters used.

Once Joel stopped barking, he intruded on Mom's gift-giving with some gifts of his own: programs from plays he and Mom had seen in London. As I started to puzzle over them, he announced that on Saturday we were all going downtown to the National Theatre, the site of my initiation with *Damn Yankees*, to see a new Broadway show.

Now he had my full attention. What was it? Did we have the record?

No, Joel patiently explained. This was a Broadway show that hadn't been to New York yet, that was stopping in Washington for three weeks on its way to New York, like a kind of rehearsal. It was called a "tryout."

Would it be a good Broadway show, a *real* Broadway show?, I asked suspiciously.

We'd see, he said, smiling conspiratorially. There was one thing, he added, that made the show likely to be good: One of the best actresses on

Broadway was in it, the very one, in fact, who'd played Lola in *Damn Yan-kees*.

My heart started pumping blood to I didn't know where. Later that af-ternoon, I pulled out the *Damn Yankees* record and took a fresh look at the photo of the woman's long, stocking-clad legs. That night I pictured her in the Senators' locker room, dropping her garments one by one, in the slowest possible motion, replaying once more the disrobing that was my favorite self-told bedtime story. The prospect of seeing her in the flesh combined with the prospect of seeing a Broadway show to produce a tan-gle of sensation that propelled me right past the jarring return of the strange man who now occupied our lives and house.

An eternity later, when Saturday arrived, I flew to a higher level of an-ticipation than even my previous theatergoing outings had taken me. The idea of seeing a show that could not be imagined in advance, in which every song, every character, every plot twist, was an impenetrable mystery right up until its revelation from the stage, was wholly new. The only clue I had as to what was to come was the title: *Redhead*.

The overture, though unfamiliar in its specifics, was true to my hopes. A low rumble of drums led to a fanfare of horns, then through a thicket of bright, busy melody until that moment when the auditorium lights began to dim to complete darkness in calibrations as fine as my private Lola striptease. At that point the music dimmed too, subsiding into what I knew must be a love song, in which the quiet purring of the strings was echoed by the brass, as if a woman were in tentative, then tender, then ecstatic conversation with a man.

Just as I became conscious that the overture was slipping by, once again too fast for me to hold on to it, my eye was caught by a motion a few seats away. I glanced over and saw that Joel was mimicking the conductor in the spotlight only a few rows in front of us, flapping his program to the beat of the music. I feared for a second that he might make a disruption, but no, he surprised me yet again. His other hand clasped Mom's hand tightly, and I could see her smile, her face illuminated in the faint glow still re-flecting off the gold curtain.

My spirits sank only a bit as I gathered fresh evidence of the bond be-tween my mother and her new husband. There was no time to think about it—the curtain was rising. Soon Gwen Verdon appeared, looking just as she did in my bedroom each night, in black tights just like Lola's. The audience roared in approval at everything she did, and how could they not? She danced around the stage for two hours, nearly always in those tights and a black leotard from which peeked the pale skin of her breasts.

"This is going to be a hit!" Joel shouted, the excitement in his voice spilling from the car's front seat as we drove home afterward. He explained that the Washington critics—writers in *The Washington Post*, the *Evening Star*, and the *Daily News* who went to plays and gave a kind of report card on them—had liked *Redhead*, and he was sure the same would happen when the show got to New York. Had we all noticed, he asked, how loud the audience's applause was?

"Isn't it always loud?" I asked. I couldn't imagine anything less; I had never heard anything less.

"This was louder than usual," said Joel. "People were happy to be seeing something new and good."

Perhaps this explained why I had noticed, as I hadn't before, how full the theater was. Or was it my imagination? Some people seemed to be standing in the aisles to watch the show. Some seemed to be leaning out of the balcony, so far forward it was a wonder they didn't fall into our laps.

The excitement dissipated, though, once we were back home. Since there was no record of *Redhead*—there would be one after it got to New York, Mom promised, and we would get it—I had no tool except the program for helping me reconstruct what I had seen. I studied it intently. I read and reread the "Synopsis of Scenes": Much of *Redhead* took place at a creepy London theater, the Odeon, where a murderer lurked. I went through the list of "Musical Numbers" and tried to remember the tunes and the words to "Merely Marvelous" and "My Girl Is Just Enough Woman for Me." I looked at the program's ads for restaurants and nightclubs in a Washington I didn't know: the Occidental ("Relax After the Theatre Over Exotic Café Expresso and Continental Pastries"), the Willard Room ("Open 'Til 1 A.M."), the Cherry Blossom Lounge ("No Cover, No Minimum"). I studied other ads for plays coming to Washington—the Old Vic Company "in a repertory of plays by William Shakespeare," *Starward Ark* ("Now that you've seen REDHEAD—see the

blondes, brunettes, and redheads picked to colonize another planet!")—
and was shocked by the ticket prices ("Orchestra: $5.50 and $4.95"), ten
times that for movies even at Loew's Palace. How would I ever afford to go
on a fifty-cent allowance?

I read "Who's Who in the Cast" about Gwen Verdon:

Stage and audience tingle at her presence and thesauruses frazzle as
critics hunt down superlatives to describe her. She burst upon the
consciousness of Broadway in the Cole Porter hit musical "Can-
Can." Her stunning performance in this show sent opening nighters
literally into an uproar. At the end of her big number, while she sat
in her dressing room backstage removing her makeup, the audience
sent up a convention-like chant of "We Want Verdon."

By Wednesday night's dinner with Dad, I was still carrying the program
around with me as if it could somehow keep alive the memory of Saturday
afternoon. I didn't know when I'd see a show again. Dad knew about *Redhead* and hoped to see it, he said, not sounding as if he really might.

After dinner, he sat Polly and me down in the living room while
Grandma and Grandpa were still cleaning up in the dining room.

He had some happy news to tell us, he explained.

He was getting married, he said.

Polly and I looked at him in total silence. We didn't know what to say.
If it had never occurred to us that Mom would get married, it had occurred to us even less, if such a thing were possible, that Dad would. I had
thought he was the saddest about the divorce, that he'd been as upset as we
were, that he was still in love with Mom.

Dad told us the woman's name: Anadel. It was a special name, he explained—for a special woman. He knew we would like her very much.
Anadel lived in New York, which is why we hadn't met her. She had never
been to Washington.

When are you getting married?, we asked.

In two months. In March.

Where?

In New York.

Are you moving to New York?

"No," Dad said, and when Polly and I said nothing else, he sighed and seemed about to change the subject. Then he took out his wallet, as if he was going to give us money to buy something during a visit to the shopping center. But instead he pulled a bunch of cards from one of the wallet's pockets and started flipping through them.

I recognized his business cards, and charge cards for Woodies and Hecht's and Lansburgh's, and the posed photos of me and Polly taken in the library that year at school. He stopped when he came to another picture. It was a color snapshot of a pretty young woman with pouting red lips and short, curly hair, her breasts outlined by a tight black V-neck sweater. I felt a pang of guilt—my heart jumped. It was Lola, and what was *Lola* doing in Dad's wallet?

"Here's what she looks like," Dad said as we all studied the small photo he had placed on the coffee table. "This is Anadel."

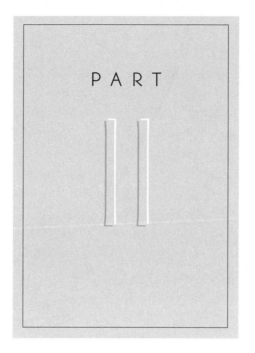

PART

II

The Plaza Hotel: I had never before heard words from my father with this New York ring, words that pulled at me as if they were music. It was at the Plaza Hotel, he said, that he and Anadel would have their wedding. He didn't have to describe the place. One night before bed, Mom had read to Polly and me a library book about a girl who lived in the Plaza Hotel, a tall white palace right in the center of New York, only a few blocks from where we had stayed that night, now an eternity of months ago, when we had seen *Bells Are Ringing*. The girl—her name was Eloise, a New York name I'd never heard in Washington—could order anything she wanted from room service at any time day or night. She could have any New York adventure she chose, she didn't have to go to school, and she didn't need parents because her family was all the people who worked in the hotel, the elevator men and waiters and maids, all of them nice, all of them glad to play with her anytime she wanted.

The girl didn't really exist, I knew that, but I knew that the Plaza Hotel did. I imagined it was a place where I could stay up as late as I wanted to every night and then, always, just when I wanted to, fall right to sleep.

Anadel didn't live at the Plaza Hotel. She lived with her mother in a part of New York called Forest Hills, a long subway ride away. She worked in an office not far from the Plaza, though, for a company that made women's clothing. Dad told us that after his wedding he was opening a new Rich's in Washington, on Wisconsin Avenue in Georgetown, where he would sell women's clothing to go with the shoes. That way Anadel would have a job once she moved to Washington.

Dad said that Polly and I could not go to his wedding—it was only for grown-ups. Not that it would have occurred to us to go, since we hadn't gone to Mom's, either. But he had a plan to take us to New York before then, for a weekend, and I was so keyed up about the trip that I stopped thinking about what might happen in the distant future when Dad was married again.

I thought we might stay at the Plaza Hotel as he and Anadel intended to after their wedding, but no, Dad said we'd stay instead at Uncle Herbert and Aunt Jane's in Great Neck, on Long Island, a suburb of New York. Would we go to Broadway and see a show? Of course, said Dad.

Two Saturdays later, Polly and I were in his station wagon, our small suitcases sliding around in the back where the boxes of Rich's shoes usually were, driving to New York as we had with Mom the previous summer. This time it was harder to figure out what would happen once we arrived there; I couldn't try to imagine in advance the show we were seeing, and then imagine it again and again, because Dad hadn't chosen it yet.

I didn't know my aunt and uncle that well. Herbert, Jr., was older than Dad, and he and Aunt Jane had two kids older than me—Bob and Wendy—and another, Nancy, just Polly's age. Aunt Jane, I had been told, was often sick. No sooner had we reached their neighborhood than I felt my familiar fear return. This was not New York as I knew it, but a quiet place of houses and trees and front yards, gray and brown and barren in the February light, an unfamiliar Somerset. Once in Uncle Herbert's house, I was even more frightened. I'd be sleeping in cousin Bob's room. All I knew about Bob was that he was a tall teenager bigger than any kid at camp.

Having put our suitcases in the rooms we'd be sleeping in—Bob's was packed with athletic pennants and trophies—we gathered in the living room with my aunt and uncle. Before I could let my fear run away with me, Dad asked, "Would you like to see *The Music Man* tonight—just you and me?" He said that Polly wasn't old enough yet to stay out past her bedtime; she would remain in Great Neck and play with Wendy and Nancy. No one in either of our households—least of all me—thought twice when Polly was routinely relegated to the role of Little Girl, unworthy of special treats.

If I didn't jump up and down in fact when Dad promised *The Music Man*, I did in my mind. I had listened to the record for more than a year. Though it had only a brief overture, which reduced its luster slightly, it did have a child actor of my age and low height who sang two songs. I had first seen this actor, Eddie Hodges, on a TV quiz show, where he identified tunes after a few notes and shouted out their names before the grown-up contestants could. He kept coming back week after week to win more and more money, until they announced that he had won the part in *The Music Man* after "a nationwide search." Unlike Eloise, Eddie Hodges was real and he was a boy. He was on Broadway. He lived in a Broadway theater, I reckoned, or nearby, and he stayed up late every night. If there was anyone in the world I could magically will myself to be, then it was Eddie Hodges, who was never far from a theater, who never had the death sentence of a bedtime.

But I'd settle for just seeing him onstage, for surely when I did I would figure out how to emulate him and get to Broadway. Was the first step being on a TV quiz show? I was good at school; I had a chance to be a contestant—didn't I?—if only I could get to New York.

My enthusiasm for *The Music Man* seemed to capture the attention of Aunt Jane, who gave me a long look from across the living room, as if she was registering my presence for the first time and wanted to say something but couldn't get the words out. She did not seem at all sick. She was a tall woman who didn't act like my other Rich relatives; when she did speak, it was in a low, regal voice, full of the gravel and quick syllables that meant "New York" to me, like the chatter of the famous guests Jack Paar invited onto the *Tonight Show*. Jane kept to her corner of the room, standing and smoking, her cigarette ashes flaking onto her lime-colored dress, while Herbert, who had sold shoes for a company in New York since leaving Washington, talked with Dad about business. Only at one point did Aunt

Jane interrupt the men; she asked if Dad would be seeing Anadel while in New York.

I had managed to stop thinking about Anadel, but my memory of the V-neck of her black sweater, framing that triangular patch of sloping pink flesh, came rushing back. Dad answered that Anadel was out of town at a relative's wedding that weekend, but would be meeting Polly and me in Washington before too long.

Aunt Jane lapsed momentarily into her private solemnity, but as Dad and Uncle Herbert resumed talking, she walked over to brusquely pepper me with questions about *The Music Man* and other shows, as if to satisfy herself that I really knew something about Broadway. Then she left the room and came back with a small stack of books. They were plays, she said, that she received in the mail each month from a book club. I took the slender volumes and examined them carefully: Their jackets matched the posters and record albums so familiar to me. I opened one, sat down on a couch, and started to read.

Sometime after that, when I was lost in the book as if I was lost in one of my records back home, Dad returned to the living room after a brief absence and said that we weren't going to see *The Music Man* after all. He had phoned the "brokers" he knew who sold tickets to shows, but it was too late to get any for *The Music Man* that night. It was "sold out"—that was the way they put it. Instead, Dad had bought tickets to another show that I had never heard of. It was in a place called Greenwich Village, which Dad explained was sort of like Broadway but in a different neighborhood.

The afternoon, I thought, would never end. I felt out of place in Bob's room, and when he returned to the house just before we left, he did little to make me feel comfortable. He asked me if I was interested in football, and when I said that my sport was baseball, I worried he might ask me to demonstrate my skills at hitting and fielding. But he just looked at me blankly while absently tossing a tennis ball between his hands and, as if to render a judgment, abruptly bolted out of the house again to be with his neighborhood friends.

Yet as Dad and I drove into what I was relieved to discover was indeed Manhattan, I felt a new rush of expectation. Before the play, we had dinner at a restaurant called Al Schacht's. Schacht was an unlikely baseball story that allowed me to cling tenuously to my own major-league fantasies. He had been a player for the Washington Senators around the time Dad was born, and though he'd never played that well, he then became a coach and baseball's beloved clown. He used to run around the base paths in the wrong direction between innings. He made everyone at Griffith Stadium laugh hysterically by wearing crazy costumes and pitching imaginary balls to batters who hit them out of the park. Then he fell down, smack on his behind, and made everyone laugh more, especially Dad, who saw him back when he was my age. After Al Schacht retired, he moved to New York and started his restaurant, which Dad always visited during his business trips.

Dad parked the station wagon on the street near Al Schacht's, which had a sign with red letters announcing its name. Inside, a bow-tied waiter handed us menus that were called "Score Cards." Dad ordered us steaks, but they weren't like Washington steaks. They were better and larger, like everything in New York. Dad had a cold beer, and gave me a taste, the way Grandpa Nat sometimes did. As Dad talked more about his memories of Al Schacht's clowning at Griffith Stadium, it was as though we were back together in Somerset, when he still told me bedtime stories.

On our way to Greenwich Village after dinner, the wintry New York streets were sparsely populated. Dad pointed out some of the office buildings where he went to buy shoes for Rich's. Though they were closed and dark now, these towers still glinted: The brass trim framing their entrances and ground-floor stores reflected the lights of the surging evening traffic, spraying the glitter in exploding patterns like Fourth of July sparklers.

The theater we reached was tiny, not at all like the ideal Broadway theater I always carried in my mind. It was in a hidden alley. There were no lights on the marquee outside, no orchestra pit within. The curtain, I soon saw, parted at the center, like the heavy curtains in our old Somerset living room.

I quickly got caught up in the performance of *The Boy Friend*, another show about men and women falling in love. I looked at the list of songs in the program, wishing they were infinite, for each finished song hurtled me toward the dreaded end of my night in New York and the return to Great Neck.

That moment came, and as Dad and I drove back to Long Island, I talked nonstop about what we had seen, actor by actor, song by song.

"Did you enjoy it, son?" Dad asked.

"I did. I *loved* it," I said.

We fell silent. Dad was busy driving, and I was busy trying to hold on to the moments of theater that had only minutes ago charged me up; they'd been in my grasp, then slipped away as they always did, disappearing into memory, where they could be retrieved only in bright splinters that could never again be made whole.

Soon enough I was back to worrying about whether I would get to sleep. My fear was compounded by the darkened house we returned to. Everyone was asleep, including Bob.

This was not New York. In New York, everyone was supposed to stay up all night to keep me company.

After Dad tucked me in to the extra bed hidden in the shadows of Bob's room and disappeared to his own room (exactly where I wasn't sure), I felt that nervous sensation—part fear, part loneliness—that always accelerated into panic. But I couldn't cry; I'd wake Bob and expose what a baby I was. I closed my eyes and waited for sunlight to come and rescue me. The unimaginable had happened: I was in New York and yet found myself wishing I were home in Rosemary Hills.

I wondered where Mom and Joel were—there had to be some way I could call them long-distance. I opened my eyes and looked at the clock. Only minutes had passed. I got out of bed. I would find Dad and tell him how frightened I was of not being able to sleep. He might have the same pills Mom had.

Out of Bob's room, I found it hard to navigate the large house. I had no idea how to find Dad. I'd settle, I decided, for finding the front door. If only I could find the front door, I could run away. But I was in pajamas, and it was cold. I had to find Dad. It had been so long since we had slept in the same house. He had to understand what had happened to me since he left Somerset. He had to hear the whole story. He had to rescue me. He had to teach me how to go to sleep. He had to teach me now, or surely I would never make it to the morning. I didn't want to go on living if this was the way I had to live.

I found myself in the living room. The lights were off, though a street-lamp sent a cold glow through the window from the sleepy, quiet street outside. I could make out a lamp on a table, and snapped it on. Nearby was the stack of play books, just where I'd left them hours earlier.

I was afraid to turn on any more lights, so I took one of the books and sat on the floor right beneath the lamp and started to read. I would read and read and read, I decided, until the sun came up.

I had read only a few pages when a noise made me jump. It was Aunt Jane, in her bathrobe, walking toward the kitchen just beyond the living room. Seeing the light, she took a detour in my direction.

She stopped a few feet from me, then paused, silent, as if to contemplate the scene. I waited for her to tell me to go back to bed.

"I'm getting a glass of water," she said finally.

I nodded. I wasn't sure what to say. "I couldn't get to sleep," I ventured at last, careful to keep any emotion out of my voice. I didn't want to embarrass myself before this woman who was more stranger than relative.

Aunt Jane said nothing. She walked over, leaned down, and started to reach toward me—or so I thought. She wasn't reaching to me, though, but to the book in my hand. She took it from me and, keeping it open to my place, held the cover to the lamp so that she could read the title. It was *The Music Man.*

"I liked that one," she said in a low voice before giving me back the book. She didn't look at me as she spoke, and before I could say anything in response, before I could even consider taking this opening to confide my fear to her, before I could ask for her sympathy or help, she was off to the kitchen. From the hall beyond the living room, I could catch the spill of the chilly fluorescent light; I heard her retrieve a glass from a cupboard, open the refrigerator, slam a tray of ice cubes into the sink.

The light was soon extinguished. I heard Aunt Jane's retreating footsteps, and then the house fell into silence again. For a moment I remembered the haunted houses my friends and I used to sneak into back in Somerset, houses like this one, empty and dark and hushed, still waiting for the new family to move in.

Somehow, in that hush, I curled up on the living-room carpet, the book still in my hands, and fell asleep.

—

Dad and Anadel were married weeks later. Anadel moved into Dad's apartment and slipped easily into our weekly routine. She came with us to Grandma and Grandpa's on Wednesdays; on Sundays, as we hung around with our books and Dad listened to his new stereo tapes, she told Polly and me she wanted to get to know us. She already knew about my interest in Broadway, and as she told me a story of going with a girlfriend to see shows free when she was a teenager because the girlfriend's father had a friend who worked in the theater, I was distracted by her perfume and the pull of her blouse against her breasts.

Anadel was nice; she could be counted on to appear in a Lola costume when I thought about her in my bed at night. And then she and Dad were gone on a long honeymoon to Italy. Just before they left, Dad showed us the pictures of their wedding party at the Plaza Hotel: I recognized a lot of the faces from Woodmont, and Aunt Jane and Uncle Herbert, and our Washington rabbi. They were all laughing. I tried to recall what I had been doing the day of the party—had I had that much fun? I couldn't remember. The pictures were strange and unexpected; I hadn't imagined the wedding while it was going on, as I had Mom and Joel's.

It was during Dad and Anadel's month in Italy that John and Sue came to our apartment in Rosemary Hills to spend an entire weekend with us for the first time. We were all sound asleep on Friday night when Joel almost danced into our room and started mimicking a camp counselor: "Rise and shine! Rise and shine!" I looked at the clock—it was after midnight.

"We're going to New York!" he continued. "And we're not waiting until the morning!"

Mom came in behind him. Yes, she added, it's a surprise trip—an Adventure!—and won't it be fun? Before we could react, she had the lights on and was busily pulling clothes from the chest of drawers. Joel had run out, then returned, his arms full of suitcases.

Mom said we could all stay in our pajamas, and she carried Polly, still struggling to wake up, to the car. Soon all six of us were packed in, speeding through the empty nighttime Maryland streets, going right through red traffic lights as we raced toward the turnpike.

"*Pocketa-pocketa-peep!*" cried Joel from behind the wheel, sounding like a boisterous character in a cartoon. This was gibberish taken from one of his favorite movies, about a guy named Walter Mitty who daydreamed he could do anything in the world.

We were all laughing, too. Joel was sweeping us to Oz as if he were a human cyclone—and in the middle of the night at that, the most magical of times. Then we passed out, caressed by the warm spring winds.

When we woke up the next morning, we were in a hotel—just down the block from the Plaza Hotel, Mom said—and then we were dressing, as fast as we could. We were going, right then, to see a TV quiz show we all knew, *Beat the Clock,* in which married couples dressed in waterproof overalls, kind of like we'd used for finger-painting in nursery school, and competed in cockeyed games where they sprayed each other with water and suds and whipped cream and fell over in conniptions while they did so. Joel had secured the tickets and was already in the lobby of the hotel waiting for us.

We were soon running to the TV theater. Once we were inside and had taken our seats, Joel stood up and started yelling at a uniformed woman with a clipboard who was standing in the aisle.

"Dear! *Dear!*" he bellowed in a voice that made the endearment sound like a threat, raising his volume until he got the woman's attention. She came over, and Joel asked how he and Mom could be contestants. Agreeably enough, she gave him a card to fill out.

After a few minutes, the lights went down a little bit and a man bounded onto the stage; a black microphone dangling from what looked like a giant, bent coat hanger bounced above his head. It wasn't Bud Collyer, the man in the gray suit and the bow tie we knew to be the famous host of *Beat the Clock,* but another man, with a deep announcer's voice, who asked us to watch a blinking APPLAUSE sign and to rehearse applauding a couple of times, which we did, as if we needed to become experts at clapping. Then, flipping through a handful of cards just like the one Joel had filled out, the announcer started doing what he called "contestant interviews."

He called out a name, and a man in the audience raised his hand—just like in school—and identified himself. Then the announcer walked over and asked a few questions about the man's job and family and hometown.

One of the next cards was "Joel Fisher," and before we knew it, Joel was standing, there was a microphone bouncing just above his head, and everyone in the theater was staring at us.

The announcer asked Joel where he was from, and when Joel told him, the man intoned, "The nation's capital!"

Then: "What is your profession, Mr. Fisher?"

"I'm an attorney."

"Is this Mrs. Fisher with you?"

"Yes, it is."

"And are these your children? How many do we have here?"

Joel identified each of us by name and age. We couldn't believe it. Our names were going to be said on network television!

"And how long have you been married?"

"Four months."

"Four months? Can you explain that?"

A chuckle rose in the announcer's throat. The audience seemed to be paying closer attention.

"No," said Joel.

The man was polite but insistent: "You can't ex—"

"No," said Joel. He smiled broadly—this was his joking face: "It's none of your darn business."

From her seat, Sue grabbed her father's jacket and tugged, as if to say, Please, Dad, don't do this. But Joel wouldn't budge. It was as if he'd been insulted by the question and would now enjoy goading the announcer in return. He stuck out his chin in defiance, smiled, and shook his head. He seemed *proud* to be part of a divorced family.

The announcer retreated. "Okay," he said, then, happily: "You and Mrs. Fisher are number five on today's list of contestants for *Beat the Clock*!" The red APPLAUSE sign flashed, and everyone clapped.

The announcer and the microphone moved on to the next name.

Our spirits wilted as soon as we were cast out of the spotlight. We knew from long experience that *Beat the Clock* never had more than two—at most three—contestants on any show. We were number five on the list. Of course we were. How would a husband and wife married four months explain that they had four children, ages almost eight to almost ten? To explain would mean talking about divorce, and no one ever talked about divorce on TV, or anywhere else. Maybe it was just as well. Much as I wanted us to be a part of one of the TV shows whose applause and laughter made me feel less lonely—a New York TV show where people were always having the happiest time, as if they were at a party—I was also relieved. I didn't want Mom and Joel to start talking about divorce now, while I was sitting in a theater, surrounded by strangers who might stare or point or laugh at us. I didn't want New York to be ruined like Washington. I didn't want to be whispered about. New York was the place where I'd somehow start life all over again, free of the humiliation that came with the stigma "broken home."

As we figured, Mom and Joel's names were never uttered by Bud Collyer once he appeared for the actual broadcast. Soon enough we were back in the bright sunlight again, chasing after Joel. We were moving too fast to talk about the show—we had to get to the next activities Joel had planned, lunch at the Gaiety, a tiny delicatessen full of screaming patrons, and a visit to a museum that had paintings Mom wanted to see. After lunch, as we stuffed our stuffed selves into a cab, Joel said we were going to a Broadway show that night: *The Music Man.*

———

Actually, Mom and Joel, having already seen *The Music Man*, were seeing a different show around the corner, and they took us to our theater early. Knocking on a glass pane of a door leading from the first lobby, where the box office was, to the second, inner lobby, Joel demanded that we be let in before anyone else. The man who answered the door disappeared to consult with someone else, then emerged with an usher to do just as Joel had ordered. While Mom waited in the outer lobby, Joel and the usher guided us to our seats, after which he and Mom went off to their theater, "on the other side of Shubert Alley," as Joel put it with a broad grin, knowing the words had special meaning for me. Before he went, he put two dollar bills in my hand for candy—as the oldest child, he said, I was in charge.

The theater for *The Music Man* was called the Majestic. It *was* majestic, the largest I had yet seen, with gold all but dripping from the ceiling and the chandeliers and the balcony above. Without parents, I was too shy to go down the aisle on my own to look into the orchestra pit, but otherwise I felt perfectly at home. I listened closely for the sounds of the musicians tuning up, their notes floating above the buzzing swarms of New Yorkers now filling the theater. The chattering audience, too, seemed to be singing to me, though of what I couldn't quite make out.

Charged up by anticipation of the rising of the curtain, I experienced only a brief pang of disappointment: In the *Playbill*, I couldn't find Eddie Hodges in the cast list. The other familiar names from the record were all accounted for, but in the spot where I knew "Eddie Hodges" was supposed to be, there was another name. Where had the real Eddie Hodges gone?

The Music Man began with a whole train car onstage, full of passengers. Several scene changes later, the new "Eddie Hodges" appeared, and I was amazed at how much he looked like the old one, as I remembered him from TV, and sang like the old one, as I knew his voice from the record. I could be *this* boy, too, I decided. It was the first time I'd seen a boy like me, my age, onstage. The boy in the show was called Winthrop, and there was something about him, besides his age, that reminded me of me—I had realized that not just from the record but from the part of *The Music Man* I had read at Aunt Jane's. Winthrop had no father, only a much older sister who was more like a mother than a sister: a librarian named Marian who sometimes reminded me of Mrs. Young in Rosemary Hills and sometimes of Mom when she was dreaming of being in love with Charles Van Doren. Winthrop's actual mother was more like a grandmother, and she cracked jokes in a hoarse voice like Grandma Lil's.

The more I watched, the faster I forgot about my real mom and my real non-Winthrop life back home. I didn't care about being apart from Mom and Joel at the theater. Happy to be on my own, I was aware of Polly, John, and Sue only at the intermission.

As they went in search of candy, I was glad to stay right where I was, not wanting to miss anything that happened in the theater even when the curtain was down, afraid to leave my seat and not be back in time for the second act, which would be even more surprising than the first, since I had fallen asleep in Great Neck before getting a chance to read to the end of the story.

Waiting for Act 2, I thought of the wonder of Mom and Joel being in another Broadway theater, having the same experience but with different ac-

tors, a different play—just around the corner. They must have been at intermission, too—what were they like with each other when we weren't
around? There were so many more theaters as well, on this block, and the
next, and the next—an infinity of Broadway. Surely the people all around
me went to one theater and then another every night, never running out of
new shows to see.

When at last the lights went down again, I momentarily thought of
Dad, as if his shadow were crossing my path. I tried to picture him in Italy,
which I could not imagine but where I knew it was already the middle of
the night.

Was it fair that I was at *The Music Man*, which Dad had so much
wanted to see—and to take me to see—just weeks ago? Was it fair that I
was seeing it without him? Was it fair that I was seeing a Broadway show
because of Joel?

But then Act 2 began, and I was back in the Iowa town where Winthrop
lived. What caught me by surprise was that in the second act Winthrop
cried onstage—cried so hard, cried as hard as I did sometimes, cried right
in front of everybody in the whole Majestic Theatre. He cried when he discovered that the Music Man, who had promised to teach him how to play
in a band with all the other kids, was a fake.

The Music Man, Winthrop had learned, didn't know anything about
music at all, just knew how to cheat parents out of money by selling them
instruments and promising to turn their children into a band.

"*Can* you lead a band?" the crying, angry Winthrop demanded to know
as he looked up at the tall Music Man. The Music Man was about to run
away, to start tricking another town before the police caught up with him.
But first he was hugging the boy, trying to make him listen to his explana-
tions, trying to make Winthrop not hate him.

"No," the Music Man answered.

"Are you a big liar?" Winthrop asked, bawling louder now, so loud and
real that the sound was as piercing and familiar as my own voice.

"Yes," said the Music Man.

Winthrop kicked and kicked, trying to escape, but the Music Man
wouldn't let him go. He had to tell the boy something else before he left
town.

"You're a wonderful kid," he said.

Winthrop calmed down just a little.

The Music Man went on: "I wanted you in the band so you'd quit mopin' around feeling sorry for yourself!"

Winthrop started crying hard again. But this time he cried because he knew that the Music Man was leaving him and his sister and his mother alone forever, and now Winthrop didn't want him to run away after all.

Winthrop was so mad—maybe frightened—that he said the opposite of what he really felt. *"Hurry up and leave!"* he yelled at the Music Man, his sobs now more hurt than sad—another sound I recognized. He wanted the Music Man to stay and be his father.

The moment seemed to last a long time—too long—and for the first time in a theater I found myself feeling a feeling that wasn't quite excitement. I didn't know what to call it. I thought of Dad. Had I moped and felt too sorry for myself back in Somerset? Maybe he'd thought that I wanted him to leave when I really wanted him to stay. Maybe I had said things to him I didn't really mean, the way Winthrop had to the Music Man. Had something I said made him move out? No one had ever explained why he left, so I could only imagine the answer.

The more I imagined, the more I worried I might cry at my seat in the Majestic Theatre just like Winthrop was crying in front of me. I couldn't let that happen. I let my eyes wander from the stage, up to the darkened ceiling, almost as if I wanted to do the unthinkable and escape the play— if only for a few seconds.

Then I looked back at the stage. Winthrop had almost stopped crying, I was relieved to see; he wasn't mad anymore—not at all. He was trying to help the Music Man now, warning him to hide, and hide fast, before the police found him and put him in jail.

But the Music Man wasn't worried about the police. He cared only about Winthrop, for he really did think that Winthrop was wonderful. The Music Man thought Winthrop was such a wonderful boy that he promised to stay right there with him and never run away. He wasn't going to be like the dead father in *Carousel*, who came back to visit his lonely daughter and then left for good again; he would stay with Winthrop and his sister and protect them forever, he said, no matter what.

That was the happy ending of the show, and it made me feel happy, too, as happy as I could hope to be, at least until it was over and we were back in front of the Majestic Theatre meeting Joel and Mom at the spot where we'd been instructed to wait for them.

The hour was late, and I thought of how much later it was in Italy. I wasn't Winthrop after all, and if there was a way to convince Dad I was wonderful, too, if there was a way to make him come back and stay with me, I had no idea what it was.

CHAPTER 2

"oday I visited the new house—nothing interesting happened," I
wrote in the diary Mom gave me as a present for my tenth birthday
that June. Mom used to keep a diary when she was a girl, and since
I liked to write stories, she thought I should start one too. She gave me a
tan book labeled "Diary" in gold lettering, with room for five years of en-
tries and a bronze clasp you could lock with a tiny key.

I tried to write in the diary every day, squeezing my words into the few
lines allotted to each date, carefully locking the book as I finished, but the
effort lasted only a couple of weeks. I couldn't write down what really happened and what I really thought. It was too complicated. I didn't have the
words I needed.

I never could have told the real story, I was sure of that.

I wanted to write in the book how much I hated the fact that we were
moving to a new house again. But to write the story down was to make it
more real, and I wanted it to be less real, not more. I wanted to go back-
ward in time, not forward.

It was getting harder and harder to remember Somerset's streets, harder
and harder to picture Mom and Dad being together there, and I was

scared that Rosemary Hills would soon fade as well. It was only a little while ago that Mom, Polly, and I moved there—and then moved again after that, once Mom married Joel. Everything was moving too fast, and I could feel the speed of events deep inside me, churning in my stomach, whirring like the old playing cards that we attached to our bike wheels with clothespins so they would click as we coasted down a hill. Wherever the bottom of the hill was now, I was too busy worrying about what I would find there to stop and write down everything I saw and felt along the way.

It was hard to imagine living in Washington. I was used to Maryland, and Washington was like a foreign country. But it was also where Joel's office was, and Mom promised we would be very happy there.

What about having to change schools and make all new friends again? No one else we knew had had to go to three different elementary schools, I complained. Mom didn't want to hear me talk about it. You *already* have friends waiting for you at your Washington school, she said—Sue and John. They lived in our new neighborhood with their own mom.

My first sight of our new house, on the day we drove into the city to take a "tour," only deepened the mystery of what was to come. It had no real front yard or backyard, and it shared a wall with the house next door. "Semi-detached," Mom called it.

I didn't want to see the house. It still needed to be decorated, Mom warned us as we got out of the car. It was much bigger than our apartment in Rosemary Hills, and we needed furniture to fill it up; Polly and I were to have our own rooms again. To overcome my resistance, Mom had promised me a "new house" present for my room—my own portable stereo record player.

John and Sue were part of the tour, too. We were all immediately taken up a narrow, twisting staircase to the third floor—the former attic—where my room and Polly's would be. In Somerset, every house had had a single story and a basement. Our new Washington house was so much taller, and there was a basement, too. What it would be like to live there I couldn't figure out. It was still a house with no furniture in a strange neighborhood with no friends.

Mom and Joel were asking the real-estate agent questions about keys and heating and money, so we four kids ran around exploring. Once we were satisfied we'd seen it all, we met up with Mom and Joel and the real-tor in the empty dining room on the ground floor.

In the center of the room on the floor was a disk with a tiny knob the size of a thick nail protruding from its center.

"What's this?" asked Sue, who sat down on the floor to examine the in-explicable knob. She was, I had learned, a curious girl who wasn't shy about investigating anything; she had once regaled Polly and me with a story of how she had tried to turn herself into a human piggy bank by swal-lowing a dime, a nickel, and a quarter.

Mom warmed to Sue's question. "This is why I love this house—it's old, it has history. That button is just like one Grandma Lil had in Brooklyn when I was a little girl," she explained. Then she instructed Sue: "If you press on it with your foot when you're sitting at the table, it makes a funny noise, and it's a signal for the maid to come out of the kitchen and bring the food or clean up when everyone's finished eating."

Sue pressed on the button with the palm of her hand, and sure enough, there was a loud buzz. Sue removed her hand, waited a few seconds, then pressed down again, proud of her experiment.

Joel stopped his conversation with the realtor and looked toward Sue. "That's enough," he said, not raising his voice but with a finality that fell through the air like a hatchet. Though Sue stopped buzzing, she kept playing with the little metal knob for a few minutes until she'd worked it out of its hole, after which it rolled across the wooden floor with a faint scratching sound, like a marble on a sidewalk. That prompted Joel to break off talking again, in midsentence. He walked the few steps to where Sue was sitting.

"I *told you* to cut it out!" he shouted down at her. Then he bent his knees and bowed slightly, as if he was going to reach down and take Sue by the hand to remove her from the scene of her crime. But instead, he raised his arm high and brought his hand down smack on her head. The blow made Sue fall over. She started crying, and Joel leaned toward her even closer and hit her again, and again, and again, on her back, her stomach, anywhere he could. "I *warned you!*" he yelled, his loud voice amplified into thunder by the hard, unforgiving walls of the vacant room.

Sue kept bawling. Her face had turned red and was wet with tears. As

Joel rose to his full height, her hands fluttered; she was trying to straighten the straps of the new white dress she had worn because Joel had told us we were going to a "good" restaurant for lunch to celebrate seeing the new house. John, Polly, and I stood frozen in place, saying nothing. So did Mom. The real-estate agent fixed her eyes on the dining-room floor. But Joel, completely relaxed now, picked up the conversation as if there had been no interruption at all.

Minutes later, we were in the station wagon, driving to lunch. Frightened, I listened, as all of us kids did, to hear what the grown-ups would say from their front-seat throne. None of us dared speak a word, not that we would have known what to say anyway. Sue's crying was now only a low, sputtering whimper. In a perfectly normal tone of voice, Joel told Mom that he planned to park in a particular lot near the restaurant because it had a special weekend-afternoon rate; Mom agreed. If either of them was worried about Sue, it didn't show. They didn't so much as glance at her. Mom wasn't her usual self—she never turned her head to look back at us, as she usually did—and yet she didn't seem sad or upset, either. It was as if what had happened at the new house was a closed chapter, and we were on to the next.

By the time we moved from Rosemary Hills to Washington a few weeks later, the incident was ancient history. The buzzer in the dining room was now hidden under a rug, beneath the heavy dining-room table where Willie Mae served us dinner.

———

Rosemary Hills soon seemed far away, already a ghost of itself.

On the last day of fourth grade, Mrs. Young had taken me aside after the final assembly and asked me to follow her back to the classroom. The room was already packed up for the summer. The blackboards were washed and spotless, the bulletin boards stripped of our classroom papers and pictures, the chairs placed upside down on our desks. The windows were wide open; the fragrance of freshly mowed grass swept in from the playground.

Mrs. Young took down a chair so that we could sit facing each other. She asked questions about my new neighborhood and house and school. I told her what little I knew by then, and she listened, smiling and nodding in understanding and maybe approval, though not saying too much. She pulled open her top desk drawer, reached in, and extracted what I immediately recognized as the "book" I had written—A *World of My Own*.

"I enjoyed this so much, I hate to part with it," Mrs. Young said, her voice as buoyant as usual. "But I didn't want to forget to give it back to you."

I took the book. The green construction-paper cover, with its uneven crayon lettering, showed the stick figure of a boy standing outside a house surrounded by flowers.

"Do you have a safe place where you can keep it when you're moving to your new house?" she asked.

"Yes," I said.

"You should write more stories, Frank," she said.

I nodded. Like Mom when she brought me art supplies, Mrs. Young was fond of saying that you could do anything with your imagination. I wasn't convinced. My imagination couldn't even take me all the way through the night.

But I couldn't say that aloud; I didn't want to hurt my favorite teacher's feelings. I still held out hope that she'd reveal a secret plan to rescue me, so I could stay with her and not have to move again and change schools and live with Joel anymore. Maybe she was waiting to tell me at the last possible minute.

"I know everything is going to be fine at your new school," Mrs. Young said.

I waited for her to say something more, but she didn't. Instead she stood up, so I did too. She walked me to the door of her classroom, and just when I thought she might lean over and kiss me goodbye, she smiled and told me not to worry about anything and to enjoy my summer. She leaned over, patted my shoulder, and sent me on my way.

I walked out of Rosemary Hills Elementary School for the last time, passing through its corridors, past all the empty bulletin boards, until I was outside, in the radiant June light. As I walked home, I clutched my book as tightly as I could, as if it were an anchor that would keep me close to Mrs. Young and everything else I was leaving behind. But whatever safe place I had in mind for it was not safe enough, and after we'd moved to Washington a month later, I could never find it again.

———

The summer was hot, and there was little to fill up the days: no camp, to my relief, but also no friends to pal around with. Joel was busy at his office. Mom was busy running from store to store as she "finished" the house. Sue and John and their mom, Mary Jane, were only a fifteen-minute walk away, and at a dead end nearby was their daily summer destination, the Cleveland Park Club. It was no Woodmont—just a small swimming pool packed to capacity with laughing and screaming neighborhood kids. Polly and I became members, with our own membership cards laminated in plastic, and spent afternoon after afternoon there, fighting for our patch of chlorinated water to cool us off from the fetid heat, waiting for our lives to resume once more with our entrance into John Eaton Elementary in the fall.

Unlike our Maryland neighborhoods, my new one in Washington felt completely deserted, afternoons at the pool excepted. You could walk out into the blaring sunlight on our street, Cleveland Avenue, and not see a single other person on the block. Some of the old houses, Mom explained, were literally empty. More families were moving from the District into Maryland than the reverse—to escape the blacks, I'd later discover. The neighbors who stayed put were often as ancient as their homes; many of them were retired military men who walked with canes and spent hours sitting idly on folding chairs in the shade outside their front doors.

Mrs. Young aside, I didn't miss Rosemary Hills. I thought of it now as the neighborhood where I had forgotten how to fall asleep. I liked my new room, which had shelves along the wall on which I could pile my books and baseball cards and records for my new record player, which, as promised, had been installed as soon as we moved in. At night, lying on the top of my bunk bed, which we'd brought from the old apartment, I could leave the door open and make out the muffled sound of Mom and Joel's TV, which Joel kept on almost all the time in their big bedroom at the bottom of the stairs directly below my room.

The only drawback was Polly: In the peculiar renovation of the attic, my narrow room served as the corridor between her room and the landing that led not only to the stairs but to our shared bathroom. To preserve the illusion of privacy, an unspoken etiquette evolved in which she passed through my room quickly and silently, as if she were blind and dumb, and I kept to the area of my bed, in a far corner, when I heard her footsteps. And though she, at least, had actual privacy in her room, she was, in a way, held hostage there, knowing that she would have to pass by me, involuntarily exhibited like an animal in a cage, when she wanted to get out. Which of us was better off in this strange arrangement was hard to say, but since I, the older child, the boy, had the bigger room, she resented it. Soon I would be as loath to cross the threshold into her room as she was embarrassed to make her mandatory traversals of mine.

I had so much solitary time that summer that reading became my paramount activity, and my greatest reading discovery was the New York newspaper, the *Times*, that Joel had delivered to our front door every morning, "for work," along with *The Washington Post*. While he was at the office, I could take it up to my room and study a single page that mesmerized me: It contained a list in small type of every theater on Broadway, indicating what show was playing there, what time the performances were, and what the tickets cost. On Sundays this page blossomed into an entire section of the paper, full of articles about these plays and advertisements that looked like black-and-white versions of the record covers I so cherished. I read every last detail, searching for the slightest changes from day to day in the fine print, as if I were studying hieroglyphs, some decipherable and others not, of a feverish civilization beyond my reach and, as yet, my understanding. Even the change of a performance time or the unexplained replacement of one name in a cast listing with another, as Eddie Hodges had been replaced in my *Playbill* for *The Music Man*, took on weighty if mysterious significance as I tried to catapult my imagination to the hectic precincts of Broadway, as frenetic as Cleveland Avenue was tranquil.

Some of the more striking ads were for a new show whose record Mom and Joel had just bought, *Gypsy*. Mom explained that the title referred to an actual person, Gypsy Rose Lee, a famous performer who used to take her clothes off onstage while dancing—she was called a "stripper"—and then, when she retired, became a writer. As Mom talked, she didn't seem to care at all whether I knew about the existence of someone so identified with sex. She had seen Gypsy Rose Lee with her own eyes, she told me, when her Aunt Dot and Uncle Sid had taken her to the New York World's Fair when she was only a few years older than I was now. It couldn't hurt me to know about Gypsy, she said—her striptease was all very funny and harmless, really, as long as you didn't take it too seriously.

Of course I took Gypsy Rose Lee very seriously. I knew more than I let on, because I had already discovered that among the books Joel had brought into our household in Rosemary Hills was *A Pictorial History of Burlesque,* full of women dressed like Lola in *Damn Yankees.* Within hours of Mom's "history" lesson, I took the book down from its new perch on the bookshelves in our den and located Gypsy Rose Lee's picture inside it. Maybe she wasn't as pretty as Gwen Verdon, but she wore the same sheer, lacy black stockings, with their tantalizing display of flesh at once revealed and hidden.

Gypsy the show, surprisingly, didn't seem to have a lot to do with strippers. As best I could tell from the description on the back of the record and the words of the songs, it was the story of a mother and her two daughters and their adventures in the theater during the Depression. Only at the end of *Gypsy* did one of the girls—her name was Louise—grow up to become a stripper, changing her name to "Miss Gypsy Rose Lee," as a Minsky's Burlesque Theatre announcer on the record proclaimed before she did her striptease. She sang a song that reminded me a little of "Whatever Lola Wants," and I could easily picture her doing on Minsky's stage just what Lola had done in the Washington Senators' locker room.

It wasn't just that one song in *Gypsy*, however, that captivated me. With my own record player, a door I could shut so no one could hear what I was doing (as long as Polly wasn't traipsing through), and with my first air conditioner, which I could turn up full-blast to envelop me in a cool protective cocoon, I had the means to listen to *Gypsy* without interruption again and again for hours at a time. And I listened more intensely than I ever had sitting on the floor in our old living rooms.

Gypsy began with an overture that was almost exhausting in its rapid-fire melodies, yanking me between the extremes of anticipation and melancholy from moment to moment; the sultry blare of the horns and the fusillade of drums at its climax left me breathless, as if I could propel myself two hundred miles by sheer will to be in the theater as the lights went down—as if I were really there for the swift rise of the curtain about to come. There wasn't a letdown on the record after that. Almost every song seemed to describe a fragment of my own life—an effect that no other story had ever had on me, whether the story was told in a book or a movie or a TV show or in the Broadway musicals I already knew.

Gypsy wasn't about a man falling in love with a woman and becoming the Most Happy Fella, or about Lost Boys running away to join Peter Pan in Never Never Land, or about a Music Man deciding to stay in town and never leave little Winthrop. No, *Gypsy*, as far as I could tell, was about a man and a woman falling in love and becoming angry instead of happy; about children of a divorced mom who want to run away from home but never live long enough in one place to call it home; about a nice man who promises to stay with Louise, her sister, June, and their mother, Rose, forever but ends up deserting them anyway.

Not that *Gypsy* made me sad. Song after song made me feel better than I could remember feeling since before my sleeplessness began. I *knew* these characters who were singing; their company made me feel less lonely. I recognized them. I could touch them, if only they'd let me—if only I could find them. And if they seemed sad . . . well, they couldn't be, because they lived in the theater, traveling from town to town doing a show. They were in New York performing *Gypsy* right now, at 8:30 every night, and twice on Wednesdays and Saturdays. The paper Joel had delivered every morning said so. *Gypsy* played in a theater in New York that was actually named the Broadway Theatre.

Of all the songs on the record, there was one I always particularly looked forward to hearing—the only one sung by a boy, albeit an older one than me or Eddie Hodges. But I would wait for its appearance in its proper sequence on the second side, never leaping ahead to it, lest I destroy my pretense that I was actually "watching" *Gypsy* in the packed Broadway Theatre rather than merely listening to the record alone in my room.

The song was called "All I Need Is the Girl," and it was performed by a character named Tulsa, who merited only a single sentence in the synopsis on the back of the record jacket. He was one of the teenagers who trav-

eled and sang and danced with June and Louise in the act their mom had
written for them. In the song, he describes how he is going to have his own
act someday, in a nightclub, with himself as the star, if only he can find a
girl who can sing and dance with him. Imagining aloud what the act will
be like, he explains to Louise the song, the dance steps he'll use, the costumes he and his future partner will wear—all the while getting more and
more carried away by the splendor of his own description. Some of his
words I found hard to understand—what did Tulsa mean by "ast-air
bit"?—but I understood the ravenousness of his desire. Halfway through
the song his feet take over, banging out the rhythm of the music in tap
shoes on the stage, as if he were preparing to take flight.

At first the rhythm of his dancing is slow—"I start easy," he explains to
Louise—then it becomes a trot—then faster still—and then Tulsa doubles
the speed again. His tapping sounds so fast that you don't think he can
dance any faster, but then, suddenly, the steps cease. Softer music takes
over, and Tulsa's voice also turns softer as he announces that his imaginary
dream girl has arrived at last, dressed "all in white," and that he is taking
her hand and leading her to the stage.

"Now we waltz—strings come in," Tulsa sings next, dancing slowly with
his invisible girl. He lifts her—so he tells Louise—and then he lifts her
again, and again. After that, the strings fade, making the sound I had
learned that violins make in movies when a dream is ending, and Tulsa's
feet start tapping again, slowly at first, before picking up speed once more.

"And now the tempo changes!" Tulsa shouts, as his tapping gets faster
and faster. "All the lights come up! And I build for the finale!" But his voice
on the record is drowned out now—by the staccato blasts of his tapping,
louder than ever, and by the horns in the orchestra pit, which are themselves shouting in joy. Somewhere in all the tapping and music you can
hear him cry out "Give me your hand!" to Louise—not the girl of his
dreams, just the girl who is his friend, the one person who is there in the
theater alley to keep him company and watch his imaginary nightclub act.
Her reply, though, is lost in the frenzy of the music, which grows louder
still until it breaks off into a silence that I imagined was being filled every
night by an audience's cheers.

Each time *Gypsy* reached Tulsa's song, I tried to fill in more details in the story it told. What did the dance look like? How old was Tulsa? What did Louise and June look like? Did he ever get his nightclub act? From there it was only a small leap to wondering if there was an act *I* could do, if there was a girl I might find to run away with. I had none of the answers, and yet I treasured the list of questions, with Tulsa and Louise and June and everyone else in *Gypsy* as my constant companions. The characters in this show, I never forgot, were real people. Their story had actually happened.

To further the illusion that I might somehow inhabit the Broadway where *Gypsy* was being retold each night, I started to cut out all the advertisements and pictures and stories I found about the theater in *The New York Times* (once Joel was finished with that day's paper) and sometimes the *New York Herald-Tribune* as well, which Joel brought home from work now and then. Mom had bought me a new bulletin board, which I set up in my room just behind the record player on the linoleum floor, leaning it against the side of my desk. Whatever record I was playing, I adjusted the clippings on the bulletin board accordingly, as if it were a sign outside a real Broadway theater. I changed my marquee so many times that the thumbtack holes left by the repeated rotation of my displays began to obliterate the fragile newsprint. I wore out the clipping of the biggest ad—for a quartet of "David Merrick Productions," one of which was *Gypsy*.

Joel and Mom shared my enthusiasm for *Gypsy*, if not my minute knowledge of it. Before long they saw it in New York, bringing me back the usual two *Playbills*. Would I ever get to go, too?, I asked. Someday, they said. *Gypsy* was "a little too grown-up," Mom explained.

"I have to agree with your mother," Joel added, not sounding as if he really agreed at all. If anything, he sounded as if he wished to take me to see *Gypsy* himself, not only because he thought I'd enjoy it but because he wanted to see it again right away. Sometimes he'd ask me to play the record on the hi-fi as he hurried through the living room to wherever he was rushing next, and when the overture began, he'd stop for a few moments to hum loudly along with it, conducting the orchestra with his hand much as he had at the theater when we'd all gone to see *Redhead*.

"This is great!" he'd call over the music, already heading to the bedroom or the den or perhaps toward the kitchen to cadge a preview of the dinner Mom and Willie Mae were preparing, his eyes dancing behind his thick black-rimmed glasses.

———

It was on one of those sultry *Gypsy* summer nights, as I would later remember them, that Joel came home from work with another newspaper he thought I might like to see: a tabloid that came to his office by subscription each Thursday, rolled up tight in brown wrapping paper, having been mailed from New York on Wednesday. It was called *Variety*, and it was known, he explained, as "the Bible of show business"—which meant that it had news about movies and plays and records and radio and TV and every other kind of entertainment. Minutes after he'd tossed it to me, I had found a section near the back titled "Legit"—which meant "legitimate theater," Joel said, the "official name for Broadway." "Legit" was five or six pages dense with type, bereft of photographs, written in a slang that I had no trouble deciphering; some of it sounded just like the lingo in *Gypsy*.

In "Legit" there were stories about Broadway shows, familiar and not, and reviews just like the ones in the New York papers. But I soon fixated on a page full of "grosses." On it were two lists: one of every play on Broadway, and one of every play in the cities beyond New York—a list called "The Road." Looking at the road grosses, I saw the National Theatre listed under "Washington," just as every city in the country seemed to have at least one theater with a Broadway show. The New York list, of course, contained more theaters than the rest of America combined. And there they were: the familiar titles of the plays whose ads I'd followed in the *Times*, each with the name of its theater and a profusion of numbers that I soon decoded as indicating the amount of money the play had taken in the previous week. What stunned me was that *Variety* boldly graded these "grosses" as "SRO" or "boffo" or "OK" or "NSG"—based on how high the amount was. "SRO" meant "standing room only" because all the seats in the theater had been sold. "NSG"—"not so good"—was for shows that had many, sometimes most, of their seats empty each night.

How could this be? How could any Broadway show have any unsold tickets? It made no sense, and it was hard to imagine actors, the actors on my records, performing one of my favorite musicals to a theater with

empty seats, with empty *rows* of seats. How could there not be enough people to fill every theater when New York has more people than any other
place in the world? Who would pass a Broadway show without going in?

It was with relief that I read in *Variety* that *Gypsy* didn't have this problem. I couldn't imagine Tulsa performing "All I Need Is the Girl" in anything other than a theater as full of people as the theaters I had been in so
far. For him to do otherwise would mean that I would have to accept his
loneliness—now interchangeable with my own nightly solitude—as permanent. Without a large audience, he would never find the girl he so des-
perately needed—for wasn't that girl somewhere in that audience?

I asked Joel why he subscribed to *Variety*, and he said it was because he
had some clients who had business in the theater. In New York? Yes.
Would he bring it home each week? Of course: "You can read it first, just
give it back when you're done."

A week later, he brought me another present: a new invention, or so he
said, called a "transistor radio." It was small, red, and shaped like a space-
ship, with an antenna you pulled out of its nose. Unlike our other radios,
it needed only flashlight batteries to work, so you didn't have to plug it in
and could take it anywhere.

For me, it was better even than a sleeping pill. Late at night, if I couldn't
sleep, I could listen to the radio and no one would know—it had an
earplug, like Grandma Rose's hearing aid. At night, after Bob Wolff's
broadcasts of the Senators games, I started listening to Steve Allison, "the
Man Who Owns Midnight," who broadcast "live" from a restaurant, "the
Black Saddle Steak House," in "downtown Washington." It astonished me
that Washington had a restaurant that was open late, just like restaurants
in New York, and that famous actors and politicians would visit there and
talk to Steve Allison as if he was an old friend. The only drawback was my
fear as I listened that I might not get to sleep before the show ended. If I
didn't, I knew I would be more alone than ever before—the last person
still awake in the entire city.

On those truly sleepless nights, I learned a new kind of terror. I could
no longer immediately seek out Mom in her room at the bottom of the
stairs, for to wake her was to risk waking Joel, and Mom seemed as frightened of that prospect as I was. If I opened the door to their bedroom, she'd

rise up from the bed with a start, her face hardened into a glare I hadn't known before, then hurry to me and shut the door behind her as quickly as she could. I was ten years old, and her patience for my sleeplessness had run out. She'd either give me a pill immediately or, if she sensed that even a tiny commotion in her bathroom might disturb Joel, order me to go back upstairs and "just try harder." Was it my imagination that she didn't hug me anymore when I needed her to?

Back in my room, I'd turn on all the lights, but I wouldn't cry as I had in Somerset and Rosemary Hills. I'd think of calling Dad in his new Washington house, but it was the middle of the night. I wasn't a baby anymore, I'd tell myself—I was about to enter the fifth grade. And besides, if I cried, who except Polly would hear me?

So I'd turn off the lights, climb back into bed, and, as had become my habit in as many homes as I could remember, surrender to the sensation of free fall that could be broken only by the arrival of dawn.

CHAPTER 3

Just as Polly and I would go to Dad's on Sunday, John and Sue would arrive first thing Saturday morning to spend the weekend with us on Cleveland Avenue, where they'd sleep in our rooms in the new trundle beds that pulled out from beneath ours. Their arrival immediately led to some compulsory activity cooked up by Joel. You never knew what it might be: a trip to a movie that had to be seen *right then*, before the prices changed at noon, or a pilgrimage to competing suburban drugstores in search of the least-expensive roll of toilet paper or AA battery.

Joel's favorite weekend excursion was a trip to Capon Springs. It was a family resort in West Virginia that he had visited often with the twins, who vouched for its fun quotient as we prepared for our first collective visit, on the Labor Day weekend before we started our new school. Capon Springs was like sleep-away camp, Sue and John said. There were activities—swimming and fishing and games and movies on rainy days—and you could get all the ice cream and Cokes you wanted.

Despite the speed at which Joel drove, the journey there was as long as that to New York. Much of it was on dirt roads that passed through farm country and parched tiny towns. When we finally arrived in Capon

Springs itself, there was no town at all—just a road that led through hills and forest until we landed at a compound that indeed looked like a camp. We followed Joel up the steps to the "main house," a large pile of gray stone and green wood trim surrounded by a huge porch. Inside, a friendly man who seemed to know Joel well loped out from behind a counter, said a loud hello to us all, and told Joel which of the buildings dotting the grounds our rooms were in: one room for Mom and Joel, another for the rest of us.

"Goddammit!" Joel snarled. We weren't in the rooms he had asked for.

"That's all I had, Joel," the man explained. "You can't make reservations so late for Labor Day."

"Come on, everyone!" Joel said angrily, stomping out of the main house as we scrambled to follow him. We got back into the car and drove the hundred or so yards to the two-story cabin where we were staying. John and I lugged most of the luggage—suitcases for us all, plus Joel's usual half-dozen airline bags full of cigarettes, magazines, candy, gum, pipe tobacco, and crumpled work papers—from the car to our rooms. We then scattered out of Joel's sight as quickly as possible—to the pool, the Ping-Pong tables, the library in the main house filled with old *National Geographics*—until lunch.

Capon Springs had lots of rules. Meals were served at a set time, each heralded fifteen minutes in advance by martial music that blasted out of loudspeakers hanging in the trees that lined the narrow road bisecting the grounds. Capon Springs also forbade alcohol, TV sets, and telephones, and if you brought a radio, it had to be turned off by ten P.M., the official lights-off curfew. That's all I had to hear to set off my inner alarm. No TV noise, no baseball on the radio, lights off at ten, a strange room in the middle of nowhere—there was no more certain recipe for panic.

What I hadn't imagined was that Joel had no intention of obeying any rules. "That crap is for the Pygmies, not us," he said, not that he explained what the Pygmies were. On our first day, he spent much of the afternoon tying up the single pay phone the management permitted, next to the red Coke cooler in the main-house office where we had first checked in. When we kids went to get cold drinks, we found him talking animatedly with some client, in a jocular shout that suggested the call was long-distance.

Wearing just his flip-flops and a plaid bathing suit, with Vesuvian ash from his dangling cigarette dusting the Brillo-like hair of his chest, Joel acknowledged our presence with a nod, then broke into French phrases punctuated by the insistent cry "Operator! Operator, *s'il vous plaît!* Goddammit!"

As we made our way out of the main house, icy soda bottles in hand, we were startled to see the nice man who ran the Capon Springs office rushing past us through the front door, his screaming, pudgy five-year-old son in his arms. The boy was bawling loudly as his father carried him into the men's room just inside the entrance. We halted for a second, long enough to hear the sound of the howling boy being spanked over and over as his dad cursed him.

Outside, we convulsed ourselves with laughter, united in our glee as we relived the scene from a safe distance. Sue and John told us that the host's kid was a spoiled brat who acted like he owned the place, and we enjoyed seeing that he was not exempt from parental punishment.

Dinner came later, preceded by a loudspeaker rendition of "Taps." Every night a different child visiting Capon Springs was selected to lower the flag to the pops and cracks that battled with the music on the recording, in exchange for which came an official certificate signed by Lou Austin, the resort's owner and patron saint. A bald and elfin old man in spectacles, Lou Austin was ubiquitous on the grounds, as was his large extended family. The Austins, Joel and Mom explained, believed that Capon Springs was not just a vacation spot but a philosophy, which was kind of like (Mom said) a religion without God. "And that's the best kind!" said Joel.

Maybe Lou Austin *was* God. In every room, there were books he had written espousing his philosophy. The grown-ups' version of the Austin creed came in a dense volume as forbidding and thick as a Bible; for children, there was the picture-book edition, filled with cartoons in what looked like a *Mad* magazine vandalization of *Peanuts* titled *The Great Me and the Little Me.* The general idea, I discovered upon flipping through our room's copy, was that you were supposed to be the nice, generous, smiling Great Me, not the mean, selfish, ill-tempered, spoiled Little Me. There was always a shining sun beaming down on the Great Me. The Little Me was shadowed by a dark rain cloud.

Joel, I realized, exulted in being a Little Me—he loved to challenge even an authority as beatific as old Lou Austin. At Capon Springs' communal "family-style" meals, I was tutored in new modes of embarrassment: Joel not only hogged the platters of food but reached with his hand into any plates that had leftover food on them, including those of the strangers at the table. He reassured any aghast victim that there was nothing unsanitary about this procedure since he paid for a manicurist to visit his office each week—and he'd show off his lacquered nails as proof.

His defiance of Capon Springs decorum didn't end there. After one dinner, Joel declared that we were driving to Winchester, Virginia—the nearest "big" town, nearly an hour away on dirt roads—to see a movie.

Won't we be coming home after curfew?, we asked. Yes, Joel said, sharing a conspiratorial smile with Mom, but don't worry about it.

Of course we could barely stay awake for the movie by the time we got there, and Joel didn't see much of it either, since he left his seat every five minutes to use a pay phone in the lobby.

The real fun, actually, was the journey back. Joel took the empty country roads at daredevil speed, and we reached Capon Springs close to midnight. With dramatic relish, he turned off the headlights and slowed the car to a crawl, negotiating the way to our cabin in the darkness, the gravel crunching under the tires the only sound. We laughed at Joel's mischief, which he accentuated with a running commentary that made each of us feel a special part of his conspiracy. We were all designated "lookouts," on guard should Lou Austin or one of his deputies leap out from behind a tree.

"The Austins aren't as smart as they think they are," Joel said as he parked, chuckling with an infectiousness that inspired us to join in.

"Why don't other families do this too?" I asked, intrigued by the notion of revolt against rules.

"Because they're no geniuses, either," Joel answered. "Most people just do as they're told and never question anything. I call it 'sex life among the midgets.'"

I didn't quite know what he meant, but I laughed anyway. He was laughing too, and I always found it safest to laugh when anyone mentioned the word "sex."

—

Many years later, Sue would tell me that it was my "big mouth" that finally conscripted me in the unending war with Joel that had always been a fact of life for her and John. What words came out of my mouth that next day at Capon Springs I no longer recall. Maybe I had simply made a wise-crack, a ten-year-old's wisecrack, when I said I was too busy to run back immediately to our cabin to fetch something (a book, pipe tobacco, an airline schedule?) that he needed at exactly that moment but had carelessly left behind five minutes earlier when we'd walked to the main house for lunch.

I might have tried to provoke him. A few weeks earlier, our dog, Patty, had been run over by a car—or so Joel had told us that Sunday when we'd returned from Dad's house, Mom sitting in silence, looking away from me and Polly, neither then nor ever after offering so much as a word of corroborating detail. Mom loved Patty too, and I thought it was unlike her to express so little response to our dog's death just hours earlier. I was convinced that Joel, who was always directing Mom to "get that goddamn mutt" out of the bedroom whenever she started barking, had killed Patty. Maybe he had smashed her with his car, just as he always slammed the garbage cans when backing recklessly out of our garage. In a moment of anger, did I accuse him?

What I do remember is this: The sun streamed down on the road in front of the Capon Springs main house, and Joel shouted, inches from my face, "I will not take any more crap from you, young man." His plaid shirt a blur blocking my vision, Joel slapped me to the ground with his huge hand. My brain felt as if it was knocking against my head. Then he grabbed me by the ankles and started dragging me up the road on my back, the dirt and gravel scraping against my skin. We were at the next building—some fifty yards away—before he dropped me in a heap in the center of the road. Through my tears, I could see that half of Capon Springs' guests, all on their way to lunch as we had been, had witnessed the scene—a humiliation more painful to me than the beating. Their stares destroyed my one illusion: that I was, if nothing else, a "good boy" who did well in school and didn't get into trouble, that I was a boy from a broken home who was not himself broken. As the onlookers hurried away, I knew that they knew I was bad, and deserved to be punished. The other children, the ones I didn't know, were laughing at me as surely as I had laughed at the boy being beaten by his father in the men's room.

I wanted to tell people at least this: Joel is *not* my father! My *real* dad is a *nice* man!

Joel stormed off in the other direction, toward our rooms: *"I'll go get my own lunch!"* Polly, John, Sue, and Mom just stood there, as immobile as I had been in the past when I'd watched Joel hit John and Sue, until Mom came over and said, in a voice whose lack of emotion was as frightening in its way as Joel's screaming, "You'll have to clean yourself up before we eat."

Clean myself up! I just lay where I was, my tears streaming into the dirt, and might have stayed there for hours had not a car soon come crawling down the road, forcing me to move out of its path. I scurried to get up, but with no help from Mom, who seemed impatient rather than concerned. I wondered if she too was afraid—afraid that if Joel returned she might be seen coddling me, the enemy. I turned my back on her and just started walking as fast as I could: away from her, away from the main house, away from Joel and our rooms, just away, past the patio where they lowered the flag each night, anywhere I could go, as far away as possible. I didn't look back. I felt as I had on that night when I ran away from Somerset, yet now I was old enough to know that there wasn't any safe haven.

I thought again of phoning Dad, but how could I do that? What would I use for money at the pay phone? Minutes later, I threw myself in defeat onto a patch of grass near the fishing creek, faintly clinging to the old fantasy that someone would care enough to worry about where I'd gone, that someone would come searching for me, that someone—Grandma Lil, Mrs. Young, anyone—would miraculously rescue me.

No one came. I stopped sniffling and, somehow sealing off from consciousness the embarrassment and fear and rage Joel's attack had provoked, made my way back to the main house. My family was sitting at its usual table as if nothing had happened, Joel included—his plan to get his own meal elsewhere having apparently been derailed by the lure of Capon Springs' scrapple. Though lunch hour was almost over, Joel, in his usual restaurant tone, shouted over to the waitress, "Dear, please bring my son a plate—there's still time for him to catch up." I ate in silence, my head down as the dining room emptied, hoping no one would notice me and stare.

Soon only Mom and I remained. We walked out of the main house together, to the nearby lawn dotted with hammocks and wicker chairs. I tried to imagine what she was thinking: How could she love a man who struck me? How could she love a man who yelled all the time and expected everyone, including her, to jump whenever he shouted an order? Didn't she think she had made a mistake to marry Joel and not be married to Dad anymore? I had never seen Dad raise his voice or so much as threaten to hit me or Polly. He didn't believe in that—he had told us so—and neither, I had thought, did Mom.

As we sat together on a bench, my effort to give voice to these thoughts trailed off. I thought Mom looked troubled, but maybe I was only imagining it. Maybe she was just squinting in the sun.

"Joel isn't like other people," she said in a neutral tone. "He has his own good points and his own peculiarities. You have to remember that he loves you and Polly very much, just as he loves me. If it weren't for Joel, we wouldn't be able to take trips to places like this—"

"I don't want to take trips like—"

"You wouldn't have a room of your own, you wouldn't have seen *The Music Man* and *Redhead* and—"

"I don't care. I don't want to live with you and him anymore. I want to live with Daddy." I was screaming, but Mom stayed maddeningly calm.

"You can't live with your father, Frank. You have to learn to have patience with Joel. He's a great man, and I love him very much. You will too . . ."

I started to say something else, but what could I say? Before I could form a thought, Mom cut it off.

"I'm going to go swimming now," she said. "Do you want to come back with me and change into your bathing suit?"

Sulking, I refused. With a sigh of resignation, Mom left me there. A few minutes later she returned, in her bathing suit now and on her way to the pool. She stopped beside me, reached into her large straw bag, and handed me a big new white pad and a narrow rectangular box full of charcoal sticks for drawing. My spirits brightened.

"I had brought these along in case it rained," she said. "There are so many different kinds of trees to draw," she went on, a touch of the old Mom back in her voice. "Why don't you try? It will take your mind off things. I always find the country inspiring when I need cheering up."

I thanked her. She moved closer and I kissed her. "I'll try," I said. As she walked away, I spread the pad out on the grass, opened the box of charcoals beside it, and started to make a picture. I hoped that if it was good enough, if what I made was beautiful, Mom would then realize that she must side with me and not with Joel.

———

The first Sunday after we were back in Washington, I asked Dad if I could speak to him alone—away from Polly and from Anadel. He seemed pleased by this novel request and, after lunch, sat me down on the living-room couch. I told him what had happened at Capon Springs, and tried to explain how it was on Cleveland Avenue. I tried not to cry, but as I searched for words to explain what my life was like and couldn't find them, the tears came involuntarily, as if to fill in the blanks. Dad's expression was one I'd never seen before: not smiling, not frowning—almost dazed, as if he was concentrating very hard on thoughts he had to keep private. When I finished, he wordlessly handed me the folded white handkerchief he always kept in his pants pocket.

"Would you like to live here—with me and Anadel?" he finally asked.

I couldn't believe he'd spoken these magic words. "Yes," I said, nodding. "Yes."

"I don't know if it's possible," he said.

"Why not?"

"Courts decide about custody, son."

"But isn't Joel breaking a law when he hits me?"

Dad sighed. "I am going to talk to my lawyer about it," he said. Then, after another pause: "Here's what you can do: I want you to write down any other incident that happens like this—just keep a list. That will be helpful."

"That happens to me—to any of us?"

"Anything you think is worth writing down."

At last I had a reason to keep a diary. If I wrote my list as carefully as I did my schoolwork, and showed it to Dad, and he took it to his lawyer, my whole life would change. I would stop lugging around this dark ache. I would have a new mom in Anadel, who on Sunday afternoons sometimes talked to me about Broadway and *Variety* and all the theater stuff Dad had no time for. Plus, Dad and Anadel's home was only slightly farther away than Mom and Joel's from my new school in Washington, where I was beginning to make friends.

My list for Dad grew quickly. Thanksgiving brought another trip with Mom and Joel—to Colonial Williamsburg, whose main appeal was that we could lock each other up in the stocks. Our first night there, when we were returning to our hotel rooms after the Thanksgiving feast, Joel yelled at John for jumping into the elevator as soon as the doors opened, before Mom had a chance to do so: *"I told you the woman always goes in and out first!"* Then—even though there were two elderly women in the elevator with us—he knocked John to the floor and, straddling him, slugged him over and over and over on the head.

The next outbreak occurred the following night on the stairs leading from the parking lot to our rooms. When I told Mom I was worried about getting to sleep, Joel started shouting that he'd had enough of my complaining, that I didn't know how good I had it. In a motion so quick I could hardly tell what was happening, he threw me down the stairs. As I tumbled, I felt as if I had been knocked underwater. I couldn't breathe, and I didn't know when or if I'd be able to regain control of my body and right myself.

Where Mom went when this happened, I never learned. She and Joel disappeared immediately. My voice echoing against the gray concrete, I just stayed where I had landed and howled. I felt more shock than pain, and once again, I felt a loss of pride—as if I'd been branded an irredeemably bad child. When other hotel guests passed through the stairwell and asked if they could help me, I stopped crying and said, "I'm okay—I just fell," so they would leave me alone.

I tried as best I could to write what happened in the diary I was keeping for Dad. If this wouldn't convince the judge to let me live with my father, what would?

—

That fall, for the first time since Mom and Dad's divorce, Mom didn't go back to school when we did. She had quit her teaching job so as to be able to travel with Joel on business. Since his foreign clients were mainly airlines, this meant, as he put it loudly, "They've got to give me passes, those bastards, anytime your mother and I want to go on a trip." He spent hours in bed, the TV roaring, his ear always pressed to the phone he yelled into, poring over his thick books of schedules, plotting routes by which he could pack in the most destinations in the shortest time. Sometimes he'd get so excited about his plans he'd absentmindedly throw a lighted cigarette into his overflowing wastebasket, setting it on fire—which finally prompted Mom to buy him a fire extinguisher as a joke birthday present.

Joel needed schedules for every conceivable activity because he didn't believe in staying in any one place too long. Even when marooned in Washington, he and Mom went out almost every night to try a new restaurant or see a movie or hear a symphony; sometimes, on a Saturday or Sunday, they'd do all three. Joel believed that the moment he arrived anywhere was the moment to begin planning a fast getaway, a lesson he taught me so well that it would take me half a lifetime to unlearn it.

The more Mom and Joel traveled, the more frantic their pace became. "You've heard of the International Jet Set?" Joel joked. "Well, we're charter members of the Cheap International Jet Set!" Almost every night Joel's secretary, Miss Adgate, would drop off a "Revised Itinerary," neatly typed on the new electric typewriter in Joel's office, on her way home from work.

The addresses were exotic: Hotel Ryukyu, Okinawa; c/o U.S. Embassy, Tokyo; Grosvenor House Hotel, Park Lane, London; Hotel d'Angleterre, Copenhagen; Queen's Park Hotel, Trinidad; the Ritz, Madrid. Joel boasted that because he never had to pay full price at any hotel, he and Mom could always stay at the best—or the best to be had "at a price where you're not getting screwed." We followed their progress by postcard—many of them now dashed off by Joel in a cryptic seismographic scrawl that often left only his standard sign-off, "All Love," legible.

They went away so often that Mom started to give us presents before she left as well as upon return. One going-away present was a grown-up book she had received in her regular brown package from the Book-of-the-Month Club: *Act One*. It was the autobiography of a man, Moss Hart, whose name I knew. He was listed as the playwright in one of the two *Playbills* (*You Can't Take It with You*) in Mom's childhood scrapbook of her trip to New York. His name was also on one of my Broadway records, *My Fair Lady*—where it said he had "staged" the production, a concept I only vaguely understood, despite Joel's and *Variety*'s efforts to explain it to me.

I opened the book, a thick and heavy one with dense print. On the first page, I learned that Moss Hart was twelve years old at the beginning of his story—just over a year older than I was—and, he wrote, "thoroughly conscious of the fact that my own dreams of glory were quite unlike those of the other boys on the block, for the fantasies and speculations I indulged in, after I had reluctantly turned the last page of *Theatre Magazine*, were always of Broadway." The pages that followed flew by so fast that I have no memory of having ever put the book down. I couldn't have read it in one sitting, but it felt as if I had.

There was much that I didn't have in common with Moss Hart. His family was poor; mine was not. He lived in New York City, not Washington. His parents were not divorced, and they rarely got in the way of his relentless efforts to find his way into the theater, first as a member of the audience and then as an assistant to a producer and then as an actor and then as a playwright. His childhood was well in the past: He was a teenager in the years before Mom was born.

And yet I grasped at the similarities, coincidental and not. My middle name was Hart, I proudly noted, and my dreams were the young Moss Hart's dreams. Early in *Act One* there was a family fight pitting the boy's father against his Aunt Kate, a kindhearted unmarried woman who lived with Moss's parents, loved the theater, and took her nephew to a show whenever she could muster the price of balcony tickets. Aunt Kate reminded me of Grandma Lil and Mom—she loved Adventures—and when Moss Hart's dad threw her out of the house, I felt that I was Moss as he stood watching this violent brawl. I was crying with him as he wondered if he'd ever again be taken to the theater. I could fathom nothing scarier—not even Joel—than the sight of Aunt Kate "dropping her beloved programs from trembling hands all over the floor" as she packed to leave forever.

Beloved: There was no possession more sacred, I felt, than a *Playbill*. Dropping programs on the floor, mutilating them, perhaps losing them: Was there any crueler fate for someone who loved the theater even more than life? Moss Hart wrote that for years he blamed his father for the loss of the aunt who was more a mother than his actual mother—much as I blamed Joel for my growing distance from Mom. But when Moss Hart grew up, he learned that he had been wrong to do so; his dad, he realized, may have been right in his argument with Aunt Kate after all. Was I wrong too? Was Mom right that I had more reason to be grateful to Joel than to be angry with him? Neither Joel nor anyone else was taking away my beloved programs; far from threatening my collection, Joel was adding to it by the score.

I couldn't answer my own questions. With Mom and Joel away and leaving us in Willie Mae's charge for weeks at a time, I found it hard to think about them too much; it was safer to daydream about Broadway than to invite another storm to break out in my head.

When I reluctantly turned the final page of *Act One*, I didn't want to leave its story behind. I went to the library to find anything else I could read about Moss Hart, so that I could learn more about what happened to him after the book ended with his first Broadway hit in 1930: *Once in a Lifetime*, the script of which I found and read. That was almost thirty years ago—would he ever write *Act Two*? The librarian at the Cleveland Park Library on Connecticut Avenue showed me a book where I could look up the titles of all Moss Hart's plays, and I read those I could find. One book led to another, until I was reading book after book about the theater, play after play, and learning about other playwrights and actors and directors whose names I hadn't known before.

Moss Hart had descended upon me, unbidden, like an angel to open up more of the world I was so desperate to see. *Act One* had validated my fantasies and speculations, which were as far removed from those of the boys on my block as his were from those of the boys in *his* neighborhood, so distant in time and geography from my own. There was a growing group of us, in my head at least: the girl who wanted to run away with the traveling show in *Carousel*, and Tulsa, who wanted to run away with his act in *Gypsy*, and now Moss Hart, who, unlike the others, with their unknown fates, had realized his goal. His name was in Mom's scrapbook, and on my records, and in almost every book I could find about the theater. I had no idea how I might accomplish what he had, but now that I had read *Act One*, which ended not with the words "The End" but with an open invitation to "Intermission," I was left with the inchoate hope that somehow I could do it too.

CHAPTER 4

n Washington, the arrival of 1960 seemed as palpable as those hokey flash-forwards in old Hollywood movies when a gust of wind blows the pages of a calendar to depict the swift passing of time. A world—a city— a childhood—that always struck me as moving in slow motion, like the bent and arthritic retired Army officers who took their daily constitutionals on becalmed Cleveland Avenue, seemed to visibly lurch forward that year. Or was I just growing up?

In Mrs. Howard's class, a combined fifth and sixth grade necessitated by the shortage of children in Cleveland Park, you could feel a stiff breeze roiling Washington's heavy swamp air. The breeze was an insistent whisper of *"Kennedy, Kennedy . . ."*—a constant Pied Piper refrain that lured even the most insulated child.

Like her parents, Mom was a Democrat. She had worshiped Adlai Stevenson much as she had Charles Van Doren. Stevenson was a brilliant man with a sense of humor, Mom had said four years earlier in Somerset when we had gone door to door to hand out "All the Way with Adlai" buttons. Maybe Mom liked as well Adlai's notoriously comic indifference to shoes: She was entranced by the famous picture of him sitting with one leg crossed over the other, exposing the hole in one of his soles. But in 1960, Mom was sure that Adlai, having already lost two races for the presidency, couldn't win. And there was something about this *Senator Kennedy*. He had even written a history book that Mom brought home from Brentano's.

We watched him on TV, marveling at his strange accent. Kennedy cared about poor people, we were told. We saw him on the news visiting the soot-encrusted men in the coal mines of West Virginia—"near Capon Springs," Joel pointed out. Willie Mae watched too; it was the first time I'd noticed her riveted by the news.

I started looking for Kennedy on the front page of the paper—the *Evening Star*—I now delivered out of a red wagon after school to make pocket money. He was always there.

Grandpa Nat gave me one of his discarded cigar boxes, which smelled just as smoky as he did, to store my growing collection of campaign buttons: Kennedy, Stevenson, Johnson, Nixon, Symington, Humphrey, Kefauver. Mom sent away to NBC News for a *1960 Convention Handbook* for me. Inside was a chart on which to write down the number of votes each candidate received when the Democratic delegates voted in July. I recorded them all, from Kennedy to Smathers, until the chart looked like one of the baseball scorecards soon to be relegated to my past: The Senators were playing their final season at Griffith Stadium before moving to a new home in Minnesota—which, everyone said, the Griffith family had chosen so that its team wouldn't have to play any longer before crowds of Negroes.

When Election Day arrived, Mom and Joel were in Italy; they couldn't vote for Kennedy because in the District, no one was allowed to vote for President at all—a strange Constitutional slight that no schoolteacher could ever coherently explain. Willie Mae had been given permission to let me stay up and watch Chet Huntley and David Brinkley, who used to be our neighbor in Somerset, on TV. I copied down all the results on a blue air letter.

Washington shifted into a still higher gear after Kennedy won. Every day the papers had pictures of Kennedy and his wife and his son and daughter as they went in and out of their house in Georgetown (right near the restaurant where I used to get triangle-shaped Danish sandwiches with

Mom, I was sure of it). In Cleveland Park, new families moved into the empty houses. They were Kennedy people, Mom and Joel said. They were Democrats coming to work in the White House, and they all had children who would be going to John Eaton Elementary, too. The city changed from a ghost town presided over by a remote, elderly man and his mute wife—all Ike did was play golf, Grandpa Nat liked to joke—to . . . well, if not New York, then at least a place where some people lived for a reason other than the accident of having been born, stationed, or marooned there.

Was it my imagination that Broadway was thinking and talking about Kennedy too—that New York was suddenly paying attention to Washington and its politics? Mom and Joel brought home the record of *Fiorello!*, a show about the man who had been the mayor of New York when Mom was young. Fiorello cared about all kinds of people, no matter how poor, just like Kennedy, Mom explained. In *Variety*, Kennedy was part of the Legit section every week, as if he were a producer or a star. Ike never went to the theater, *Variety* said, but JFK, as it always called him, loved to see plays: "JFK had a standing order for years for four tix for National openings. The other two were almost always used by RFK and Ethel." A month after the election, Kennedy went to Broadway. It had been announced he was planning to see *Camelot*, the first show directed by Moss Hart since *My Fair Lady*. But instead he went to a play about politicians running for president—one of the characters was Adlai Stevenson given a fictitious name, Mom told me—called *The Best Man*. There were so many policemen guarding Kennedy—even on the turntables of the show's scenery— that *Variety* wrote, "If Abraham Lincoln had had this kind of protection, he would have been around to applaud the final curtain of 'Our American Cousin.' "

As 1960 melted into 1961, Christmas and Chanukah were almost forgotten. No one in the city could talk about anything but the inauguration, and no holiday could compete with it. Once the big day approached, Dad was as animated as I'd ever seen him. Like Mom and Joel, he talked admiringly of Kennedy all the time: how smart he was, how heroic he had been in the war, how rich and how young (just three years older than Dad) he was. He told Polly and me that we could watch the inaugural parade with him and Anadel at a party in a friend's office on the high floor of a building flanking Pennsylvania Avenue. The way I felt about plays was the way Dad felt about presidents and senators: He liked seeing them up close, as often as possible. He and Grandpa Herbert always talked about the times, some of them before Dad was born, when Theodore Roosevelt and William Howard Taft had ordered shoes from the old downtown store— and sometimes first ladies, too, like Mrs. Harry Truman. At Rich's, they kept every order and letter ever sent from someone in the White House— and a copy of every bill. Now Dad and I together were going to see every politician in Washington, and half the leaders of the world, march right up Pennsylvania Avenue to celebrate our new president.

The day before the inauguration, Washington had one of those snow-storms that threw the city into a snarl, closing all the schools and snuffing out whatever life there was on its streets. I was nervous that Mom and Joel would not be able to go to the other big inaugural event—not the inaugu-ration itself but the inaugural eve "gala" at the Armory. Surely the storm couldn't prevent them from attending this extravaganza full of stars from Hollywood and Broadway. They had bought the tickets through Lyndon Johnson himself, Joel said. The new vice president had been a friend—"I taught Lyndon a thing or two about Washington"—since after the war, when Joel had worked at the Commerce Department for Henry Wallace, a man who had also been vice president. I pictured Joel side by side with Johnson: They were both tall men with booming voices.

As the day of the gala wore on, though, the snow swirled more and more densely in the ferocious blasts of wind. Polly and I and our friends ran around the neighborhood, which was hushed except for the scraping sound of chains on a struggling car's tires and our yelps as we hurled snow-balls or sledded down the white hills on the National Cathedral grounds. The *Evening Star* truck couldn't get through, so I was liberated from my paper route. All of Washington was on holiday. Did this mean Mom and Joel would not be able to drive to the show?

"Of course we can!" shouted Joel, his smile at its widest, his eyes beam-ing through his thick glasses. It was freezing that evening, and still snow-ing; you could hear icy spray splatter our windows. Yet he and Mom were getting all dressed up as if there was no problem. In his tuxedo, Joel looked glamorous, as if he were stepping out of one of those newspaper photographs of all the Kennedys going to a Georgetown party. Mom wore a light-blue dress she said was made of satin; her hair had been in curlers all day, and now a perfect brown wave swept upward from her forehead like a princess's crown.

Joel promised that they would make it to the Armory no matter what, even though it was miles beyond downtown, because he had the strongest chains a car could have, and because he knew a special route, and because, "Goddammit, no one stops Joel H. Fisher!" Soon they were in their red Mercury and gone.

The next morning, Inauguration Day, I woke up early. The snow had stopped; from my third-floor window I looked down on the mountainous drifts. I made my way to the kitchen; Mom and Joel were already there, drinking coffee as sunlight streamed in the kitchen windows.

"We have a present for you," Mom said, handing me a large Inaugural Gala program with a navy-blue cover that had engraved gold writing on it and a tasseled loop of gold braid along its binding. She also gave me her ticket stub—for Box 42, Seat 3.

As Mom described what she'd seen, her voice was soft and musical— the same way she'd first talked about her visit to Broadway as a little girl. She explained how long it had taken to drive to the Armory with all the stalled and abandoned cars and impassable streets; the show's curtain time had to be delayed two whole hours—it didn't start until almost eleven— because some of the stars and Washington celebrities were forced to hitchhike after their limousines were stalled by the ice and the drifts. A show in Washington that went on late at night—it was hard for me to imagine.

Joel didn't interrupt Mom as much as usual, except to make a joke or two, as if he, too, was under the spell of her storytelling. She told how she shook the president's hand, and how she had spotted so many famous people: Kay Thompson, who wrote the Eloise books and whom we'd seen in the movie *Funny Face*, and Leonard Bernstein, who conducted the Young People's Concerts on TV and wrote *West Side Story*, and Gene Kelly, who was in *Singin' in the Rain*, and the singers who had been her and Dad's favorites (though she didn't mention Dad), Frank Sinatra and Ella Fitzgerald. Ethel Merman was there, too, and sang "Everything's Coming Up Roses" from *Gypsy*. It was as if all those voices we had listened to and all those people we had seen in movies and on TV were in the kitchen with us now, as if we were back in Somerset on one of those afternoons when Dad's records were on the record player and Mom strolled into the living room while she was cooking, just for a second or two, to sway to the music and sing along.

Dad picked Polly and me up a little later—Mom and Joel slipped out of sight when he rang the bell, as usual. On our way to watch the inaugural parade, the treacherousness of the snowy streets didn't seem to faze him. Even the blizzard seemed a part of the Kennedy magic that was transforming the Washington landscape and, with it, the country. The new president was striding so confidently into the future that it would take more than a storm to deter him or anyone else who wanted to be a part of his New Frontier.

From our perch in a Pennsylvania Avenue office building, we had a clear view of the president as he passed by in his open limousine, his wife beside him. The parade was saturated with color, like Dad's eight-millimeter silent home movies. You could see Kennedy's smile as he waved to the bundled crowds lining the street, and the rich chestnut of his thick hair, glinting in the harsh winter sun.

—

Maybe it was because of the new president: The National Theatre seemed busier than ever. Maybe it was because I was older: Mom and Joel took me there more frequently than they ever had before, and sometimes to Washington's smaller theater, Arena Stage, too. On one Saturday afternoon in February, we watched Bert Lahr, the clown who was the Cowardly Lion in *The Wizard of Oz*, play a man who turns into a donkey in what Mom announced was my "first Shakespeare." In March we saw another musical on its way to Broadway, following the same path *Redhead* had, and I knew its plot in advance. The show was based on a movie we'd seen, *Lili*, about a young woman with only a suitcase to her name who runs away to join the circus.

Variety was full of news about this musical, *Carnival!*, as if it, too, were part of the new Kennedy administration. Tickets were so hard to get that "Mrs. LBJ" had to go to the National in person, knock on the door of "the house manager, Scott Kirkpatrick," and beg for seats for herself and the vice president. "Lyndon should have called me," said Joel when I showed him *Variety.* "Your mother and I are taking you and Polly and Johnny and Sue on Saturday afternoon." I was beside myself. Joel could get tickets the new vice president couldn't!

How?

Joel smiled slyly. "Remember this lesson: You can always get into anything if you try hard enough."

As I waited for the Saturday matinee of *Carnival!* I thought the week would never end. Finally, at the theater, I saw what all the excitement was about. Like the new president, this show was different. When we walked into the auditorium, the curtain was already up, revealing an empty stage with a sky-blue background. As the lights dimmed, stagehands and performers trickled into view and started to set up a circus before our eyes — raising a tent, practicing their stunts, trying on their costumes — until finally the stage was filled with a throng of people, all singing in full voice. There was no overture at all: The band, which at first sounded as if it contained only a few instruments, sang out now too, as loud and festive as any Broadway orchestra. Only then did all the lights in the auditorium go down.

It was like watching not just a circus but a Broadway show being constructed step by step, and even as *Carnival!* continued I couldn't get those opening minutes out of my mind. After the performance was over and we drove home, I went up to my room desperate, as always, to relive the experience. Improvising, I took one of the extra Rich's shoe boxes I had lying around and, taking colored paper, pastels, and scissors from my art supplies, sat down to reconstruct *Carnival!* in miniature, building and placing its scenery as if the Rich's box were a stage.

I had noticed that the shows I saw often had curtains with scenes painted on them — I knew now to call them "drops." Sometimes a drop would rise to reveal actors and three-dimensional scenery hiding behind it. Sometimes a drop would become transparent, revealing the action even before it rose — a magic trick I was eager to re-create. If I took my desk lamp and shined it from behind the drops I was making from the torn pillowcases Mom didn't want anymore, would it look just like what I had seen at the National? Hours passed as I tried, and I lost all track of time. When I finished later that night, I invited Mom up to my room to see my *Carnival!*—scene after scene, just as we had experienced it at the National hours earlier.

Mom sat on the floor. I turned off the lights in my room one by one, so that we could pretend we were at the theater and the show was getting ready to start. Soon she was laughing and applauding at each of my effects; if I had any doubts of their authenticity, she didn't. We were carried away together by the joy of my shoe-box theater. The show we had seen was with us on Cleveland Avenue, it seemed, and would never leave. When, inevitably, it ended, Mom gave me a hug, almost crushing me with her excitement. It was only later, after she had gone back downstairs, that my spirits plummeted. I may have created my own *Carnival!*, but there was no more audience for it after Mom. I did the whole show one more time, for myself.

Meanwhile, the real *Carnival!* was departing Washington for Broadway after its three weeks at the National, and I felt as if I were being abandoned. I couldn't explain why, but the thought of this show leaving reminded me of Dad moving out of our house in Somerset. Once *Carnival!* was on its way to New York, I put my shoe-box replica away on a shelf, where it sat like a lamp that had been unplugged. What use was growing attached to a play, spending hours thinking about it, if it was going to move on to another neighborhood far away? If only I could follow *Carnival!* to Broadway, my own suitcase in hand like Lili when she joins the circus, and be with it every night.

———

At school, I didn't have any friends who shared my fantasies about the theater. (Luckily I did find one, Scott, who shared my passion for girls—I'm confident that every neighborhood in those days had one boy with access to a stash of *Playboys* carelessly tucked away by his father.) Polly, Sue, and John enjoyed seeing shows well enough, but rarely remarked upon the experience afterward. The only people who understood my hobby, which only later I would realize was an obsession, were Mom and Joel. They went to the theater nearly as frequently as I aspired to. And if there was any way they could take me with them, at least in Washington, they did. I knew it was Joel's idea that I go, but I was baffled as to why he would give me the thing I wanted most in the world and still scream at me in the car on the way there and back. I couldn't figure it out, any more than I could figure out how I would ever go to the theater if I moved to Dad's—for Dad almost never went to shows.

Did this mean it was worth being hit by Joel? Whenever I started to think it was, I would halt in midthought—for surely I wanted to live with my own dad more than anything, didn't I?

Once, with Joel's encouragement, Mom even took me to the National on a school night—an unexpected breach of a previously ironclad rule. She told me the play was about a Negro family that tried to move into a new neighborhood but was kept out by white people who didn't want to live around any Negroes. I had rarely heard about such incidents, though I knew that my grandparents sometimes talked about "the colored" as if they were a different breed of human from the rest of us—not bad, just different and, well, perhaps a tiny bit inferior. I knew as well that the new vice president, Joel's friend, lived in a neighborhood that didn't allow either Negroes or Jews. But it was not a prohibition many questioned.

On the way downtown, Mom told me how Washington used to have separate sections at theaters for white people and Negroes—separate white and Negro schools, too, when she was growing up. She made it sound like ancient history, but I was confused: I never saw Negroes at the theater now and rarely saw any at John Eaton Elementary School, either. The only Negroes we encountered were the singers and ballplayers on TV, and the maids and workmen in our neighborhood.

The play at the National, A Raisin in the Sun, was as sad as Mom said it would be, but it took place in Chicago, not Washington. Surely nothing this sad could happen in the nation's capital, I figured. Since I liked A Raisin in the Sun, Mom took me to another adult play at the National, Sunrise at Campobello, which told the story of another three-initialed Democratic president, FDR, and his struggle with polio. More ancient history: As we were told when Dr. Lachman gave us our shots every fall, polio had been cured by a Jewish doctor named Salk and no one had to worry about catching it ever again.

For all my theatergoing, I never got my fill. A play only had to end for me to immediately start worrying about when I'd see another one. And because we usually went to plays with Mom and Joel on Saturday afternoons, Saturday nights became a kind of torture. After dinner, back in my room, I counted down time until eight-thirty—when I could imagine the last few stragglers entering the National to see the same show I had just seen, only now without me, whose presence in the theater that afternoon was already forgotten and who was powerless to return. I'd pull out the program and try to pinpoint exactly when each scene I'd watched at the matinee was reoccurring. If Mom and Joel had gone out for the night, I might screw up my courage, go downstairs into their bedroom around eight o'clock, and call the National box office to see if there were any tickets still left for that night's performance. Or, more daringly, I might use the tie-line—a special phone line a client had put in for Joel to speak directly to New York without paying for long-distance—to call one of the Broadway box-office numbers listed in *The New York Times*. I'd hesitantly ask the angry-sounding man who answered "Imperial" or "Broadhurst" or "Forty-sixth Street" the same question I'd asked the man at the National. If the answer was not a swift "Sold out" (and I couldn't resist calling the SRO shows, to see if they really were) I'd ask what price tickets were still left, and it was almost always "Balcony at three-eighty"—unless the man added "There are a few singles in the orchestra, but hurry up" or a flat "Standing room." Fearful that Joel would walk in at any minute, discover my misuse of his precious phone line, and punish me, I'd slam down the phone as guiltily as if I'd been caught leafing through A *Pictorial History of Burlesque* and run as fast as I could upstairs to my room.

Maybe Joel wouldn't have minded so much; he was impossible to predict. But he wouldn't be my problem much longer anyway. I kept turning over to Dad my descriptions of his behavior: Of how one night, when Joel and Mom took us to the restaurant where Steve Allison did his late-night radio show, Joel started a fight with the waitress and made her cry, forcing us to leave without eating, before the Man Who Owned Midnight arrived. Or of how Joel once tipped over John's chair when John mumbled an answer to a question about school. Mom didn't know I was making this list for Dad, but I wondered if she had guessed. If she had, did she see Joel's crimes against us as an indictment of her as well?

One night, Mom announced after dinner that in honor of my graduating from John Eaton that spring, she was taking me to New York for the weekend—me and no one else—to see three Broadway plays: one Friday night, one Saturday afternoon, one Saturday night. When she told me what the shows were, I was incredulous. I knew from *Variety* that at least two of them were SRO week after week.

"You can thank Joel for that," she said. "We can only take this trip because he got the tickets—the plane tickets, too."

Was this her way—and his—of apologizing for all that had happened? When we arrived at our hotel two nights later—it was the first time I'd gone to New York by plane—Mom let me open the three separate small envelopes containing our tickets: yellow for *Fiorello!* at the Broadhurst Theatre that night (Orchestra $9.40), pink for *Do Re Mi* at the St. James Theatre the next afternoon (Orchestra $5.50), and white for *Camelot* at the Majestic Theatre Saturday night (Orchestra $9.40). The tickets were shiny and smooth, Crayola-bright. We examined them together as if they were talismans, worldly signs of a miracle.

We had dinner at the Automat, then walked to the Broadhurst. I looked at Times Square through different eyes than I had almost three years earlier, when Polly and I had gone with Mom to *Bells Are Ringing* at the Shubert. Now I knew the name of every show and its theater and what its poster looked like. The welcoming images on the billboards, as familiar as the clippings on my bedroom bulletin board, seemed to rain down upon me like the waterfall in the Pepsi-Cola sign. In between the signs heralding plays and products were marquees for movies, the same movies that played in Washington, of course, but here the signs announcing them were elaborately painted, with color artwork of gargantuan proportions— not just white letters arranged like tiles against a black background. It was as if these movies would play in perpetuity in Times Square, never closing, unlike those that just passed through F Street on their way to the suburbs.

Walking down Broadway, I looked to my right at each intersection to see the playhouses' marquees lined up like jeweled pendants on the side streets. At Forty-fifth Street, Mom asked, "Want to take a shortcut through Shubert Alley?"—knowing she needn't wait for my assent.

I grabbed Mom's hand. The parade of theatergoers was thick now in the spring night, moving forward briskly as curtain time approached. We reached the alley, turned into it, and walked past the row of posters: *Toys in the Attic, Irma La Douce, Wildcat, A Taste of Honey, Gypsy, Advise and Consent, Tenderloin, The Tenth Man, An Evening with Mike Nichols and Elaine May, The Miracle Worker.* Soon we were right where we had been on that hot August night: at the stage door to the Shubert. But *Bells Are Ringing,* as I knew, was no longer there—*Bye Bye Birdie* had taken its place. We turned again as we passed the Shubert's front entrance, and there, without warning, was the Broadhurst right next door, its marquee proclaiming *Fiorello!*

So many people were pushing into the lobby, as small as the Shubert's, that it was hard to see how we could fight our way inside. Mom reminded me we were ten minutes early.

"Then can we stand and watch for a minute, Mom?"

"Of course, dear," she answered, and looked skyward as I did, sharing my appreciation of the sights.

I took a deep breath. All the shows we were seeing between now and the next night were in this same block on Forty-fourth Street—and this was just one block's worth of Broadway theaters. Across the street loomed a huge red-and-black sign for *Do Re Mi,* with a three-story-high cartoon by Al Hirschfeld of *The New York Times* depicting its star, my favorite TV comedian, Sergeant Bilko himself—Phil Silvers. Right past the Broadhurst was the Majestic, still vivid in my memory from *The Music Man.* The marquee was now a glowing white sign with Gothic calligraphy from King Arthur's day spelling out *Camelot.*

Years later, when I would think of Mom on that weekend, I would remember that she kept telling me how much she missed Joel, and how grateful we must be to him. I nodded in magnanimous agreement. As long as we could enjoy the fruits of Joel's largesse without the man himself, it was fine with me. But Mom really did seem to miss him; she called him long-distance during almost every spare moment—even from a phone booth the next morning, when we were out having an Adventure, visiting Mom's favorite bookstores, Scribner's and Brentano's, and the big public library on Fifth Avenue. We ran from our Adventure to the Saturday matinee of *Do Re Mi,* and when that was over, I started to feel as I usually did after Saturday matinees at the National—anxious and melancholy. But this time my mood made no sense: I was in New York, and that night we were going to see yet another show. Still, I was already anticipating the next show being over too, and having to return to Washington after that. I didn't want to go back to the hotel and take a nap before dinner. I didn't need a nap. I didn't want to leave Broadway.

Okay, said Mom. How about *another* Adventure? She suggested that we look at all the theaters we would not be going to over the weekend, starting on the next block—Forty-fifth Street. She could not have thought up a better idea—she seemed to guess my own feelings and leaned over a bit so I could kiss her in gratitude. As we made our way back across Shubert Alley to begin our tour, I could feel my heart beating: I was about to see the theaters that up until now had been only names in the *Times* and *Variety*—theaters whose actual façades existed only in fantasy, but whose box offices I had called, surreptitiously, on Joel's tie-line. Not only was I going to see what these theaters looked like, but I would be able to examine their marquees, the photographs in front, the box offices and the lobbies and the people (all New Yorkers, surely) waiting to buy tickets. "List 3 Alternate Dates," said all the advertisements for plays in the *Times*. Would the people in line to buy tickets have to list three choices too?

I found out quickly enough. On Forty-fifth Street was a huge marquee for *Carnival!* at the Imperial Theatre—it would be opening in New York the next week, having already traveled from Washington to Philadelphia, where (I knew from *Variety*) it was playing its last pre-Broadway performance tonight. We walked into the lobby and found a long line of people waiting to buy tickets.

"See," said Mom. "They've heard what a hit it was in Washington!"

We walked back out and looked at the pictures of the show—just what we'd seen at the National. I yearned to visit it again, next week, in New York.

"Let's see what else we can find," Mom said, taking my hand and leading me up the street. She sounded like Grandma Lil in the Somerset days when we used to drive to the country and get lost on purpose.

But I wasn't lost. I knew the geography by heart, as if I had known it my whole life, without ever having been there. The theaters presented themselves to us as naturally and predictably as I had imagined them; they were living things, not mere buildings of brick and stone:

The Morosco, where JFK had seen *The Best Man* only five months earlier.

The Music Box, the same theater Moss Hart had called "the Money Box" in *Act One* when, in the last chapter, he and his playwriting partner, George S. Kaufman, had their first opening night there, *Once in a Lifetime*, thirty-one years before.

The Golden, where Mike Nichols and Elaine May were performing the comedy sketches we had laughed at on *The Ed Sullivan Show*.

Then we slipped around the corner to Forty-sixth Street. There was the 46th Street Theatre, home to *Tenderloin*, a new show by the same writers as *Fiorello!* And next door, at the Helen Hayes, *Mary, Mary*, by Jean Kerr, the author of a funny book I'd read and movie I'd seen, *Please Don't Eat the Daisies*. And across the street, at the Lunt-Fontanne, was Mary Martin — no longer Peter Pan — in *The Sound of Music*, the new show by Rodgers and Hammerstein, who'd also done the songs for *Carousel*. From there it was only a short walk to the Winter Garden and *The Unsinkable Molly Brown*, by Meredith Willson, the same author as *The Music Man*; and *My Fair Lady*, by Lerner and Loewe of *Camelot*, at the Mark Hellinger; and *Wildcat*, with Lucille Ball of *I Love Lucy*, at the Alvin. Lucy, Mom told me with an ambiguous expression, was now divorced from Desi.

"Mom," I asked, pulling at her sleeve in front of the Alvin, "do you mind if I take these *Playbills*?"

In a wire trash can on Fifty-second Street, I could see *Wildcat* and *The Happiest Girl in the World* and *A Taste of Honey* — discarded *Playbills* from that afternoon, from plays I'd never see and some that Mom and Joel hadn't seen either. Why would anyone throw away a *Playbill*?, I wondered.

"Do you think they're clean, honey?" Mom asked.

"Look!" I was already leaning with half my body into the basket, stretching my short arms toward my quarry. The *Playbills* were mine!

Mom laughed. "They can't kill you as long as you don't eat them! Why didn't I think of that when I was your age?" she asked.

"Yeah, Mom — wouldn't that have been great?"

"Should we go look for more?" Mom offered, her eyes bright now. Taking my hand, she led me across Fifty-second Street, to another trash can, where I scooped up *The Miracle Worker* and *Advise and Consent,* a play about Washington that even had the Capitol on its cover.

"Make sure you don't miss any!" Mom said as I stretched and stretched to reach to the bottom.

So we continued all the way back to the hotel, sharing laughing fits as I made a show of diving into every trash can except those filthy with mustard and other remnants of Times Square lunches—with Mom always standing watch to protect me from strangers and even giving me permission to check out ("Carefully, dear") those overflowing cans on the boundary between the safe and the unsanitary.

We returned to the hotel so late that we barely had time to eat dinner. Entering the Majestic just before eight-thirty, Mom and I were euphoric when it turned out that the legend "AA" on our tickets meant that the usher would lead us all the way down a steep, long aisle until we had descended to the first row. I could touch the orchestra pit with my foot when we sat down. The curtain towered so high above us that it seemed twice as large as that of any theater I'd ever been in. It was bathed in golden light that matched the marquees outside on Forty-fourth Street.

Mom clutched my hand, as excited as I was. "Remember you have Joel to thank for this," she said.

"I know," I said, gladly. "I will."

———

When we returned home, I had three shows to build in shoe boxes, two full days and nights of memories to pick apart and examine and reassemble and replay at will, a pile of *Playbills* to examine down to the finest print. I clung to these remnants of my trip with Mom as if they were a kind of Salk vaccine inoculating me against the present reality of my return to Washington.

As Mom had schooled me, I thanked Joel as soon as we walked into the house, and told him about all the shows while Mom looked on. He'd seen them all before—as had Mom—but he didn't seem to mind hearing about them again in what must have been excruciating detail.

"Don't worry, Frank," he said. "There are many more trips where this one came from."

I went upstairs to play the records of *Fiorello!*, *Do Re Mi*, and *Camelot*, reliving the shows scene by scene. Only Dad's nightly phone call jolted me back to the present and to Washington.

I told Dad about the weekend in a shorthand version of my earlier account to Joel, but talking to Dad was like talking to Polly: He listened, then indicated his approval of my pleasure without experiencing any of it himself.

I got off the phone, returned to my record player, and gently lowered the tone arm to where I'd left off *Fiorello!*, near the end of the first act. A woman, a tall and pretty blond woman I now studied avidly in the souvenir program that Mom had bought me in the Broadhurst's lobby, sang softly in waltz time:

> *Twilight descends,*
> *Ev'rything ends*
> *'Til tomorrow, tomorrow . . .*

And I remembered just how it had been that first night of our trip only forty-eight hours earlier, when, a few minutes after the woman sang that song, Mom and I had walked out of the Broadhurst, Mom to smoke her Parliaments, me to gaze up at the lights, waltzing in our own way in the luxuriant night air of a Broadway intermission.

CHAPTER 5

hanukah Heights. Something told me the term was not meant affectionately when Joel lobbed it into our dinner-table conversation, not long after he had let go with a long, spiraling fart—which he pretended to ignore (and which we had no choice but to ignore or risk a parallel eruption of his temper).

Mom laughed at the mere mention of those two words, her eyes moist with merriment. Joel gestured toward me with his fork: "You are about to meet the idiots Helene and I have spent a lifetime trying to avoid. . . ." He was trying to prepare me "psychologically and sociologically," he announced, for Alice Deal Junior High, which I, as the oldest child, was about to enter.

"They're the kind of people I grew up with after we moved here from Manhattan Beach," Mom interjected. "The kind my mother kept pushing me to be friends with—you know, the 'in crowd'—who were better off than we were. The ones who belong to Woodmont and the Washington Hebrew Congregation—"

"Nat and Lil go to Woodmont and Washington Hebrew," I said.

"It's not the same," Mom countered. "In their generation, they didn't have a choice. But *my* generation could rebel and—"

"And join a Unitarian church, like you and Dad," said John in a rare kamikaze dive into the conversation.

"Exactly, Johnny!" said Joel, egging on his son and farting again. "As Dr. Fisher is fond of saying," he went on, "the Jews didn't kill Christ—they just worried him to death!"

Hypersensitive to all other sounds and sights, to the point of constantly anticipating imagined slights and berating relatives and strangers alike when their smirks were still in embryo, Joel was uncharacteristically poker-faced as he delivered his intestinal symphonies, his expression as innocent as that of a TV ventriloquist pretending he was not responsible for the words emitted by his dummy. "Gas" was Mom's euphemism for these constant eruptions, and she'd invoke it with a smile; as always, she seemed to be hoping that either a bemused tolerance or outright denial of her husband's most ferocious effusions could elevate them into whimsical eccentricity.

"The people in Chanukah Heights," Mom continued, as she, too, ignored the sulfurous smell engulfing the table, "care about *possessions*, material things, *chazerai*—who has the most money and the latest cars and the right clothes and all that crap. Believe me—you'll see."

I had sufficient memory of Woodmont to know what she was talking about, though I hadn't fully understood the order of materialistic magnitude I would encounter at Deal. It was a whole new Washington I hadn't seen before.

And the more I saw of this new Washington, once seventh grade began, the more I wanted to see of it. For if everything Mom and Joel said about Chanukah Heights was true, they'd left out one crucial element that outweighed all its defects: the girls.

After two years living in the sparsely populated Cleveland Park—which, I soon learned, was viewed as a possibly malevolent precinct of downtown by the Deal kids who lived on leafy Chanukah Heights streets with Anglophilic Somerset-style names like Albemarle and Brandywine—I was almost overwhelmed by the endless supply of Lauries and Lindas and Marlas and Carols in my seventh-grade class. They were not like the girls I had met at Eaton, many of whom, including almost all those belonging to the new Kennedy administration families, deserted the public-school system after sixth grade for Maret, National Cathedral, and Sidwell Friends, the private schools of Cleveland Park.

The girls at Deal were louder than those I left behind, and they didn't pretend that they weren't interested in boys. The Deal girls' bras peeked insistently through their translucent, creamy blouses. They had freckles not just on their noses and cheeks but, as in my treasured photo of Doris Day from *Boys' Life*, on that triangle of skin their blouses exposed below their necks. Their burly white ankle socks only accentuated the sculpted pink contours of their legs, which were enticingly revealed by plaid skirts compelled, alas, by school edict to drop below the knee. When the girls changed into gym clothes and bounced down the halls in shorts on their way to volleyball, you could see above the knees too and speculate about what was beyond that.

They lived in grand houses that made mine look puny and bohemian. Some of their homes resembled English castles, complete with turrets out of an illustrated fairy tale. Others were Oriental pavilions, doubles for the Moon Palace restaurant on Wisconsin Avenue, though far grander, and some had swimming pools in back bigger than the one at the Cleveland Park Club. After school, we boys would follow the girls home; their mothers, dressed with a starchy formality so different from Mom and smelling thickly of hair spray, were always afoot, ready to help their uniformed Negro maids serve cookies and milk. The moms smiled vacantly at our harmless teenage antics, then took to their bedrooms somewhere in the vast upstairs.

The dads, meanwhile, had driven to work in wide, leather-upholstered Cadillac Eldorados and Lincoln Continentals for a day of running their shops or car dealerships or "doing real estate" or manning the doctors' offices on Eye Street, where they treated the errant ears, noses, and throats of the entire metropolitan area. Most of these men, like their wives, had gone to high schools in neighborhoods farther downtown, as Dad had, back when those schools were still officially all-white. Now their lives revolved more and more around the suburbs, where their stores were expanding into one new shopping center after another north of Chevy Chase, well beyond Rich's early suburban foothold in Wisconsin Circle. Almost no dad in Chanukah Heights worked in the government: Those transient families who did, even the wealthy ones, lived on either side of Chanukah Heights but never in it. They belonged to another, and separate, civilization—one with fewer Jews, different clubs, different cars (some of them foreign), different summer homes. Government employees—whether exalted congressmen, cabinet members, and Supreme Court justices or lowly Labor Department bureaucrats—were all merely fly-by-night customers as far as the Jewish mercantile and medical aristocracy of Washington was concerned.

No one in Chanukah Heights was divorced, either. As far as I could tell, there was only one other seventh-grader who shared my predicament—a girl named Pauline. She was the most beautiful girl I'd ever laid eyes on, with springy blond curls, large blue eyes, and skin as pale as paper. She didn't dress as elaborately as the Chanukah Heights girls—she didn't wear Villager sweaters, said another girl unkindly—because her father was a beautician and didn't have much money. Like me, she lived a bus ride away from school—farther downtown than Cleveland Park, in an apartment hotel on Dupont Circle.

Pauline was the only student at Deal who lived in an apartment: a distinction as unenviable as my anomalous semi-detached house. Her parents' divorce had left her with a father but no mother. I could never quite learn why that was so as I tried to coax information out of her at lunch in the cafeteria, and then after school at the snack shop where we and our friends bought Cokes each day while waiting for the bus at Connecticut and Nebraska. When I told Pauline that my parents were divorced, she smiled and turned away, dismissing the whole subject as a joke she didn't quite get but which was, in any event, unworthy of further discussion, especially in a bustling storefront hangout where we might be overheard. Pauline didn't want to talk about *her* parents at all, I realized, so I dropped the topic.

I followed Pauline around every chance I could, trying not to look like a puppy dog, trying to strike a spark of conversation out of any slender verbal kindling that presented itself. It wasn't easy. She was shier than I was. She didn't want to talk about . . . anything, really, except what we were going to order at the snack shop and the songs we all listened to on WEAM, the top-40 radio station that supplied us with rock and roll. I too had become a devoted WEAM listener, eschewing my collection of Broadway music to listen to "Runaround Sue," "Johnny Angel," "Wanderer," and *"Duke, Duke, Duke, Duke of Earl"*—the latter a familiar chorus in gym as a joking tribute to our good-natured star athlete, Earl Swindells. Earl wasn't Jewish, but neither were any of the Deal jocks. It was as if Deal had decreed that what Grandma Lil called the *goyim* be good at sports and Jews get the good grades. Almost everyone was white, except for a couple of tall Negro boys who popped up in basketball games but, mysteriously, not in class.

Mom was startled to learn that I had some of the same teachers she had had at Deal, back before the war. At first she thought I was joking. Nor was it clear if any of the textbooks had been updated since then. Mom explained that this was because the D.C. public schools, unlike those we'd left behind in Maryland, were on a starvation budget: The city was governed by the House of Representatives' "District Committee," which, she said contemptuously, "doesn't want to give money to a school system full of Negroes." With the exception of Deal, the high school it fed into, Woodrow Wilson, and a handful of others, every school in Washington was all-Negro. Mom said that Congress spent less on kids in D.C. schools than was spent on the poorest children that President Kennedy had visited in West Virginia. Nonetheless, she insisted we'd learn "more about life" in public schools than at the fancier alternatives I walked by every day on my way to catch the D.C. Transit bus for Deal.

Life perhaps, but little else. With undemanding courses and huge classes, school seemed mostly a pretext for socializing. Dissecting frogs in biology class was not so much a scientific experiment as a heaven-sent means for contriving ghoulish pranks to catch the attention of girls. Classes were often spent passing notes making fun of the more elderly teachers. One forgetful veteran from Mom's youth, nicknamed "the Twitch" for the slapstick that ensued whenever she attempted to apply chalk to blackboard, gave us the same test repeatedly, a syndrome we were not about to correct. For every teacher who worked hard to inspire us— like Mrs. Glaser, the history teacher who taught us how to understand the news—there were at least two relics from a Washington that had gone out with Ike, if not Truman.

When I wasn't passing notes myself in Deal classes, I spent much of the time scribbling on the subject dividers of my loose-leaf notebook, drawing exact replicas of the ads for new Broadway shows I'd seen in *The New York Times*. A whole new roster of shows was opening that fall, and I added each in turn as I followed the season's progress. Late at night I found that if I fiddled with my radio patiently enough, I could bring in signals from New York—faint, but still audible. I strained to hear these distant stations, hoping that one of the chatting voices would have something to say about the new shows that were arriving almost every night on Broadway or, failing that, at least keep me company until dawn. To hear just a few words about an opening night, beamed to me directly from Broadway by a "host" with a name like "Long John" Nebel, intimate and live at that exact instant, was as titillating as envisioning girls (especially Pauline) as I tried to fall asleep. When I'd get up in the morning, though, and turn on the radio to the same spot, the New York station would always have vanished, as if it were a phantom visitor, as evanescent as the girls of my dreams.

By Thanksgiving of 1961, the new Broadway season was so hectic that I followed the openings, reviews, and grosses as avidly as I had the Senators and the election the year before. To my surprise, Dad announced that he would do just what Mom had done last spring: take me to New York to indulge my "hobby." Polly was coming too, and so was Anadel, and so was her five-month-old baby, whose name might as well have been "your new sister," since that's the way Dad always referred to her in my presence, especially when explaining that he and Anadel were moving into a new house in Washington so that "your new sister" could have a room of her own. The lack of mention of a room of *my* own, or of Polly's, at the new house was, I figured, only temporary; though Dad visibly flinched at my accounts of Joel's behavior, he said little, not wanting to tell me a concrete plan for the future, he said, until his lawyer told him the time was right.

The Thanksgiving trip was good news enough for the time being—the prospect of a trip to Broadway was like a huge blinding light, obliterating everything else in my path. By the time it arrived, Mom and Joel were in Rome, leaving the usual trail of itineraries and air letters in their wake. I could hardly contain my excitement about my trip with Dad, and wrote Mom and Joel on Thanksgiving morning from my step-uncle and aunt's house on Long Island, where we were staying:

Dear Mom and Joel,

Tomorrow I'm going to go shopping on Broadway and Fifth Avenue. I will try to get tickets for "Sail Away," "Milk and Honey" or something else, depending on luck. I will go to the box office all by myself while Dad is working in the Empire State Building. In the afternoon, I'll be on 5th Avenue and see the N.Y. Public Library again, Brentano's, Scribner's, etc. Saturday, after the play, I will make my trash-can raiding session. I hope you are having a wonderful time in Rome. I miss you—

The next morning Anadel, Polly, and "your new sister" stayed behind while Dad and I drove into the city in his station wagon. Dad wanted me to accompany him first to an office on Broadway, not far from the theaters, to visit a company called Capezio, whose shoes he sold at Rich's. I liked the idea of going to work with Dad; it made me feel that I was grown-up. Besides, I would get an idea of what the New York part of Dad's work was.

It wasn't what I had expected. The elevator doors opened onto a dazzling white corridor with framed Broadway posters everywhere, huge ones, the same as those in Shubert Alley. Dad explained that Capezio made all the shoes that dancers wore in Broadway musicals, and I listened with renewed respect for his business. Dad explained my interest in Broadway to his business friends, who smiled and promised to mail me some extra posters. Then a secretary entered with lunch for all of us—a tray piled with sandwiches and potato chips and Cokes. In New York, anything was possible: An office could be like a restaurant and Shubert Alley all at the same time.

After lunch, I went on my way. Could there be anything more exhilarating or precious than the freedom to walk down Broadway by myself? I was proud that I wouldn't need a map to figure out my route. *Sail Away*, after all, was at the Broadhurst, practically an old haunt to me now. I would rush from there to Brentano's. I had fifteen dollars from Dad in my pocket, enough for two Saturday-matinee tickets, with money left over to buy a book.

I had been given an hour and a half for my solitary adventure, to be clocked on the new "self-winding" watch Dad had given me for my twelfth birthday. It was hard to know what to do first—search through trash cans for *Playbills*, or go to the box offices.

I decided to retrace my walk from my last visit, one block at a time. But not only was Mom absent this time; so was the April sun, replaced by the chill slate sky of late autumn, and so were many of the theatrical landmarks Mom and I had toured together. Seeing the changes with my own eyes, rather than just reading about them in the paper, I was struck by how life moved so fast, almost cruelly, on Broadway. *Fiorello!* had fled the Broadhurst to make way for *Sail Away*, as if it had never existed. I studied each such metamorphosis with contradictory emotions of excitement and loss. With their new marquees and posters and glass-encased displays of fresh photos, the theaters promised a teeming bounty of surprises. But there remained not a shred of their previous tenants, who were gone forever and mourned by no one, perhaps, except me. When shows left the National, I knew they were going on to Broadway or at least to another town on the road. Where did the plays that left New York go?

Even more disconcerting was to revisit the shows, still running, that I'd walked by with Mom in the spring but that had since changed their casts. The theaters looked the same, and the photographs out front showed the identical scenes and poses, but the names on the marquees and posters were different, the faces in the photos unfamiliar. *The Sound of Music* was still at the Lunt-Fontanne, but it wasn't Mary Martin holding a guitar and singing to the Trapp family children in their sailor suits; it was a stranger named Martha Wright in exactly the same dress Mary Martin had worn, her face fixed in the same expression, but with a whole new covey of children. The cover of the *Playbill* had the new photo too, wiping out *The Sound of Music*'s previous family portrait with the finality of death. The same was true at the Imperial, where Lili in *Carnival!* was no longer Anna Maria Alberghetti but Susan Watson, and at the Majestic, where King Arthur and Queen Guenevere weren't the Richard Burton and Julie Andrews whom Mom and I had loved but actors I'd never heard of. It was astonishing and weird, like a dream, that new actors could entirely displace those who came before, as if no one would know the difference or care.

Was this what had happened in Somerset and Rosemary Hills when new families had moved into the homes we'd abandoned? I didn't want to be forgotten, either, and yet I knew that I had been.

The Broadway cast changes filled me with that unsettling old feeling, as old as that first visit to the National and *Damn Yankees*, that the happiness of being at a play, the most joyous sensation I knew, could not be had without the punishing realization of how finite and unrepeatable each visit to a theater was.

Not that I dwelled on that thought. I was having too much fun waiting in line with all the other ticket-buyers at the box offices of the shows I wanted to see the next day. If the people ahead of me were impatient to get to the window, I was anything but; I listened intently, doting on each customer, trying to hear each request and how it was dealt with. But my eavesdropping foretold my own fate: a brusque "Sold out" from the man behind the box-office window, who looked dismissively past me to the next customer, as he had past the preceding theatergoers who had been so frivolous as to shop at the last minute for a holiday weekend.

I couldn't hide my disappointment from Dad when I reported back to him that I'd failed to find tickets for any of our choices. "That's the way the ball game goes sometimes," he said, with half a smile and no visible disappointment. He had little sense, I felt, of how crushed I was at the notion that we'd traveled all the way to Broadway and yet might fail to see a show. But his Capezio friend announced that he would have his secretary call his ticket broker—a rescue that was for me as dramatic and unlikely as a prisoner's last-minute reprieve from Death Row. Within minutes—though it seemed like hours—his secretary came in to say we were all set with tickets the next afternoon for a mystery called *Write Me a Murder* that had just opened on Forty-fourth Street, at the Belasco.

And so we went to the Saturday matinee, just Dad and me together again, and I was as content as I would have been had we succeeded in getting tickets to one of the shows I'd set my mind on. This seemed to be the kind of play Dad would like, too—so I hoped—but though afterward he said he'd enjoyed it, he didn't have the same enthusiasm that I—or Mom—or Joel had. When Dad saw a play, he always liked it—no more, no less. On our way to the parking garage, I asked him if I could search through trash cans for *Playbills* from other shows, as I had with Mom. He said yes, but that we must hurry, so that we could get back to Long Island— and to Dad's second, new family.

———

It was late afternoon, and no one was home when I returned to Cleveland Avenue on Sunday. Willie Mae was off, and Mom had left a note on the hall table saying that she and Joel had gone to the movies. Polly had decided to continue on with Dad and Anadel for dinner. With the place to myself, I went right to my room to settle down with my *Playbills* and records.

I was soon interrupted by phone calls coming in for Joel on our three regular lines and on the tie-line to New York, which had its own insistent, high-pitched ring; I wrote down the messages very carefully, as I'd been instructed to do. I hadn't been home an hour when a rarity occurred: a collect call.

"Selma Fisher is phoning Mr. Joel Fisher from Baltimore," the operator said.

"Mr. Fisher is not in," I said in the voice I'd perfected for Joel's business callers.

A distraught woman's voice cut in, speaking over the operator: "Can't you accept the call? Please! I'm Joel's sister."

I knew Joel had a sister, but though Polly and I had been introduced to all the new step-relatives that had come with Anadel, we'd never met any family members on Joel's side except Sue and John.

What could I do? Anxiously, I told the operator I'd accept the charges, and she left me alone on the line with Selma Fisher.

"Who are you?" she said.

"Frank."

"Are you Helene's son?"

"Yes."

"You have a nice mother."

I didn't know how to respond; Mom had never mentioned Selma; I wanted to speak as rapidly as I could. If the call went beyond the three-minute long-distance rate, Joel's wrath would be guaranteed. "Do you want me to take a message?"

"Tell your father Selma called."

I had long since learned it was too complicated to correct anyone who said Joel was my father. "Okay."

"How old are you, young man?"

"Twelve."

"I live in Baltimore, you know."

"Yes . . ."

"Do you know what is happening in Baltimore?"

I didn't know about anything that happened there except the Orioles. It was just a city we drove through on our way to New York.

"Please listen!" she said. "You must tell this to Joel and Helene as soon as they're home—do you know when they're going to be home?"

I guessed around seven to seven-thirty, based on Mom's note.

"They have to call me as soon as they get home. You see, they're killing all the Jews—"

"What?"

"Tell them this," she repeated urgently. "They're killing all the Jews in Baltimore."

I listened in silence, not knowing what to say.

"Did you hear me?" she asked. She had started shouting into the phone, the way Joel sometimes did.

"Yes."

"Will you leave your parents my message?"

"Yes."

"I have to go now," she said, now speaking rapidly, her voice another octave higher, as if she were fleeing a pursuer. "I really have to get out of here, I have to get out of here fast. Joel will know how to find me."

Before I could say anything else, she had slammed down the phone.

I didn't know what to do. How could I rescue Selma? There was nothing to do except wait and hope that Joel or Mom might call in at some point. But they didn't. When they finally came home, I told them the story of the entire call.

Mom shot a look toward Joel.

"Don't worry," Joel said to me, sounding neither upset nor angry. "They're not killing any Jews in Baltimore. That's Selma. She has a mental illness, and she's in a hospital—"

"A very nice hospital," Mom interjected.

"A hospital in Baltimore. If she calls again, you are not to accept the charges."

Still fearful that Joel might boil over, I protested: "I didn't know what to do. If you had told me—"

"You'll know for next time," Joel said quietly, cutting me off and closing the subject.

———

At Deal, my heart continued to quicken at any sighting of Pauline, but trying to talk to her on the phone was futile. Her father discouraged any calls by commanding her to the phone grudgingly, in a thick accent; that's all it took to sap the courage I'd needed just to dial her number, the only one I knew with a DUpont exchange in a world of EMersons and FEderals.

One day after school at the snack shop on Connecticut Avenue, I noticed that she had written my name in blue ballpoint pen on her white sneakers. Like a boy's gift to a girl of his I.D. bracelet or the writing of a name on the light-blue cover of a loose-leaf binder, this was a Deal ritual signifying that Pauline and I were going steady.

My classmates, male and female, mocked me—but with curiosity and smiles, not ridicule. The jokes were lewd, and I didn't mind. I knew that my name on Pauline's Keds meant that I had crossed an official barrier: This was my permission to kiss her as soon as possible, instead of waiting interminably and perhaps in vain for us to be brought together by the Spin the Bottle games we played in the unsupervised rec rooms of Chanukah Heights in the afternoons. Maybe it was permission as well to get to what all the Deal boys referred to as second base—to touch the bra beneath Pauline's blouse and, through it, the pale white breasts whose increasingly fantasized proportions I dreamed of each night.

But how? Where? When? Pauline never invited any of us to her apartment. Her home was far removed from the Deal neighborhood, and she made it clear that her dad didn't want her friends around anyway. The weekend parties thrown by Deal seventh-graders were also a dim prospect; unlike our afternoon soirees on school days, these were heavily chaperoned by mothers wielding platters of Ritz crackers and cheddar-cheese spread. There was no way to kiss anyone there—you had to settle for grazing your lips on the curve of a girl's neck in the shadows as the party's host set the 45 r.p.m. record player to repeat "Soldier Boy" until the restrictive confines of the song and the zone of petting induced a claustrophobic nausea. With such restraints on my lovemaking intentions, I needed another plan. My *Evening Star* paper-route cash mounting up into double digits, I resolved to send away for tickets to a show at the National Theatre and then take Pauline there on a Saturday afternoon all by myself. I ached to go to a Broadway play without my parents, and in my imagination I pictured Pauline, who had never seen a play before and didn't seem to quite know what one was, falling in love with the theater even as she fell in love with me. She was unhappy living with her dad—I could tell that. I would make her happy—she would make *me* happy—and we would run away together.

To where? At that point the fantasy trailed off. Not that I needed to think it through that far. *All I need is the girl!*

I knew just what play to take Pauline to. *Bye Bye Birdie* was arriving at the National after its long run on Broadway. The show's story would surely be irresistible to her, since it described life as we knew it at Deal. Its characters were teenagers who wanted to go steady, just like us and like the teens we watched on TV's *Many Loves of Dobie Gillis*.

As soon as the first ads for *Bye Bye Birdie* appeared in the Sunday Washington papers, I broached the idea with Mom and Joel at dinner. I would buy tickets with "my own money," I made clear. Joel cast an instant veto. "We already have tickets for you and Polly and Sue and John for the last Saturday matinee," he said. Then he added, as if to preclude any possible rebellion on my part. "We are going *as a family*, and that's it."

Well, I could find another way to kiss Pauline. Not even sex could distract me for long from news of an imminent visit to the National. I could barely absorb the other news Mom announced at dinner: a story in the *Times* that Moss Hart had dropped dead in New York. Moss Hart was "young," Mom said—"only fifty-seven"—though that didn't seem young to me, since Mom was thirty-five.

I read the article after dinner, but I had already studied the life of Moss Hart so exhaustively that I learned little from it. His death didn't make me feel sad so much as lost. The two times I had been in New York since reading *Act One*, I had convinced myself that I would turn a corner on Broadway and there would be Moss Hart, standing in the lobby of his old Music

Box theater—or at the Mark Hellinger or the Majestic, where his *My Fair Lady* and *Camelot* played every night. I would tell him how his book had changed my life and how much I wanted to be just like him. And he would shake my hand and take me into the theater, where we would sit in the empty house and talk about his plays and what we had read in *Variety*.

Now I knew that this meeting would never take place, but his death was otherwise hard to fathom; I had yet to experience the death of anyone I knew. If I couldn't meet Moss Hart, would I ever meet anyone who could explain to me how the theater worked? Many of its mysteries, large and small, were not contained in books, and I was confronted by more of them at *Bye Bye Birdie*. Early on in the show, a black drop rose to reveal a huge, Crayola-colored jungle gym that then moved forward so quickly I thought it might keep advancing until it sailed over the orchestra pit and into the auditorium and my lap. That didn't happen, but the gyrating sensation generated by the onrushing tableau kept gathering momentum just the same. The giant set, divided into cubicles, was filled with teenagers, boys and girls, singing into pastel Princess phones about "going steady" as they danced maniacally, flinging their lithe bodies against the walls of their confined "rooms." The sight of all these bodies undulating in sync with their telephone cords, combined with the words they were singing and the brass of the orchestra in the pit, made me levitate in my seat. The girls were all cute, as cute as any in Chanukah Heights, and I couldn't tell whether I was more excited about the show or about the cresting waves of sex that seemed to wash over me from the stage—or whether both of my favorite stimuli had by some alchemy merged into a sensation that was greater than the sum of its alluring parts.

"Can we go again tonight?" I asked on the way home, surprising myself with my outspoken greed but suspecting that I might find a sympathetic patron in my stepfather.

"No," said Joel, the merriment in his voice echoing my own enthusiasm, despite the cold water of his answer. I knew my wish was ludicrous, but I also knew that Joel didn't follow the normal rules and routinely saw plays and movies over again—maybe sometimes in the same day.

But my disappointment galloped forward anyway; I didn't know how I'd get through this Saturday night. The thought of *Bye Bye Birdie* playing its last performance in Washington without me there seemed unbearable. How could the actors in whom I had invested all my affection that afternoon now go on as if I had never known them? How could they be so fickle as to give the same performance for a whole new audience from which I was excluded? If I could have leapt out of the car at a stoplight and run back to E Street on my own, I would have.

I put on my *Bye Bye Birdie* record as soon as I was in my room, careful not to raise the volume to the point where Joel and Mom might hear it. But soon I heard Joel yelling anyway. I opened my door to confront the tirade wafting up the stairs, only to realize that Joel was yelling at Mom, not at me.

"This is your goddamn fault, Helene," he said.

I kept still, trying to hear what they were saying in the bedroom below me. Then Joel slammed the door to their room so hard that the shelves on my wall rattled.

As if I were listening to a stereo with a speaker missing, I could hear only him, not Mom.

"Christ, you always do this, Helene, no matter how—"

Then silence; she must be interrupting him.

"I'm sick of your crap!"

More silence—a longer one.

"I don't want to hear any more about it—"

A short silence; I could hear Mom's angry voice but not her words—just a tone, a muffled but high-pitched siren sound.

Then Joel again, louder than ever: *"That's the way you want it—well, that's the way you'll have it!"*

Suddenly the door to their room swung open, smashing against the wall.

Now I could hear Mom crying loudly. The sound was familiar—I recognized it all too well. She sounded like me back in Somerset, when I'd sobbed so hard that I felt I was having convulsions and couldn't stop, couldn't ever stop. She was trying to say words while she was crying, just as I used to do, but they were drowned out by choking and coughing.

I heard Joel stomp down the hall and clatter down the stairs.

Then I heard something I'd never heard before: Mom screaming, her voice escalating in hysteria with each word. *"Where are you going? Where are you going, Joel?"*

Joel was now two floors below me. I could hear his enraged fumbling with the ring full of car keys that he always left in a brass bowl on the table by the front door, but his voice was still loud and clear.

"I'm just getting out. It's none of your goddamn business where I'm going!"

"It is my business," Mom said between sobs. *"It is . . . "*

Mom was out of her bedroom now, on the second-floor landing. I don't know if even *I* had ever cried so hard. Mom was trying to speak, but the sobs kept cutting off her words. *"You . . . can't . . . leave . . . You can't leave, Joel!"* She started toward him down the stairs, sobbing and shouting at the same time.

Then there was another huge slam—the front door now, and so hard that it, too, shook my room at the top of the house.

In the wake of Joel's departure came an eerie hush. I could hear Mom crying quietly, so much more quietly now, like a last brief downpour of rain after a storm has passed. I heard her walk slowly up the stairs to the second floor and along the hall to her room; then she firmly closed the door behind her.

Did she assume that I hadn't heard anything because I was asleep? Did she expect me to come downstairs and talk to her? What would I say?

I didn't know what I could say to anyone about this. If I told Dad, he might not care. Grandma Lil would want to change the subject. If Joel caught me telling anyone, I could imagine all too well what the reprisal would be.

I was gripped by the thought that Mom was going to get divorced again—and then what? Could I leave Mom and move in with Dad then? Would Mom have to move again? Where would we live? What school would I go to next? I couldn't leave Mom.

I wished that the next day was Monday, not Sunday, so that I might be with my friends at Deal, instead of with my family, whatever was left of it. I really didn't want to see tomorrow.

I wondered what Mom was doing. I listened hard but couldn't hear anything. Creeping in the dark, I started down the stairs. But when I reached the lowest steps, just above the landing, all I found was more darkness. Mom's door was still closed, and as there was no light or sound seeping underneath the door, I knew that she was either asleep or lying in bed alone, awake, in the dark.

There was nothing to do. Standing on the steps outside Mom and Joel's room, I didn't feel like crying as Mom had. I felt angry, so angry that I started to fantasize how happy I would be if Joel died. I hated him so much that I wanted to kill him.

But then the hatred and the anger turned into another, familiar feeling, an unfocused seething—that old, old fear of the darkness that scared me most—the darkness of not knowing what was going to happen next.

I was too terrified to concentrate on a book, or the radio, or even my *Bye Bye Birdie* program. There was nothing to do once I climbed the stairs but get into bed with all the lights on and wait until it was time to deliver the Sunday newspaper.

CHAPTER 6

At first I thought I must have imagined it, in the haze between sleeping and waking that I inhabited until my alarm clock went off at dawn. But when I went downstairs Sunday morning on my way to pick up the thick Sunday *Stars* for my paper route, I knew I had not. There *had* been a huge thud at some later hour—and more screaming—but so faint I couldn't identify its source—or perhaps the sound had been muffled because I had been sleeping, albeit fitfully, after all. The evidence was in the living room. There, in the steely February dawn, were two chairs lying broken in a corner, a pair of casualties left on a battlefield, their dark wooden backs ripped from their straw-covered seats in splintered, jagged tears. They were like family, these chairs: They had been in every house we'd lived in, starting in Somerset. I wondered if Mom and Dad had picked them out together before I was born, on a shopping spree at Hecht's downtown. I tried as best I could to picture how Joel had reduced them to their current state. Then I tried to stop thinking about it, as if I could hide away a shard of pain to retrieve and examine some other day.

When I returned from delivering my papers an hour later, the chairs were gone, their disappearance never to be explained. Walking swiftly past

the living room on my way to the stairs, not eager to call attention to myself, I glanced down the corridor to the kitchen, where I saw Mom and Joel
eating breakfast, as if nothing had happened.

I was a coward, I would come to realize. I never did quiz Mom fully
about that night—or about any of the many nights like it that followed. I
didn't want to know too much. Maybe I was too preoccupied with saving
myself to rescue her. Maybe I didn't want to save her out of the selfish fear
that another divorce would hurt me more than Joel hurt Mom. Maybe I
couldn't have saved her even if I'd tried—I was the child, after all, and she
was the adult, and I could not interject myself into her marriage any more
than I could have kept her and Dad together.

Maybe, I would sometimes wonder, she didn't want to be saved. When
Mom and Dad divorced, it was not only our home that had been broken,
and me and Polly, but Mom and Dad too. Mom wanted her life fixed now,
and Mom wasn't good at fixing things—not Joel's temper, not my insomnia, not Polly's growing shyness, not herself when she felt overwhelmed by
the world. She tried hard always; she loved us and would do anything to
help us if she could, to help us before she helped herself, to help us even
if she couldn't help herself. But more often than not, she'd be frustrated by
the effort and retreat into a sadness I didn't know enough to understand.
She'd become quiet then, and she'd burn the food at dinner, not in a far-
cial *I Love Lucy* kind of way that we could all laugh about later but in a
catastrophe that would lead to tears.

With Joel around, she didn't have to be the fixer anymore. He had pills
for me, and there were always restaurants for dinner. The Broadway shows
and museums and trips she longed for, and that she had rarely visited with
Dad, were always there: Like a magician, Joel could pull them out of his hat.

Was his magic worth any price, even his rage? No, I told myself. But
then I would think of how young and happy Mom looked when she came
back from a trip—I would think, too, of how happy I was when Joel sent
Mom and me to New York to see all the shows we wanted to see. Mom had
been imprisoned in Somerset, perhaps, and if her new marriage, too, was
a kind of confinement, she was nonetheless doing all the things she
wanted to do, all the things that were in the scrapbook she kept of her visit
to New York when she was my age. And I had to admit to myself—if only

for a second—that they were the things I wanted to do too, and that if we'd stayed in Somerset, and had Mom and Dad stayed married, we wouldn't be doing them.

After that first brawl, Joel more and more treated Mom as if she were one of us kids—a child to be barked at or slapped whenever she didn't do exactly what he demanded, whether it was bringing the Tabasco sauce or pickles from the kitchen to the dinner table with his food, or getting into the car on time when heading to a restaurant or theater, or instantly retrieving the *TV Guide* or the shirt or the newspaper that he lost on a daily, if not hourly, basis. Out of such tiny lapses he would weave a tapestry of recrimination in which Mom's failure to be "competent" was an indictment of her entire personality—from her inability to stick up for herself with her mother or a department-store clerk to her inability to "do anything right"—a malignant internal haplessness that I sensed Mom always believed she had.

That was Joel's method, I was beginning to realize: to find the most vulnerable aspect of whomever he wanted to attack and target it—and then to come to the unexpected rescue of the very person he had just hurt. (Was this why he was a successful Washington lawyer?) And so he zeroed in on Sue's insecurities about fitting in at school, Polly's sullen shyness, John's abstracted daydreaming. With me? He didn't attack my athletic incompetence (and actually made patient efforts to give me the remedial coaching Dad never had time for) or my slight stature; if anything, he encouraged my insolent attitude toward Deal and my addiction to the theater. Could his idea of my vulnerability have been that I was too fearful of losing Mom? So it would seem, for when Joel came down on me most violently, it was by forcing Mom to choose between the two of us, by wresting her away from me, as he had at Capon Springs. And yet why did he then turn around and make it possible for Mom and me to go to New York together, without him? There was no logic that applied. Magicians don't explain their tricks.

Increasingly, Joel's fights with Mom, like those with the rest of us, were not hidden behind closed doors. He lashed out at her as uninhibitedly and spontaneously as he farted, without any pretense of self-censorship. After a while, Mom didn't seem to care if we heard her yelling or sobbing, and had no way to prevent us from hearing even if she did care. Joel's explosions often detonated while we were all at dinner—at which point he would throw back his thronelike chair with a crash and bolt from the house altogether, jumping into his car and driving downtown to his office. Polly, Mom, and I would just sit in silence, contemplating the ruins of the evening before us. We would try to finish our meal as expeditiously as possible while Willie Mae hovered in the background, platter in hand, to offer seconds, surrealistically upbeat amid the gloom. Mom would quickly excuse herself, leaving Polly and me to eat alone while she climbed up to her bedroom to collapse. "Oh, that Mr. Fisher!" Willie Mae always said, like a comic maid on a TV show, as if the tension could be diffused with a joke.

Once dinner was at last adjourned, Polly would scurry upstairs to her room and hide. Sometimes I would follow right behind her, and we'd band together on the third floor to compare notes on the latest cataclysm. For a few minutes, as if we were reconstituting our old cardboard-box home, our attic would be a safe, private haven from all the warfare below us. But in a way, Polly had long since given up hope for Cleveland Avenue; she had moved to Dad's in spirit if not in fact and left me behind, even as I was still planning my move. Not that she confided in me—I had to guess. As so much about our family was different from other families, Polly and I had never been close in the easygoing way of siblings around us, not from the start. By the time Mom and Dad separated, I realized long after the fact, we had unintentionally mimicked them with our own separation. Instead of bringing us closer, our shared hatred of Joel sealed our divorce.

On one of these nights, I let Polly run ahead while I knocked on Mom's door on the way up to my room. She told me to come in, and there she was, lying down fully dressed the way she used to when she wasn't feeling well on those Somerset afternoons when she was still married to Dad. I knew she'd been crying hard because her face was bright red, her eyes bloodshot. I fumbled around for something to say, but Mom cut me off.

"All husbands and wives have fights, Frank," she told me.

"You and Dad didn't."

"We should have. It's healthy to get it all out instead of letting things fester inside."

"Are you sure you're all right, Mom?" I asked, moving closer to her side of the king-size bed. On the covers next to her, in the indentation left by

Joel's hulking body, was the collage of his paraphernalia: the magazines and newspapers, the tiny Olivetti he typed on in his lap, the bowl-size ashtrays overflowing with cigarette butts, cigar stubs, and used pipe cleaners.

"I'm fine, honey," she said, raising herself slowly as if waking from a deep sleep.

She could see I didn't believe her. "You worry too much," she added. "I wish you wouldn't pick up my worst traits—I'm a big worrier, too, so I know what it feels like. I wish I could get back all the time I wasted worrying about things that there's no point in worrying about. You have to promise me you'll stop doing it. You're too special to fall into that trap, honey."

Was that the problem—that I worried too much? Maybe she was right. Maybe this happened in other houses, not just my own, and I just took it more seriously than my friends did. How could I find out? Like Mom and Dad's divorce, a marriage like Mom and Joel's wasn't on TV, or in the movies, or in the books I read. Yet I still had my memory of *Carousel*, where Billy Bigelow hit Julie Jordan and she kept loving him anyway. "What's the use of wond'rin'," she sang on Dad's old record, "if he's good or if he's bad? He's your feller and you love him—that's all there is to that."

Was that all there was to this? I didn't want to make Mom feel worse. But I had to say *something*. I decided that the safest approach was to limit my complaints to *my* conflicts with Joel—hoping that this might be a cue for her to talk about her own. But she never did. She was never disloyal to her husband.

Her explanation was the same as always. I came to know it by heart: "Joel loves you very much, just as he loves me very much. I know that he doesn't behave like other people—but that's what I admire about him. He isn't a conformist. He doesn't care what other people think, like all the other people I know, and my parents, and most of the people I grew up with."

"But, Mom," I argued. "It's not fair. Joel—"

She didn't deviate from her usual text. "Everybody loses their temper—you do too. Someday you'll understand better. Joel didn't have an easy childhood. He had to overcome a lot." She told me that Joel's father had died in an accident when Joel was still a boy—falling down an elevator shaft.

"Frank, you have to think of the good things, not just the bad. If it weren't for Joel, we wouldn't be living in this house, you wouldn't be going to the theater whenever you want—"

"*Whenever* I want?"

"You go plenty. Look around at the other kids your age—don't you see how lucky you are? How exciting your life is by comparison?"

At that juncture, I gave up. I was too confused. I *was* better off than many of my friends, I guess. I *did* see plays, I *did* go to New York, I wasn't confined by the boundaries of Chanukah Heights. Did this mean I had to be terrified half the time, tiptoeing around my own house to avoid the land mines Joel deposited there without warning or reason every day?

"I want to live with Dad," I said petulantly, a threat. Mom snapped back, her voice as sharp now as it had been soft: "I'm not stopping you. Go ahead!" And then I started crying, because while I was sure I wanted to live with Dad, wasn't Mom, by inviting me to leave, saying that she didn't love me anymore?

She started crying again too, as if, after all, she thought it might be the worst thing in the world if I moved out. She reached out for me, and cradled me against her. Did she need me as much as she needed Joel?

"I didn't mean it," she said. "When people get angry, they say things they don't mean." After that, we both calmed down, each of us grateful to forge a truce, and Mom said, so gently it was impossible to object: "You've got to give Joel more of a chance—you've got to look at his good side." I nodded, just to get my surrender over with, and she continued: "Get yourself together and come downstairs. Maybe we'll go to a bookstore tomorrow . . ."

And so the next Saturday afternoon we would wander through the rambling Saville bookstore in an old house in Georgetown, stopping for a sundae in the garden at a nearby ice cream parlor. Or we'd go to the Phillips, where Mom would talk to me about the Rothkos and Klees, because she'd read about them in the encyclopedia of art that had arrived volume by volume from the Book-of-the-Month Club. In those stolen hours together, we'd share the unacknowledged safety that was ours when Joel was away in his office on K Street—at least until Mom checked in with him by phone, at which point he'd either insist on meeting us wherever we were or summon us to join him immediately in *his* next plan, whether it was filling up both cars with gas or making a pilgrimage to a late-afternoon movie.

Even as Mom and Joel fought more and more often, there were just as many nights when the coiled tension of Joel's anger would dissipate, throwing the entire household into a celebratory mood. Sometimes Joel and Mom threw dinner parties in the same dining room that was often the site of their rows, with what we were told were important guests, Kennedy Washington guests: a Supreme Court justice named Bill Douglas, whom Mom admired as much as she did Adlai Stevenson, and an ambassador to India named Ken Galbraith—so tall he towered even above Joel—who had taught at Harvard and written books that Mom proudly displayed on her shelves in the den.

Polly and I ate earlier with Willie Mae, but we were always summoned downstairs to say hello to the visitors, a ritual that allowed us to see Joel in a rare moment of polite docility, pouring generous drinks and telling the elaborate priest-minister-rabbi jokes he loved, while Mom chatted tentatively with the wives, showing off pieces of pottery and art she had picked up on her travels. On these occasions, Mom talked more slowly than usual, her voice almost a Southern drawl, as if she was embarrassed that she was not part of what she called "Washington Washington," the Cleveland Park and Georgetown of the Kennedy people; and not part of the Chanukah Heights Washington or the gentile Spring Valley Washington, either; and had not gone to a "fancy college" but to the University of Maryland, the best school Nat and Lil could afford after the Depression struck.

Sometimes on these nights, Mom wore clothing she'd brought back from her trips to India: silken saris in sherbet hues that looked like something out of the exotic adventure movies I knew from Saturday double features at the Avalon. Mom's dresses, like her Scotch-lubricated party smile, sparkled in the flickering light of the many candles she painstakingly dispersed throughout the living and dining rooms before the guests arrived. As the evenings grew late, past my bedtime, I'd descend from my room to the second-floor landing to eavesdrop on the company as they had coffee in the living room. Then I'd hear a more relaxed Mom, sounding like herself and laughing now, though it would be hard to make out what had struck her as funny, so animated was the conversation; even Joel's words were difficult to discern over the general jovial din. These parties sounded like television to me; I always slept better if I knew there was company downstairs. I also knew that when they were over, Mom and Joel would be too tired to fight. If I was up particularly late on those nights, I'd hear them talking quietly as they got ready for bed, in the low, congenial voices I imagined normal husbands and wives used when their children are supposed to be asleep. "When the Children Are Asleep"—I had learned about that peaceful feeling from a song in *Carousel* too.

What happy couples sounded like in real life, as opposed to in a show, I didn't know. Dad and Anadel never fought, and yet I rarely saw them have a conversation that wasn't about logistics: My new sister was crying, or some crisis had to be dealt with at the store, or Dad had a problem with the flashgun of the camera that served as his omnipresent third eye on his Sundays away from Rich's. In the hubbub of their new house, they were always calling to each other from different rooms while Polly and I watched TV in the living room, or I hid away with a phone, monitoring my social life at Deal, trying to remain aloof from the chaos of the household.

Some of the logistical to-and-fro was about my forthcoming bar mitzvah, which Dad was organizing with grudging help from Mom, who hinted to me that the whole exercise had been mandated against her will by her and Dad's divorce agreement. *My* main interest in the event was prompted by Temple Sinai's new synagogue, a modern building on Military Road. The ark from which I would fetch the Torah had been designed by Boris Aronson, an artist whose name I knew from my *Playbills*; he had also designed the gaudy scenery of *Do Re Mi*. How Boris Aronson ended up working for a congregation in Washington where no one but me seemed to have any idea who he was, I couldn't fathom. But when I squinted at the ark during High Holiday services—while older congregants wilted and sometimes fainted in the heat and younger ones listened to the World Series through transistor-radio earpieces—its design looked just like the kaleidoscopic settings of the musical still running at the St. James Theatre.

For me, Boris Aronson's ark was the closest thing Temple Sinai offered to a spiritual experience. Yet even this otherwise uninspiring synagogue was considered more religious than its Chanukah Heights rival, the inaccurately named Washington Hebrew Congregation, prized by many of its members precisely because it had stripped most Hebrew from its services, in case Washington might think anyone in attendance could actually be Jewish. No such luck at Sinai: I had to master enough of the Old Testament in the original to get through the big event. My parents were no help. Neither of them knew Hebrew—and Joel had intentionally forgotten his once he had disowned his Orthodox upbringing in Brooklyn and Baltimore to become a Unitarian (which, as he described it, sounded like Reform Judaism without the Marc Chagall lithographs in the lobby). It was a relief when the rabbi decided to perform a radical circumcision on my Haftorah portion because, he said, "It's not the kind of thing our congregation should be exposed to before lunch." I wasn't quite sure what he meant until one of my more knowing religious-school classmates looked over the unexpurgated version and cried out: "Hey, they've given you a rape!"

My major concern about the bar mitzvah was that of my peers—the party that would take place after it was over. Woodmont was out of the question—too expensive, and Mom wouldn't hear of it on principle, anyway. Also verboten was any kind of family party, since it was no more possible for Mom and Dad to coexist at a social event than it was for the United States and Khrushchev's bellicose Soviet Union to do so at the United Nations. The Talmudic solution we arrived at was a party for my friends, and no adults, at the National Press Club, which was in the same building as Loew's Capitol on F Street downtown. Dad was proud of being a member there: On special occasions, if I was off from school on a weekday, he'd take me to its dining room for a sandwich, and I would linger as long as possible to study the teletypes banging out the news. For my party, I was given money to buy all my favorite 45s at the Super Music City on Thirteenth Street, so that my friends and I could play and dance to the latest hits until eleven.

Pauline, though, was no longer part of my fantasy for that night. As abruptly as we had started going steady, we stopped: One day at school I found that my name had been erased from her sneakers, its place usurped by "Duke Duke Duke Duke of Earl" Swindells's. Was this how it felt to be replaced in a Broadway show—to turn up one day and find another face where your face had been in the picture outside the theater? Or was this worse, like divorce? Though Pauline and I had never had a conversation that went longer than five sentences, my elimination from her life hurt more than I could have anticipated. Just being acknowledged by her each day, each smile an implicit promise of the greater intimacies I believed were my due, was as much a part of my well-being as the good grades that I had long before convinced myself could protect me from ridicule. I felt as if I'd been punched, as if *I* had been divorced. An old feeling ambushed me, an unexpected and unwanted memory of Somerset, of visiting Dad, so quiet and alone, in his room in his new home after he moved out of our house.

I was determined to do anything I could to neutralize my social deformity. I tried to blend seamlessly into the crowd at Deal, as if the stigma of being from a "divorced family" could be eradicated with time and a new school. I made a joke of my novel household—I was always ready with a wisecrack about having two moms and two dads, hoping that humor would turn my embarrassment into a virtue.

Knowing that none of my classmates' parents knew my stepfather, I painted a romantic, if not inaccurate, picture of his exploits when I spoke to my friends of him: flying to Germany in the dead of night for a two-hour meeting to fix a problem for the government, or speaking three different languages at dinner parties, or buying an entire cow (cut up, thank God) for a freezer we kept in the basement so we'd never run out of steak. Of course, though the events were not exaggerated, the mood surrounding many of them was not as festive as I let on. And to some extent, I succeeded: The Chanukah Heights kids seemed to find me and my largely unseen family an amusing curiosity, in our "almost downtown" neighborhood, in a house with no lawn, in a family where you needed a scorecard to tell the players. Girls, I discovered, were intrigued.

If only they knew what my Cleveland Avenue life was really like—what would they possibly make of that? If only they knew I had still another secret life on top of my life with Mom and Joel—the life of my room, the life of my records and *Playbills* and New York newspapers and faraway radio stations, the life of my nightly struggles to drown out the battles at the bottom of the stairs.

Despite Pauline's defection, I was still determined to go to a play by myself, without Mom and Joel, and I had picked one—the latest musical to have a "tryout" at the National on its way to Broadway. I didn't know much about the show—A *Funny Thing Happened on the Way to the Forum*—except that it starred a man with a funny first name, Zero Mostel, whom Mom and Joel had told me all about when they saw him on Broadway in a show where he played a rhinoceros.

With Mom's permission, I mailed in to the National nine one-dollar bills and sixty cents in change from my paper-route takings. I enclosed a self-addressed stamped envelope and the requested "three alternate dates": each one of the show's three scheduled Saturday matinees a month hence. A week later, the envelope I had addressed to myself came back—with a small envelope inside and, inside that, two tickets, just like those on Broadway, for my first choice, the final Saturday matinee. I had picked the last Saturday because I knew that by then all the changes would have been made to improve the show for its next stop, New York.

Who would want the second ticket? I had believed that Pauline, the only girl at Deal who knew what it was like to have divorced parents, could enter my theater world too—and that for the first time my two secret lives wouldn't be secret anymore. Now I was back where I started: There was no other girl at Deal who could understand my broken family. At least I might find a girl who would share my secret life in the theater, but who? My infatuation with the stage was a lonely one.

There was another hitch as well. When A *Funny Thing Happened on the Way to the Forum* opened in Washington, the critics in all three newspapers pronounced it not just dreadful but "lewd." At a Passover seder, my Great-Aunt Bert looked askance at Mom: "You're really going to let Frank go to that filthy thing? The papers all said it's a burlesque show!"

Burlesque!

I feigned innocence as the adults debated around me.

Burlesque! I thought of the book on that top shelf at home, and of *Gypsy*—I knew that one of the authors of this show had also been one of those of *Gypsy*—

"Don't worry, Bert," Mom concluded, much to my relief. "He's old enough to handle it."

By the time the day came, I had settled by default on Nancy, the sole girl at Deal who I knew had been to the National before. On the bus downtown, I tried to rally her enthusiasm by boasting that we had really good seats—fourth row center, thanks to the alacrity with which I'd sent in my mail order. Once we were at the theater, I felt terribly grown-up as we were led by the usher to Row D. But there was something wrong: Unlike on my previous visits, the auditorium, with its sweeping orchestra floor and two balconies, was not full of excited patrons. I craned my head and saw that not a single person was sitting behind us in the entire place.

Surely it was because we were early, I told myself. But when at last the lights dimmed for the overture, I peeked around and saw that not only did the seats behind us remain empty but that those in front of us were merely scattered with theatergoers. I'd never seen anything like this, except in the pages of *Variety*, where I would occasionally read of Broadway shows with tiny grosses, usually just before they closed, and worry about what it might be like at a theater where only a few people had shown up to see the play. The mental image of an empty house filled me with both wonder and grief. Part of me longed to be in such an audience, if only to fill one seat that might otherwise be vacant, to be there to offer some comfort to actors who might be as lonely as I was so much of the time. And now that I was having that experience, I almost wished Nancy were not there, so that I could have the performance to myself, to uninhibitedly display my solidarity with the cast.

The conductor turned up in his tiny spotlight, and then I was listening intently to the unfamiliar music, expecting it to be as lousy as the Washington reviews and the pitifully empty National Theatre promised. Yet it *was* an overture, the overture of a musical going to Broadway, with all those familiar sounds I had learned to recognize since *The Pajama Game* (which, I noticed in the National's program, had the same producer as this show), and it *wasn't* lousy. Once the overture ended and the theater had been completely plunged into darkness, the curtain rose on the sight of four colorfully dressed clowns who proceeded to sing and dance. They didn't seem sad at all; they didn't seem to notice that the theater was deserted. Soon they were joined by a cast of tall women wearing clothes as scanty as those in *A Pictorial History of Burlesque*—all of them playing characters who were (I could hardly contain myself) prostitutes. They were doing dances that left less to the imagination than Lola's in *Damn*

Yankees, and when they weren't, the other actors were cracking risqué jokes better than any I'd heard at Deal and racing through a giddy plot that was itself constructed like a joke. When the curtain came down at the end of the first act—with an ingenious gag whose punch line was, to my delight, the word "intermission"—I turned to Nancy and was relieved to see that she was enjoying herself too. But once the lights were up I also saw the indifference of the others in the theater. They stood by their seats, slouching and chatting quietly while impatiently consulting their watches, as if they weren't even at a Broadway show. How could they be so ungrateful, so blind to the magnitude of the occasion?

The same was true when the show ended. The applause stopped before the curtain fell. Was there something wrong with me that the most enjoyable play I'd ever seen was what *Variety* called a "flopola"? When, a few weeks later, A *Funny Thing Happened on the Way to the Forum* opened at the Alvin Theatre on Broadway, I begged Joel to take me to the out-of-town newsstand at Eighteenth and Columbia Road to buy all the New York papers. To my astonishment, the critics in New York agreed with me and Nancy, mere seventh-graders, and not with the rest of Washington. Had the show been rewritten between its closing at the National and its opening at the Alvin? Not really, said Joel—that would have been impossible. "The fact is, Frank, it was a funny show. Washington critics didn't understand it. That's what I mean by sex life among the midgets."

Joel's assessment made me feel good—maybe I knew something that really mattered, not like the stuff in school. Yet at the same time he confirmed my fear that Washington was about as far away from Broadway as you could possibly be. *I* lived in another universe entirely, where people were scandalized by A *Funny Thing Happened on the Way to the Forum* instead of being entertained by it.

———

As my bar mitzvah approached, Dad took charge—"That's your father's department" was Mom's refrain—even though he seemed more and more distant. Anadel was pregnant again, and Dad was busier than ever, having to help run her small clothing store next to the Rich's in Georgetown when she was overburdened with children present and future. Dad seemed to have forgotten about our plan for me to move in with him and Anadel. Sometimes when I was alone with him, I'd ask about his lawyer, but he was noncommittal, almost nervous. "Wait and see," he'd say, as mildly as if he was talking about where we would eat on Sunday. I wondered how much Anadel knew about our plan; she didn't say, but I knew she had to be an ally. Eager to be closer to her, I decided to get her a special present for her birthday, and I sent off my first Broadway mail order, buying her a mezzanine ticket to a new play based on one of her favorite books, A Passage to India; I picked a Wednesday matinee—the only performance I could afford—on a date when I knew she'd be in New York for her store. I felt that Anadel—like Mom, when she had been married to Dad—wanted to see plays more often than she could.

When she returned from her trip, Anadel thanked me and told me how much she loved A Passage to India, even if it wasn't quite as good as the novel, and brought me back the Playbill. But she still said nothing about my living with her and Dad. The more I waited, the more my frustration turned to anger.

The day I realized that I was never going to escape Joel and move to Dad's house was the day that Dad and I had a meeting with the rabbi at Temple Sinai. A few weeks earlier, my Hebrew-school teacher had stunned me by announcing before the entire class that I didn't take my studies seriously because I had been "raised in a broken home." After letting the slight fester for a couple of weeks, I'd written the teacher an angry letter, defending my "very happy life despite your slurs"—so determined was I to maintain the illusion that I had the same ideal existence I assumed all my classmates did. But when we met with the rabbi about it, he bullied me in a voice that sounded like Joel's, and Dad just listened, never speaking in my defense.

I knew that if Dad wasn't going to stand up to Rabbi Lipman, there was no way he and his lawyer would fight my stepfather. This realization wasn't sudden—in retrospect, I could pick up earlier hints—and yet the finality of it still stung. As Dad drove me back to Cleveland Avenue after the meeting with the rabbi, I seethed in silence. Maybe Mom was right that it's better to get anger out of your system, but I couldn't.

The weekend of my bar mitzvah, I prayed only that my parents wouldn't start an embarrassing fight while on rare display to all my friends. They didn't. Joel and Mom beamed from their side of the invisible wall splitting the sanctuary, as did Dad and Anadel from theirs. The sole awkward moment came when Joel read his assigned English text at three times the decibel level and twice the speed of any other adult: Would my friends notice that one of my parents was so strange a beast? But no one did; by then, most of my friends' attention had been extinguished by the torpor of the passionless service.

Even if Joel had mortified me, he had chosen a bar mitzvah present to preempt any possible complaint: another theatergoing trip to New York with Mom, to be taken on my way to sleep-away camp in New England.

I had gone away for camp each of the previous two summers. To my surprise, my Inverness travails had not reoccurred; even more incredibly, I proved to be the only junior camper who was not homesick for a single second. But now that I was a teenager, if not the man my bar mitzvah had allegedly made me, Mom had found a new camp after an assiduous search through the advertisements in the back pages of *The New York Times*'s Sunday magazine. Certain that I was not outgrowing my interest in the theater, she sent for brochures from each camp that had the words "stage door," "acting," or "theatercraft" in its ad.

She had chosen a place called Indian Hill, whose brochure described it as "a new experience and an exciting summer vacation for boys and girls in music, art, dance, theater." Indian Hill was located in "a beautiful Berkshire estate, one mile from the historic village of Stockbridge, Massachusetts," with "proximity to Tanglewood, the Berkshire Playhouse, Jacob's Pillow, the Berkshire Museum in Pittsfield, the Adams Theatre in Williamstown." As well as to girls: "Indian Hill senior girls live in the 'mansion,' with women faculty members"—no counselors here!—while junior girls lived "in up-to-date cabins, especially designed for their needs and comfort." This sounded too good to be true.

Instead of the other camps' glossy pictures of kids in greasepaint, Indian Hill's brochure featured encomiums from famous practitioners of the arts, including Charles E. Ives, "American composer," and S. N. Behrman, a playwright whose name I recognized from my theater books. Behrman had sent his son David to Indian Hill because it allowed "a teen-ager of specialized interests to find out that there are others like him." By "specialized interests," it was clear that Behrman was not talking about sports; an out-of-focus snapshot of a basketball game was relegated to the bottom of the brochure's last page, where it was dwarfed by a giant shot of a hootenanny led by Pete Seeger.

No one from Washington went to Indian Hill; the parents Mom phoned as references were all strangers in New York, which is no doubt why the camp bus left from in front of Pennsylvania Station. Joel had planned for Mom and me to fly up a day early and had secured us tickets on departure eve to *No Strings*, a new show Mom and I both longed to see. On the shuttle to New York, however, I hatched another plan: With my own money, I asked Mom, could I buy a ticket to another show for the matinee that day, a Wednesday?

"What a Joel kind of idea!" Mom said, her voice rising in approval. Once I reassured her that I would know how to walk from the theater to our nearby hotel, she agreed. Having checked the grosses in *Variety*, I knew I could secure a ticket to *I Can Get It for You Wholesale*, a new show that had received so-so reviews and was not SRO. In its cast was a teenage singer, Barbra Streisand, who had been so funny on the *Tonight Show*. "And" I said to Mom, "it's playing at the Shubert Theatre, where we saw *Bells Are Ringing*—so you'll know just where to find me."

I almost drove myself insane, however, when it became clear that we would not get to the Shubert Theatre in time for the two o'clock Wednesday matinee curtain. Our taxi was stalled in traffic. Was there any crime more heinous than missing that instant when the curtain rose on a play? I begged Mom for permission to get out of the cab and run, and when she gave it, I threw my arms around her.

Then I was off, racing like a New Yorker down a sunlit Forty-fourth Street, into the Shubert lobby and its box office. There was no one in line, and through the closed doors in the lobby I could hear the sound of a Broadway show, just out of reach. I asked the man if I could still buy a ticket, and he said, "Yeah—curtain's been up for ten minutes." Even that didn't matter now. I gave him a precious five-dollar bill and was handed twenty cents change and a ticket for a seat as good as I'd expected, based on my reading of *Variety*'s numbers: center orchestra, about five rows from the back. As I climbed over other theatergoers to get to my place, the usher's flashlight illuminating my way in the dark house, I was so exhilarated I didn't care about what I had missed. Nor did I care that two members of the cast had been replaced by understudies, their names printed on little slips of paper that fell out of my *Playbill* to the floor like pressed leaves when I stood up for intermission.

No matter. I was seeing my first Broadway show by myself, with my own ticket bought with my own money. When it was over, I decided I wouldn't rush right to the hotel: I stood outside the same stage door where Mom, Polly, and I had once waited in vain to be greeted by Judy Holliday, and joined the few other stragglers who asked the exiting cast members to sign their programs. After getting a single autograph, I found myself distracted, studying the actors as they streamed out of the theater to go wherever they were going before that night's performance; I wanted to see how they dressed, how they spoke, how they walked—I didn't care how they signed their names. I noticed that while they wore ordinary clothes when they emerged into Shubert Alley, they moved with a speed and a sense of purpose that set them apart from the audience members who blocked their paths. It was as if the actors belonged to a world exclusively their own, which they were in a hurry to get to for the few hours until they became part of the *I Can Get It for You Wholesale* family again.

Where was this world? What happened there? I took the long way to meet Mom back at the hotel, passing stage door after stage door, hoping to gather any clue I could even as I scooped up the *Playbill*s in every trash can on my route. But no matter how hard I looked—into the window of a delicatessen sleepwalking through its late-afternoon languors, into the dank subterranean dark of a bar, into a narrow enclosed alley bordering the battered rear exit doors of a movie palace that fronted on Broadway— I could not figure out where the people who lived in the blaze of light onstage had dispersed after the curtain fell.

CHAPTER 7

On the bus to Stockbridge, I read my book while kids who seemed to know one another, many of them obviously already in high school, jabbered around me, fully at home in a glamorous argot whose code I'd have to crack. They went to New York schools with exotic names like Walden and E.I. and New Lincoln and, most tantalizing of all, Performing Arts and Music and Art. Imagine going to a school called Music and Art! Only in New York could they come up with an idea like that.

Many of the boys had arrived on the bus with black guitar cases strapped over their shoulders. Instead of the madras plaid Bermuda shorts and chinos wardrobe that had been sent up ahead of me in my trunk, they wore white T-shirts and black jeans. Most of the girls on the bus also wore jeans, with tight black leotard tops through which their white bras showed even more clearly than the view afforded by the blouses of Chanukah Heights.

I was a long way from Washington—a prospect that, as much as I welcomed it, was nonetheless intimidating. After all this time spent willing myself to New York, here I was with New Yorkers, not at all certain I would fit in. It was a relief when we arrived at camp and were immediately led past the "mansion," a rambling stone-and-wood building that looked like the main house at Capon Springs, and then across a large, hilly lawn to our bunks. So maybe the cabins weren't entirely up-to-date and especially designed for our needs and comfort, as the brochure had said—a description that had prompted me to imagine they might resemble the Manhattan penthouses in *Bells Are Ringing*. But it was reassuring that the cabins at Indian Hill were not much different from those at my previous camp, except that they were shaped like tepees and, blessedly, had electricity.

Everywhere I turned, there was a kid sketching some view in charcoal or practicing a clarinet with a music stand precariously set up under a tree, or a cluster of dancers heading toward the barn that served as the dance studio. In this environment, I for once wasn't the odd man out. These campers didn't look up to jocks but to kids who wrote poetry without capital letters and rhymes, like e. e. cummings, or aspired to be folksingers, like Bob Dylan. Dylan's best imitator among the campers was Joady Guthrie, named after the poor Okie family in *The Grapes of Wrath* and, like his older brother, Arlo, and sister Nora, a child of Marjorie Mazia, the no-nonsense doyenne of Indian Hill's dance faculty, who was divorced from the folksinger Woody Guthrie.

Nor were the Guthrie siblings and I the only Indian Hill kids with divorced parents. Divorce was practically a fashion. When one camper talked about a mother and father who were still married to each other, he was quizzed in detail, as if his home life were an anthropological novelty akin to being raised by aborigines. No one I met found anything peculiar about my infinite horde of step-relatives; they were shocked only that I wasn't seeing a psychiatrist. But I was normal, wasn't I? Why would I need that?

Virtually the day I arrived at Indian Hill, I found something I'd yet to find at Deal: a best friend. Harry was a wiry teenager, not much taller than I was, whose teeth, eyes, and Brillo-pad black hair always looked clenched, making him resemble a fox terrier. He wasn't among the more typical campers: His mother and father were not divorced, and he was not from the city but from a New York suburb. Yet the suburb's pseudo-Gallic name, New Rochelle, sounded far more sophisticated than Washington's humdrum Chevy Chase and Silver Spring, and, as if to make good on the Indian Hill brochure, he was actually the son of a playwright. Not a playwright I had heard of, but a Broadway playwright just the same, Joseph Stein. Harry reeled off the names of his father's shows—almost all of them musicals with vaguely familiar titles predating my discovery of the theater. Only his father's recent *Take Me Along*—Jackie Gleason, of *The Honeymooners*, had been its star—was represented by a record in my collection.

Harry scoffed. "That was the biggest piece of shit my father ever wrote." Indeed, Harry didn't seem to have a high opinion of any of his father's theatrical endeavors, none of which had been hugely successful. "I secretly fear my dear Dad may be a hack," he said, as if it was all a joke.

Harry, like me, was in the drama group, so we were both in the charge of a counselor named Logan, a professional folksinger who had acted Off Broadway, and his assistant, Betty, a graduate student in French literature at Brandeis University who also taught junior lifesaving. Betty held us spellbound: The persistent though never consummated daily struggle of her huge breasts to escape the captivity of her tight bathing suit was more dramatic than most of our rehearsals.

The play they taught us was the strangest I'd ever encountered—it was written entirely in impudent jokes that sounded like those of Mel Brooks, the 2,000 Year Old Man, whose comedy record Harry and I had deemed our favorite. We didn't know what any of the play meant, from its title, *The Bald Soprano* ("There is no bald soprano, that's the whole point," said Logan), to its plot ("There is no story, that's the whole point," said Betty), except that it was about two bickering married couples, the Martins and Smiths, who could hardly remember who was married to whom half the time. I was Mr. Smith, Harry was Mr. Martin, and Nora Guthrie was the maid.

On "Production Weekend," as visiting day at Indian Hill was called, we performed *The Bald Soprano* to so much laughter that we could hardly believe it. The play that had made no sense to us really was funny after all. The audience's gales of hilarity buoyed us, as did our intense preparation (we'd rehearsed so hard that we couldn't have made a mistake if we had wanted to—though with this play, no one might have known the difference if we had). At the curtain call, we bowed and bowed, not wanting the show to end. As far as I was concerned, we could go on and play it another five hundred times, like the Broadway hits listed in *Variety*—which I was keeping up with, thanks to Joel, who had secured me my own eight-week summer subscription for the duration of camp.

Mom and Joel and Dad and Anadel had all come up for the weekend. Since neither set of parents talked to the other, I ran back and forth between them before and after the show participating in the same conversation twice, as if I was giving back-to-back performances in yet another role in a whole other play. At the picnic lunch afterward, I shlepped my paper plate back and forth across Indian Hill's football-field-size front lawn like a runner in a relay race.

As Saturday wore on, I found myself favoring Mom and Joel. Dad had brought his usual weekend worries with him—whether the light was right for taking pictures—while Anadel fretted about how my new sister was faring with her mother, with whom the baby had been deposited in New York. My one-sided romance with my stepmother, I realized, had ended with the arrival of her own child, but at least she still nodded knowingly, like Mom and Joel, when I dropped such names as Munch, Monteux, Chekhov, Duke Ellington, Ted Shawn, and *Rashomon*—with all of which I now claimed a casual familiarity, as though I'd feasted on the Berkshires arts scene for a lifetime. Whatever else Indian Hill taught its campers, it was peerless in bringing out our as yet untapped talent for being pretentious assholes.

It was a relief when all the parents left, though as soon as Production Weekend was over I was particularly cognizant that the summer's clock was running down. I didn't want camp to end. I wondered if I had ever had so much fun, or felt so at home, as I had at Indian Hill. There hadn't been a single night all summer, I realized, when I had had trouble falling asleep. After lights-out in our tepee, Harry and I just kept talking about the adventures of that day until there was nothing more to say—or until he declared, "You know, I think the time has come for me to beat off!" He was the first friend I ever had who cared as I did about the theater and novels and movies and TV, not to mention the heretofore covert art of masturbation, of which he claimed to be, as he did everything else, an expert. Harry could turn anything, I would learn, into a fiercely competitive sport.

—

Once back in Washington, I didn't have to leave Harry behind. Joel let me use the New York tie-line to phone my new friend, so long as I didn't overdo it. Most Sunday nights, after I came back from Dad's, I fought the usual gloom that crept in by calling Harry so that we could catch up on our respective weeks, almost all of which involved either the theater or girls. We punctuated our overlapping tales with an array of Mel Brooks–isms and Indian Hill–isms, a comic language no one else shared.

Citing the example of Harry, whose parents allowed him to take the train from New Rochelle to New York City on his own, I lobbied Mom for the right to see more plays at the National by myself. I had fixated on the tryout of *Mr. President,* which *Variety* proclaimed the biggest show of the Broadway season—a musical that Irving Berlin, the man who wrote "God Bless America" and *Annie Get Your Gun,* was working on about a fictional president who seemed very much like JFK. I wanted to send a mail order for the final Washington matinee, as I had for *A Funny Thing.*

But Joel showed me an article in the *Post* saying that there would be no mail orders for *Mr. President* at all. Four thousand people had mailed in blank checks over the summer without even waiting for an advertisement in the paper, and Scott Kirkpatrick, the National's manager, announced that he had returned them all and would sell tickets only at the box office. The seats would go on sale Labor Day, so that business-day downtown traffic wouldn't be tied up by the throngs certain to descend on E Street.

"Don't worry," said Joel. "You'll see *Mr. President.*" Though he and Mom were going to the opening night, when the Kennedys would be there, he'd already secured four seats for the kids for the first Saturday matinee.

The Washington papers ran stories about *Mr. President* almost every day before the premiere and, as I had expected, featured pictures of the president and the first lady attending opening night. The Secret Service, the papers said, had brought JFK's rocking chair to the National and put it in the box on the left side of the stage. The president's brother and three of his sisters were there too, Mom and Joel told me at breakfast.

The show? A clinker, said the critics. Joel concurred. "You'll see for yourself on Saturday," he said, "but this one needs a lot of work. Kennedy's no fool—he skipped the first act." The president had arrived late so that he could watch the Liston-Patterson fight on closed-circuit TV at the White House.

Still, I expected that the show would be better than the reviews said, just as A *Funny Thing* had been, and so it was. This time, though, a packed house cheered despite the bad reviews—a puzzling contrast to the reception given Zero Mostel and the other clowns the spring before. Washington loved *Mr. President* and was even unfazed by its one slightly lewd song about how the president's daughter could never make out with her boyfriend "because the Secret Service makes me nervous, and I can't."

What entranced me most, however, was the extravagance of scenery and costume, the men in tails, the women a rainbow of silk ball gowns, simulating the White House and all its storied occupants, the city's federal royalty. I had driven by the president's house countless times but had only been inside once, to see the plebeian room or two unveiled for elementary-school tours; I might as well have lived in another city, for any Washingtonian who didn't work in the government had no more access to its illustrious buildings than did the visitors who flocked in from thousands of miles away. Now the White House materialized like a mirage in the picture frame of the National's proscenium, its interior as blue as a cloudless sky, only to give way to a huge yellow tent for a party scene in the White House's backyard where all the characters danced the Twist. I had no idea if this was what the real place looked like, but the show abetted my fantasy of the capital's hidden glamour.

When Joel picked us up in his car after the matinee, he listened to our favorable opinions, then said, "I'll be curious to see what they do with it. They say they're going to make a lot of changes in Washington."

We weren't home long before I started plotting how I might satisfy my own curiosity about those changes; I was determined not to let *Mr. President* slip by as every other show had done, after a single visit and before I could make a proper farewell.

A plan presented itself right away. If Mom would let me take the bus downtown, maybe I could get into the show by buying standing room. A clandestine call to the National's box office filled me in: There were thirty standing-room tickets, costing $2.50 each, and they were sold each morning, first come, first served, when the box office opened. Could I get Mom to go along with my scheme? She said yes — "if you don't mind waiting in line" — and before I knew it, I was back at *Mr. President*, at the next Saturday matinee, the first of several visits.

I had wondered whether I would mind standing at the very rear of the theater. I was barely tall enough to see over the rail separating the standees from those in the orchestra seats, and I knew that the first balcony, suspended above me, would cut off my view of the top of the stage. But instead of regretting that I wasn't close up, I felt as I had when acting at Indian Hill; I was more than a mere spectator at the theater. With adult strangers on either side of me, and no idea of who they were, I felt independent. With a full view of the seated audience spread out before me, I could study the sort of people who went to see shows — an audience that maybe, like me, wanted the performance to last forever.

I was alone, but not alone. I was in Washington, but not in Washington. I lived with Mom and Joel, but not right now. Not as long as the curtain was up. Though years later I would realize that *Mr. President* was, at most, a theatrical footnote — the fiasco that drove Irving Berlin away from Broadway forever — I was enchanted by it. A viewing or two later, I figured out it wasn't a great show, and yet that didn't matter. I was never bored studying the slightest gradations of the revisions at each performance. I studied each new emphasis in an actor's delivery, each cut line and added one, each altered costume and set, each reworked plot twist in the mild comic narrative of a president's bumptious efforts to befriend the Russians. The revisions were some kind of map, I thought, charting the backstage lives and minds of the theater people who made the show. Was *Mr. President* getting better? I wasn't sure, but at least it was a living organism, different at each performance. I didn't want to miss a single permutation and would have gone every night if my finances and school obligations hadn't made that impossible.

One night as I studied the show, I was subliminally conscious of a stillness among the standees around me. I glanced away from the stage to the right and located its source: Standing in the deep shadows at the rail a few places down were five older men, uniformly stone-faced. My pulse raced as I spotted them, for I recognized their faces from the pictures that had been in the Washington papers: Irving Berlin, Russel Crouse and Howard Lindsay (who had written the show's script and, I knew, *The Sound of Music* before that), Leland Hayward (the producer, who had done *Peter Pan* with Mary Martin), and the director, Joshua Logan, whose name I had first read on the cover of Mom's old 78s of *South Pacific*. How, I wondered, watching their grim expressions, could they be unhappy even as the audience showered their show with affection?

When I came back a week later to stand for the final performance—the first show I ever saw alone at night—I looked around expectantly for another glimpse of these Broadway men—famous men who would surely have known Moss Hart—certain they would be back again to survey their final changes. But they were nowhere to be seen. Had they already gone back to New York? Were they backstage? Were they packing at their hotels? Once again, I felt abandoned. Though at last I was at the National for a final performance of a show that was leaving town for Broadway, I was no more a part of it than I had ever been a part of any show. *Mr. President* would flee Washington as soon as the curtain fell—much as the rarefied occupants of Washington's real presidential pageant fled whenever a term came to an end—leaving me behind to return to Cleveland Avenue and its nightly theater of slamming doors and raised voices.

Mr. President moved on to New York in that October of 1962 with the largest advance sale in the history of Broadway, but the New York reviews were no better than those in Washington, and *Variety* soon chronicled the doomed decline of its grosses. I found it hard to picture that New Yorkers didn't have to line up early for standing room as I had done but could just walk up to the box office at the St. James Theatre and buy a seat at any price for any performance. Did the actors feel as despondent as I did?, I wondered. Did it sadden them that the full houses of Washington had given way to empty ones now that they were back home in New York?

———

The fizz of Kennedy's Washington seemed to evaporate visibly that October too, as if cued by the exit of *Mr. President*. One day I returned from school to find Joel home from work early, unpacking huge brown boxes containing silver cans of "purified water," whatever that was. Mom and Joel spoke darkly of the crisis in Cuba, and declared that our dim, windowless basement on Cleveland Avenue, heretofore the laundry room, was now our fallout shelter.

Like every other kid I knew, I had seen what the A-bomb and the H-bomb could do. The world had ended several times in *The Twilight Zone* on TV, and in the movie *Dr. Strangelove*. Only a few months earlier we'd stood in line for an hour to get into RKO Keith's on Fifteenth Street to see the mad Dr. No, probably a Commie, try to blow up the world in the first movie about JFK's favorite spy, 007.

But would purified water really save us if the Russians dropped the Bomb? Our home bunker was as preposterous as the air-raid drills that had lately supplanted fire drills at school, in which we hurried into a basement supply closet that was now, according to a yellow-and-black cardboard sign, a fallout shelter. Wouldn't Washington be bombed first in a nuclear war? If so, what good would it do to crawl into the cellar of our creaky old house, no matter how large the supply of water, Campbell's chicken noodle soup, and Chef Boyardee spaghetti? "Face it," said Harry from his safe distance in New Rochelle, "you're going to be Silly Putty." I was afraid to raise these doubts with Joel, however, for fear he might throw a can at me.

School droned on as usual. Washington's agitated adults were mocked at Deal, and the urgency in the president's and our parents' voices, on TV and in the headlines, did not roil our social rituals. If the world was going to explode, there was nothing to be done anyway. Could we at least get to second base in whatever time was left before a nuclear holocaust?

When the world didn't end, and the danger was over, the whole dreamlike episode deflated in an instant. We were back in our usual crisp Washington autumn, with Porter the handyman rhythmically raking the crunchy leaves in front of the house, and Willie Mae doing the wash in the decommissioned fallout shelter. Joel decided it was safe to leave us behind and go away for business. He was also leaving behind tickets for *The School for Scandal*, a play that had come from London with two actors Mom told me were among the greatest in the world, John Gielgud and Ralph Richardson. Would I like to go with Mom on opening night?, Joel asked, smiling in anticipation of my answer.

Joel didn't know that this was going to be as special a Washington opening as *Mr. President*'s. Once Mom and I were seated at the National that
Monday night, she nudged me with her elbow and rolled her eyes toward
the row of seats behind us. I turned to look—"You're a teenager, you're allowed to stare," Mom whispered—and there, so close I could touch her,
was the wide face and large eyes of Mrs. Kennedy. Next to her was Adlai
Stevenson, and then the prime minister of England and some other
important-looking men we couldn't identify. Once the play started, I would
have sworn I could hear Mrs. Kennedy's familiar voice right next to my
ear, joining in the rest of the audience's laughter as we watched characters
in powdered wigs, with names like Sir Oliver Surface and Lady Sneerwell,
speak lines in which every syllable mattered, each word piling on top of
the one before like a precisely balanced house of cards until the whole delicate edifice tumbled down in comic hysteria.

At intermission, we stayed in our seats while the first lady and her
friends disappeared. By the time Act 2 was ready to start, the word of her
presence must have spread: Looking up, I could see that people had gathered at the edge of each balcony and in the boxes below the balconies, all
craning forward to get a look at her. Once Mrs. Kennedy did walk down
the aisle, the tiers of theatergoers, all of them standing in the yellow half-
light of the dimming auditorium like doll-size figures on the world's largest
wedding cake, applauded and cheered.

Mrs. Kennedy smiled and sat down so that the show could begin; you
could hear the herds in the balconies galloping back to their seats in the
dark. Once the curtain went up, the actors onstage took a few seconds for
the house to quiet, but they never betrayed any knowledge that someone
so important was watching their play. They were so funny that I didn't
even notice when the president slipped in sometime later, taking a seat on
the aisle at the end of his wife's row, to see the second act. Only at the end
of the play, when we turned around to stare at his wife, did I spot him
there. As his thick brown hair had caught the silver winter sun on his Inauguration Day, so it now seemed to ripple in the reflected gold of the curtain call.

When the lights came up, the president stood to leave, turned, and with
a modest wave of his hand acknowledged the continuing applause of

everyone in the theater. As the rest of the audience stayed in place, he gallantly waited in the aisle until his wife could reach him from the middle of the row, at which point she took his arm and they and their entourage exited in what seemed a precise recapitulation of the elegant style of the play we had just watched.

—

It was only six months later that JFK was taken from Washington as abruptly as he had seemed to conquer the capital three years before. His murder came on a Friday afternoon when the public schools were closed for a citywide teacher's meeting. I was in the Deal gym with David, the affable class president known for his golfing skills at Woodmont, as we taped up our homemade decorations for a much-awaited social windfall that night. By mailing in the largest number of postcards exclaiming "We love WEAM!," Deal's ninth grade had won a free dance hosted by disc jockeys from our favorite radio station.

The entire school was deserted except for David and me and a Negro janitor who wandered into the gym not because he knew us or we knew him but perhaps because he just had to tell someone. He spoke with little audible emotion, almost shyly, and his low voice barely registered: "I heard on the radio—someone shot the president." Expressionless, he slipped back into the bowels of the shuttered school as silently as he'd materialized.

I wanted to leave immediately to investigate. If the president had been shot, wouldn't the school cancel the dance? David wasn't sure. "It sounds very bad, but I really think people will have forgotten all about it by tonight."

We left Deal together, agreeing to confer later by phone. I walked toward Nebraska Avenue on my way to catch a bus home. Yet suddenly I couldn't move. Time seemed to stretch like elastic and trap me where I stood. The cars that normally sped by were moving at a crawl, as if in slow motion. As they stopped for a red light, I gingerly stepped off the curb to ask a driver whose radio was on what was happening. The woman at the steering wheel turned toward me with a start, as if my presence at her windshield had frightened her.

"Oh," she said, sounding relieved to see a mere fourteen-year-old boy. "The president," she said, absentmindedly. "Yes—the president. They think he may be dead."

The light changed, she lurched away, and I stood there, frozen. Home was too far; I couldn't wait that long to find out what was happening. I decided to visit Linda, my current girlfriend, who lived right across the street. Linda wasn't interested in the theater, but she was the one girl at Deal I could also imagine at Indian Hill. Her parents were Quakers who talked all the time about books and art and civil rights, and they were the only family I knew who, like Mom and me, had joined the largest crowd I'd ever seen downtown, Kennedy's inauguration included, to be part of Martin Luther King, Jr.'s, civil rights march, with its vast sea of Negroes, at summer's end.

Linda spent her spare time drawing intently in a sketchbook she always carried with her. We went to movies together sometimes on Saturday afternoons, debated the meaning of *Lord of the Flies*, and listened to the same Folkways records of the Weavers and Woody Guthrie. What I most liked about Linda, however, was that she admitted to being unhappy sometimes. She wasn't sure why, and I couldn't figure it out; her parents were the gentle mom and dad I wished I had. Maybe it was something in the books we shared. She was the first girl I'd known at Deal who would rather read than rehearse the cheers of the Pep Club.

She answered the door when I knocked. She was sad now, she said, and I was sad too, I decided, because I knew that's how I was supposed to feel. It didn't seem truly possible that the president could be dead, so I found myself acting as I had at Indian Hill, simulating an emotion more theoretical than real.

Linda's parents weren't home. She didn't want to stay in her house and suggested we take a walk. We ended up strolling around the deserted Deal football field, then up the hill that arched behind Wilson, the adjacent high school we'd be entering the next year. Though it had been sunny and unseasonably warm when David and I had emerged from Deal an hour earlier, it was gray now and nippy.

Cautiously—once I was convinced that no one was around who could spy on us—I put my arm around Linda. To my relief, she responded immediately, burying her head in the crook of my neck. I stood frozen again, but not for long. She looked up at me, then removed her glasses—the first time she ever had in my presence—and fixed her eyes on me with an expression I didn't recognize. Was this just how she looked when her glasses were off, or did it mean something else? She wasn't smiling, and she wasn't crying; she seemed to be dreaming with her eyes open. I guessed what it meant and kissed her on the lips, harder than I ever had before. She kissed me back and we kept kissing until time seemed to stretch and warp again, past the point where I could keep track of it.

Whenever it was that the kissing stopped, Linda pulled back just a little and gave me another expression, similar to the last, yet with a change in calibration as detectable as an altered inflection in a line of dialogue in a Broadway tryout. I had to guess again what she meant, and I wasn't wrong. I reached my hand inside her cardigan sweater—there were a few open inches between her neck and the first buttoned button. I touched her breast through her blouse, and when she sighed I followed the dictates of my rising pulse and moved to stick my hand underneath the material. Linda reached a hand toward mine so swiftly that I jumped; I thought she was about to push me away. But her hand went instead to her top button, which she undid in an instant. Then she unbuttoned another and another, and I waited, my blood rising so quickly I felt flush, until she had stopped doing however much she was going to do herself. There was no ambiguity now. I reached in and slid my fingers under her bra. As she whimpered slightly, I felt for one breast, then another, then went back for another tour of both, savoring every inch of the terrain I had hungered to touch for as long as I could remember.

Time was completely askew now. When we came down from the hill, holding hands and walking in silence, it was dark. I told Linda I might see her at the dance later, but she was as doubtful as I was that it would take place.

Once I was home, I found Mom and Joel lying in bed, watching TV, though Joel was, as usual, on the phone with a client. The dance had been called off, Mom told me. Polly was seated on the floor, and I sat down beside her to watch the longest and most mesmerizing TV show I'd ever seen. It just kept going and going, supplanting all other programs, further scrambling my sense of time. I tore myself away only to call Harry on the tie-line. "You mean you used Kennedy's assassination as an excuse to feel up Linda?" he said. "That is genius!"

The assassination show continued on and on. Life had halted in Washington as it did during a blizzard, and Mom didn't care if I watched late and fell asleep in front of the set. I was sitting alone in the den a day later—or was it two?—when a man in a hat barged into the grainy black-and-white image being broadcast from Texas, gun in hand, and shot the man who everyone said had killed Kennedy. I ran down to the basement to find Willie Mae, the only other person in the house, and tell her. She had seen it too, having moved the portable TV from the kitchen so she wouldn't miss anything while she did Mom's ironing.

"I can't believe it!" she said, her voice accelerating into a weird hysteria that made it impossible to tell if she was going to laugh or scream. Then she shouted: "You're not scared now, are you, honey?" I assured her I was not, and I wasn't. But here was another new feeling, as novel as my exploration of Linda's breasts, that couldn't be instantly assimilated. I had seen a murder on TV, and yet it seemed less real than the fake murders in movies. The pops of Jack Ruby's gun sounded no louder than the small red firecrackers we used to set off in Rosemary Hills—or a cap gun, maybe, in Somerset before that. And yet these shots, like those of two days before, had changed Washington in ways that I knew were enormous (so the men on TV kept saying) but could neither understand nor absorb. I didn't feel my usual fear or anger or grief. Could it have been—and I couldn't admit this to anyone—a kind of excitement? The tactile memory of Linda's body intermingled with the tumultuous images beamed in by TV, through which I was watching the entire country and world share in the experience of the president's death, with all its characters and unexpected plot twists and drama. I was part of the largest audience ever gathered, all of it together watching the same show, everyone staying up late to see how it came out, everyone taking off from school and work, everyone watching as intently as I did when I stood in the back of the National Theatre.

It was so thrilling—albeit in a mournful way, I kept reminding myself—that I was utterly taken aback when right in the middle of the weekend Joel said we were going to the theater that very night. "I called Scott Kirkpatrick," he said. "He's put away tickets." The show at the National was one

I had never thought about seeing: a touring company of a comedy that had enjoyed a modest run on Broadway the previous season. Now I had to think for a second: Did I want to see *Seidman and Son*—even if it starred Sam Levene, the actor Mom and I found so funny when he sang "Sue Me" in *Guys and Dolls*—more than I wanted to watch television's unending cavalcade of dramatic assassination news? The dilemma didn't last long: Of course I'd go to the theater.

When we arrived at the National just before curtain, I was surprised to find that the show that had been playing to half-empty houses, so *Variety* said, was SRO that night.

"Frank, people just want to get out of the house," Joel said when I pointed out the standees. It made sense in a way. Certainly *I* could identify with that impulse, but I was startled to learn that seventeen hundred other people who lived in Washington might feel the same. Except for Mom and Joel, almost no one I knew went to the theater on a whim; they dutifully went "on subscription," as if they were trudging off to High Holiday services, if they went at all.

My mind was too full of what I'd heard and seen over the past thirty-six hours to focus on the play, which told of a Jewish dress manufacturer who worked on New York's Seventh Avenue. Seidman was married but was falling in love with a sexy young woman in his office—someone like Anadel, whose last name had in fact been Seidman when she worked on Seventh Avenue and met Dad. My mind drifted to Linda, and when I wasn't thinking of her, my eyes would sometimes stop short of the stage to look at the seats a few rows ahead of where I sat now—those that Jackie and JFK had occupied at *The School for Scandal* in April. But now the Kennedys were mere Washington ghosts, displaced by the ordinary Washingtonians who sat where they once had.

When the curtain call came, I applauded gratefully, as everyone around me did, but with a slight reserve. I was at the performance and yet removed from it, looking at the stage through a scrim of dense meditation. The actors smiled nervously as they took their bows; they seemed to want to say something to the audience—but they didn't. Maybe they wanted company themselves on this night, their last in Washington, before they moved on to the next town.

The lights came up, and we filed out in silence. As the audience spilled onto the E Street sidewalk, the painted marquee had already been changed, as was the National's custom when a show ended its run on Saturday night, to the one heralding the new play that would open Monday. But Joel said that the National's next opening would likely be postponed, just as Deal's WEAM dance had been rescheduled, because only a few steps away from the National, on Pennsylvania Avenue, Monday would bring the show everyone knew must come next: the president's funeral.

CHAPTER 8

ariety, which had celebrated JFK's entrance onto the national stage as if he were a Hollywood star breaking box-office records, was just as dogged in counting the house after he made his premature exit. BIG SAT BIZ, said one story, reporting that attendance at legit shows throughout the country, not just *Seidman and Son,* was up after the assassination. Mary Martin, starring in a new musical called *Jennie* in New York, was reported to have "stepped out of character to make personal talks to the audience" for the first time in her career. "We in show business are schooled in the discipline that the show must go on," she told the crowds at the Majestic Theatre. "I cannot ask you to forget, but perhaps we can help each other for the next few hours." Another story said that the script of *Mr. President,* which had closed at the St. James in June after only a six-month run, was having its Kennedy references "laundered" before being offered to summer-stock companies. In other words, not even an assassination could stop the theater from picking itself up and moving forward. What else in life could be counted on with such certainty?

Washington wasn't so resilient. But at Deal, and in Chanukah Heights, life didn't change perceptibly—or pause for long. Few of our parents worked in the government. That President Kennedy had been removed from our lives with such finality was now a part of current-events discussion in homeroom, a fixture in the newspapers, a source of constant where-were-you-when-you-heard-the-news? anecdotage. The sorrow everyone talked about, though, was an abstraction: The televised images of the little Kennedy children waving goodbye to their father were already becoming iconic, fixed forever—history as immutable as the rest of the Washington monuments we'd known as far back as our memories could take us.

Life turned ordinary again. Dad's main preoccupation was his and Anadel's new baby, "your new brother." Though Polly and I didn't live with our half-siblings, Dad had us pose as a family for a professional photographer from an advertising agency. In the picture, we are living statuary—kneeling in rigid poses on the floor, surrounded by open shoe boxes. Polly and I are each holding up a shoe, as if we are expertly scrutinizing the goods, while our "new sister" crawls in front of us and Dad spies on us from behind, peering through a French door that's been left ajar. FRANK RICH KNOWS WHAT GOES OVER WITH DAD, said the ad when it was printed in *The Washington Post*. "If you feel that Father knows best, then give a Rich's gift certificate." The caption noted that our new baby brother had "crawled from camera range." The question of who might be the mother of children of such disparate ages was skirted by simply leaving out any mention whatsoever of a mom.

With so many children underfoot, Dad barely noticed if I didn't turn up at his house on Sundays, if I'd chosen to study or visit with friends instead. Sometimes I would also skip Wednesday-night dinners at my grandparents, where the furnishings were now almost hermetically sealed in vinyl as protection against the onslaught of babies. Polly increasingly represented both of us in Rich family events. She gravitated toward Dad's new family as I did not, at last able to play on a part-time basis the role of the oldest child that I had hogged from birth. This was the culmination of her slow but steady retreat from the house on Cleveland Avenue and all its occupants, even as she officially remained its third-floor hostage. Washington's public-school bureaucracy allowed her to distance herself from Sue, John, and me by attending Gordon Junior High instead of Deal, and once

there she constructed a separate life that the rest of us were not encouraged to enter. If she had a special passion of her own to escape into when
we hid out in our aerie, as I did the theater, she never revealed it.

Because Joel "knew Lyndon," he seemed busier than ever after the assassination. He stopped keeping regular office hours like other fathers, instead driving back and forth between K Street and Cleveland Avenue
several times a day. Though Mom had decided to go back to work, if only
part-time — teaching remedial reading to students at Cardozo, an all-
Negro high school in the ghetto — she'd drop it all on a moment's notice if
Joel rushed home with an exotic travel plan to be carried out in the next
twenty-four hours.

On some school vacations, we kids would go on trips too. In first class
on Air France or Air India, Joel would commandeer the caviar and Champagne for our benefit and Mom's more than his own. Like Mom, he didn't
care about luxury at all: The mere act of getting something for nothing was
an end in itself; the desirability or value of whatever that something was
didn't matter. "I live to serve," he joked — but he meant it, because he didn't
really crave anything for himself except attention. If Mom wanted to go
tour an archaeological site and it wasn't open, he'd figure out a scheme to
get her in. In London, he secured tickets for every West End play that
caught my eye and made our driver (wheedled gratis from Air India) criss-
cross the Oxfordshire countryside to find Sue a crumpet just like the ones
she'd read about in a schoolbook. Long before the prized object was finally
secured, Sue had withdrawn the request, begging her father to end the
scorched-earth search, but Joel wouldn't think of quitting until he had humiliated the driver and yelled at Sue to eat every last crumb of the goddamn thing she no longer hungered for. His largesse was real, but it came
at a price that we, unlike Mom, found steep.

The schemes by which Joel did the impossible were intricate, dishon-
est, and ingenious. He had stationery printed for a "Washington Travel
Service" that, he bragged, existed only on paper and yet entitled him to
travel discounts in addition to those he received as an airline lawyer. He
also commissioned various laminated photo-identification cards naming
him as an executive of a myriad of companies and government agencies,
and driver's licenses from at least five states; the I.D.s came in useful for

getting the "government rate" on a variety of goods and services, the licenses for bargaining with traffic cops to whom he purported to be an out-
of-town visitor unfamiliar with the local ordinances. For my own trips to
New York to see Harry, Joel presented me with an I.D. identifying me as
an attorney for an airline called Flying Tigers, just in case anyone questioned my right to a shuttle pass. Since I looked no older than my actual
age of going-on fifteen, who would possibly believe it?

"My rule," Joel was fond of saying, "is never pay unless the bastards give
you no other goddamn way out."

For the post-assassination Christmas, Joel decided that we'd take our
longest trip ever to New York: a week at the Astor hotel, literally in Times
Square, with Broadway shows jammed in as densely as possible. Given the
holiday performance schedules, we'd be able to do many more two-show
days than just the typical Wednesdays and Saturdays. The week before we
went to New York, though, a new tryout opened at the National Theatre,
and for the first time since I had been reading the critics, they were unan-
imously ecstatic in their praise. Joel announced we'd see *Hello, Dolly!* before we left. "Don't let anyone ever say I failed to spoil you rotten!" he said,
as Mom smiled in approval. I was beside myself about seeing it, not so
much because of the good reviews but because I knew that the Broadway
people who did *Hello, Dolly!* were some of the same ones who had done
Carnival! and *Bye Bye Birdie.* I still replayed in my mind that scene in
Birdie where all those gyrating teenage boys and girls were propelled
toward the audience as if by magic, all but falling into my lap as they
whipped up a sexual hurricane.

In *Hello, Dolly!,* I would soon discover, there was a similar scene. In the
second act, when the title character walked into an elegant restaurant in
New York, the waiters, all wearing crisp white shirts and black pants like
the waiters at the Broadway restaurants I'd been to, sang and danced with
a speed I'd never before seen. At one point they literally leapt over the orchestra pit, high up into the air, landing on a slender curved ramp that had
been built into the audience, necessitating the removal of some of the National's orchestra seats. As the dancers touched down, the ramp lit up with
little lightbulbs along its borders like those on an airport runway. The set
behind them blinked with lights too: a crimson restaurant with a towering

staircase as tall as the proscenium that Dolly, wearing a crimson dress to match, had just descended. It didn't matter what the song was—it just repeated the show's title over and over—because the audience was in pandemonium. When the actress playing Dolly, Carol Channing, a woman with the highest blond hair I'd ever seen, appeared on the ramp with the waiters who were serenading her and then joined their dance as well, people started standing up individually and in groups all over the theater and waving at her, as if they knew her. They didn't, I realized—they just wanted to. The eruption looked like the old TV pictures of JFK being deluged by crowds; now that he was dead, Washington had found someone else to go crazy about. *Hello, Dolly!* was like a buzzing alarm clock, waking up the solemn town and bringing it back to life.

Even Mom and Joel were agog at the spontaneous frenzy at the National. They didn't stand up, but Joel was beating out the time of the song with his *Playbill,* as though he'd been singing "Hello, Dolly!" for years. The whole theater seemed to rock on its moorings in response to the swaying of the dancers and the sound of the band.

What was the big deal about Dolly going to a restaurant? It didn't matter, I saw. The effect was like that of the dancing teenagers in *Bye Bye Birdie:* The movements of the people onstage, their leap right into the heart of the audience, got us all excited before we could figure out exactly what it was we were getting excited about.

Leaving the theater after the show was over, I didn't feel my usual letdown. *Hello, Dolly!* was staying in Washington while we went to New York, and it would be waiting for us when we got back at the end of the week. For once, I was leaving a Broadway show behind in Washington, rather than the other way around.

—

It was freezing in New York that December, and the Astor, a fraying yet ornate Winter Palace, was stuffy with heat. The hotel took up an entire block, housed its own movie theater, and was adjacent to the thickest clusters of Broadway shows. Incredibly, we were in a room overlooking Shubert Alley itself: The word BOOTH, spelled out in small white lights on black scaffolding on that theater's roof, was right outside the window.

When we looked down, we could see the New York crowds rushing through the Alley, surely to get to the box offices nearby.

I wanted to join them, of course, and the day after we arrived, Tuesday, when we had no play scheduled for the afternoon, I asked Mom if I could go to a show on my own. I had picked *Jennie*. Except for its star, it had received dismissive reviews and was closing at week's end, having run just two months, but I longed to see Mary Martin onstage. I'd seen her only on television, where every year they rebroadcast her old *Peter Pan*.

Mom and Joel didn't object—as long as I was back in time for dinner and the next play—so I went to the Majestic Theatre, bought the cheapest seat I could, and climbed the stairs to the nearly deserted balcony. Soon the lights dimmed and the music started, but the overture was muted compared to the others I'd heard. Was this really the same theater where I'd seen *Camelot* and *The Music Man*? To my amazement, the audience scattered around me didn't listen to the orchestra with intense anticipation but just kept on talking as if there was no overture at all. Was this because the show was a flop, or because I was so far away from the pit, which I could see into from my perch high above? When the curtain rose, the experience was also new. I was conscious of how flat the dialogue sounded, as if it were reaching me through an echo chamber, and of how lugubriously the actors moved around onstage. The scenery seemed pale next to the florid hues of *Hello, Dolly!* It was a show I would never be tempted to rebuild in a shoe box.

In my restlessness, I tried to picture that night a month before, a day after the assassination, when Mary Martin told the audience to "help each other for the next few hours." I could picture her saying it in a spotlight at the edge of the stage in her best Peter Pan voice, just as if she were asking everyone watching her to clap as hard as they could to bring Tinker Bell back to life. Well, she couldn't bring Kennedy to life, and *Jennie* seemed moribund as well. There was no urgency in Mary Martin's performance, and she seemed to turn her singing on and off like a faucet. The applause at the end of her songs petered out quickly every time, and the show lumbered on.

Jennie was only about forty-five minutes old when I was wishing I had chosen another show. Five blocks away, at the Eugene O'Neill Theatre, was *She Loves Me*, which starred an actress Harry and I worshiped, Barbara Cook, whom I had first seen as Marian the librarian, little Winthrop's big sister, in *The Music Man*. She was blond and sang in a voice that made you feel as if she cared about whomever she was singing to more than she cared about anyone else in the world. She was the kind of woman—blond and stacked, too—whom Harry and I planned to fall in love with someday.

She Loves Me had a three o'clock curtain—an hour later than *Jennie*—and I decided after intense internal debate to spend the extra money to see it. It had never occurred to me before to leave a show early, and as I left the Majestic, I felt guilty. Now I was deserting a show, just as I had previously imagined they all deserted me. As I walked quietly down the balcony stairs, I stopped at the back of the theater—at the railing where there would have been standees if *Jennie* had been SRO. I watched a few minutes more, but from this perspective as well the show still seemed to be sealed off in its own ether on the other side of the footlights.

I knew that this was the same theater where, the year I was born, Mary Martin had been in *South Pacific*, the musical Mom had wanted so much to see and never had. "It was impossible to get a ticket," Mom told me, offering an explanation of why Dad hadn't taken her. Now there were plenty of tickets. It seemed heartless to watch Mary Martin on the same stage, acting before an audience that greeted her with polite indifference, as if she'd never had her triumph fourteen years earlier. The whole vast theater seemed to sigh in a collective yawn.

But once on the street I put *Jennie* out of my mind and ran full-speed to *She Loves Me*, arriving just in time to get a three-dollar balcony seat as the show was starting. From then on, the week passed too quickly, with each high point spilling into the next—from the real rain that doused the stage at the end of *110 in the Shade* to the nasty wrestling match between a big tomboy of an actress named Colleen Dewhurst and a dwarf actor named Michael Dunn in *The Ballad of the Sad Café*. I was so keyed up that in between shows I could do little but constantly reshuffle my *Playbills* and ticket stubs into stacks of varying significance.

Late on our final afternoon, Mom and Joel at last heeded my persistent claims that I was entitled to special privileges befitting the eldest child. Since I'd proved that I could "handle my independence" in New York, they decided that while they and the rest of the kids ate at the hotel with a relative of Mom's from Brooklyn, I could go my own way, dine alone, and meet them at the theater just before eight-thirty. Joel sent me to Frankie and Johnny's, a steak house on Forty-fifth Street, on the same block as the Morosco, where we were seeing *The Private Ear and the Public Eye.*

Mom gave me a ten-dollar bill, more than enough for me to have a steak and something to drink, and to leave a tip. In a way, I was as pleased about having my own dinner as I was about seeing the show that would follow. If I didn't think about it too hard—if I could just keep my mind from venturing into the blackness that loomed on the other side of the trip, when, tomorrow morning, we'd return to Washington—I could imagine that I actually lived in New York and wasn't just a visitor there.

At seven o'clock, with the crisp bill tucked into the wallet I'd been given for my bar mitzvah, I eagerly headed toward the restaurant. But I took the long way there, stopping first at a newsstand at another hotel, the Manhattan, to spend a quarter of my own money on the latest *Variety.* It was a luxury, since the same issue would be waiting for me back home, but I didn't care. The night was alive to me in a way it had never been before; I wanted to possess everything in it.

As I paid, the newsstand man gave me a quizzical look, seemingly puzzled that a kid would read *Variety.* "Do you know Eddie Hodges?" he asked. I was taken aback. In fact, I had encountered Eddie Hodges from *The Music Man* one more time, when he turned up in a movie I saw with Dad, *A Hole in the Head.* In this movie, Dad's favorite singer, Frank Sinatra, played a single father (a widower, not divorced) dating pretty women like Anadel in a search for a new wife. Eddie Hodges played Sinatra's son, a boy who didn't want to lose his father to a new "mother." I felt once again that Eddie Hodges was a mysterious proxy for me, though the movie was just too awkward for Dad and me to talk about.

I told the newsstand man no, I hadn't ever met Eddie Hodges, but by my eager response made it clear that I was in the know—I knew that Eddie Hodges was the famous actor whose singing of the song "Gary, Indiana" I had mimicked countless times to the accompaniment of the original cast album, back in the days when Mom was single and I fantasized that I might by some magic become him. What a city New York was! Even the newsstand men seemed to care about the theater as much as I did.

At Frankie and Johnny's—the restaurant used to be a speakeasy like those Nat and Lil went to, Mom had told me—I climbed the stairs to the second-floor entrance and was greeted by a waiter dressed just like those at Dinty Moore's and Al Schacht's, "my" New York restaurants. I mentioned Joel's name, as he'd said to do, and the waiter showed me to a table. My feet didn't reach the floor when I sat down, but could he see that? He asked if I wanted the children's menu. I paused, then found the courage to say no, and he brought me a huge slab of New York restaurant cardboard that had to be unfolded like a box to be read. There was nothing like it in Washington, where the menus were more often than not printed on the paper place mat.

Within minutes—or maybe a half hour, since I was too enthralled with the professional bustle of the waiters, with my glittering fellow diners all around, with the Broadway posters on the wall, to keep track of time at first—they brought my sirloin steak and french fries. I painstakingly devoured my newspaper, the food, and a glass of milk, certain I had ample time to make it to the Morosco. When there was no choice but to pay and leave, I asked the waiter for the check, studied it carefully, then left a meticulously computed tip (fifteen percent of the total *before* they add the tax, Joel had instructed) and walked down the stairs back to Forty-fifth Street and up the block to the Morosco, where Joel was impatiently waiting in the lobby to take me inside to our seats.

At intermission, I told Joel what I had read in *Variety*. It seemed that not just *Jennie* but half the plays in New York were closing that night, fleeing town just as my family and the rest of the tourists would be, as if Christmas on Broadway were a charade put on exclusively for our benefit. What happens when a play closes?, I asked. To which Joel replied, catching Mom's eye as he did so: "Why don't you find out?"

He was serious. What followed after our play ended was like one of Mom's Adventures—but this time I would have the Adventure without Mom, who was going back to the hotel with Joel and the other kids. As long as I promised to be back in my room no later than midnight—an hour hence—I was free to explore Times Square, to see what happened at the theaters where the shows were closing and to scoop up any discarded *Playbills* that I had as yet failed to secure over the week.

I waved a joyous goodbye as soon as we were among the crowds spilling out of every Broadway house. On each block I found long vans parked in front of the theaters—like those that had come for our furniture in Somerset and Rosemary Hills—with men lounging about them. The sets of the closing plays were about to be "struck," as I'd learned at Indian Hill, then loaded into the trucks and taken away.

Most of the action was on Forty-fifth Street. Half the shows on the block were closing, including a comedy called *Love and Kisses* at Moss Hart's Music Box and, at the Royale, a French play called *The Rehearsal*. Outside the Royale, the photographs of *The Rehearsal* were still brightly lit in their glass cases: actors in period costumes and powdered wigs, like those in *The School for Scandal*, bowing and kissing in sumptuous rooms that looked like the palace we had visited with Mom and Joel at Versailles. The doors to the theater were still open, the empty auditorium bathed in an amber half-light, and I could peer in from the deserted lobby and see that stagehands were dismantling the walls of one of the rooms depicted in the photos out front. The set was coming apart easily, piece by piece; the furniture was being packed into boxes just like our moving boxes, and so were the costumes, carefully placed on hangers, the way Mom's clothes had been when the trucks came to take our things from Somerset to Rosemary Hills.

Then the backdrop hanging across the rear of the stage came down— that was the sky.

Only a few hours earlier, I thought, there had been people talking and laughing and crying on this stage as if their lives would never end. Now there was nothing but what looked like a giant night-light. It stood at the center of the empty stage: a tall black pole with a single lightbulb at its top, a solitary lamp casting stark shadows everywhere. What was its point?, I wondered. Instead of filling the stage with color and excitement like regular stage lights, it accentuated the drab desolation of the empty house. I knew nothing about this play, this *Rehearsal*, and yet I ached for it in some strange way—for its stilled heart, for the naked light that stood where the actors once had. Years later I would learn that this light was called a "ghost light," and that was surely the right name for it. There were ghosts everywhere.

Where were those actors from *The Rehearsal* now? They didn't stay around to watch what happened to the house they were deserting any more than Mom and Dad had. And yet the house was haunted by them and by all the audiences who had seen the play during its run.

Watching the sets being struck was nonetheless an antidote to the gloom of a show's closing. The exposure and dismantling of the play's illusion seemed every bit as theatrical to me as the creation of that illusion. Plays came and went, but the theater stayed. Even an empty playhouse had drama, intense and perhaps momentous.

Only at one closing, a block away, could I not see the dismantling of the scenery: The stage door of *Jennie* wasn't visible, seemingly hidden by a long passageway that led from it to the sidewalk. As I arrived at the Majestic, it was perilously close to midnight. The vans were pulling away, their engines heaving and belching with exhaust. The neighborhood that I had never imagined as anything other than hectic was starting to look deserted.

A lone young man was still standing at the street exit of the Majestic's cul-de-sac, dwarfed by the dark theater behind him. He clutched a stack of *Playbills* even larger than my own. His eyes were large and liquid, and he seemed a breed of person apart, residing completely in this world that I could visit only as a tourist.

I stopped a few feet from him on the sidewalk, eager to see if anything was going on; my curfew was approaching, and I had to be fast. Perhaps recognizing a somewhat kindred spirit—or simply protecting his own, carefully staked-out turf—the man said hello and struck up a conversation, explaining that he loved *Jennie* and was waiting to get Mary Martin's autograph. There was a hunger I recognized in this man, as if he were starving for company. I didn't have the heart to tell him that I hadn't liked *Jennie* and didn't think Mary Martin was going to turn up at this hour, now that the theater's marquee had dimmed.

The giant marquee across the street still burned with incongruous intensity. It was the St. James Theatre, home of *Do Re Mi* and then *Mr. President* and now a play called *Luther*. The young man pointed at it and informed me in a whisper, as if he was imparting the darkest secret, that the producer David Merrick was about to move *Luther* to another theater so that he could bring his new production, a musical, to the St. James the next month.

To the man's surprise, I told him that I had seen that musical, *Hello, Dolly!*, in its tryout in my hometown the week before I came to New York. And though he was a total stranger, I couldn't stop myself from venturing an opinion: Buy a ticket to *Hello, Dolly!* in advance, I told him. "It's going to be a hit," I said, startling myself with my outspokenness.

I couldn't tell if he believed me or not when he said that he just might send in a mail order. Maybe he'd read the bad *Variety* review of the tryout and thought I was a fool. All but swallowed up by the shadowy theater behind him, he was still waiting for Mary Martin as I said good night and turned to hurry back to the hotel.

I wondered if he was as lonely as I often was. If so, I felt sorry for him, because I didn't feel lonely that night, not at all. It had been only a little more than a month since Kennedy's funeral, and I was soon returning to Washington, but I felt indecently happy. Broadway seemed a place where no matter what happened in the rest of the world, a closing would always be followed by an opening, an empty house would always become full again.

I tried not to think of Cleveland Avenue, of Deal, of the long drive home in the morning during which Joel would yell at Mom and she would cry while we four kids cowered in the backseats of the station wagon. As a chill wind whipped me up Forty-fourth Street to the Astor, I felt terribly grown-up, as if I were being propelled into the future by the great and mysterious promise of the incipient new year.

CHAPTER 9

A s winter turned to spring, I returned to the National as often as I
could, usually buying standing room for the Saturday matinee, enjoying my solitary afternoons in downtown Washington as I had
my freedom in New York over Christmas. The play I most eagerly awaited
was one I had read a year earlier, when Mom bought me the paperback
book of its script. It had a joke title she had to explain to me when it first
opened in New York—Who's Afraid of Virginia Woolf? But it wasn't funny.
It was the first play I knew of in which a husband and wife had arguments
onstage.

Reading the play hadn't prepared me at all for what it was like to watch
it in the theater. There, for all to see at the National, were the conversations in my own house, just below my bedroom, loud and clear. But while
Mom and Joel nodded in agreement when I enthused about Virginia
Woolf, they said nothing to indicate that they recognized its characters.
They were mainly impressed by my ability to stay alert for such a long play,
and they decided to get me a ticket for the next, even longer play coming
to the National: King Lear. It was a special production traveling from the
Royal Shakespeare Company in Stratford, England, with a famous actor

named Paul Scofield as Lear, and it was playing only four nights before going to a new theater called Lincoln Center in New York. I'd go alone, since the other kids weren't "ready for it yet" and Mom and Joel would be in Paris.

Mom suggested I try to read *King Lear* before I saw it, as I had *Virginia Woolf*, and she took me to Brentano's to buy a paperback copy. By the time the night of the performance came, two weeks later, I had made my way through only half of it and was anxious that I might not be able to figure out what was going on. The play was a tragedy, I knew, but just what was a tragedy?

What was clear when I arrived at the theater was that this was a night unlike others at the National. *King Lear* was not a part of the Theatre Guild subscription series, and the audience didn't look like a regular Washington audience — or a New York one, either. The house was full but quiet before the lights went down, as if people had come to a library or a school, rather than to see a show. Sitting next to me was an elderly woman far removed from my grandparents' crowd — a tiny, bent figure with a beaklike nose and a balding gray head who struggled to lower herself into her seat and didn't take off her thick, stained coat once she had done so. When the play began, I noticed that she was quietly mouthing every word the actors said; the script that was too long for me to finish she knew by heart! Far from finding her a distraction, however, I appreciated her as a comforting companion. As the night wore on, the constant, monotonous, birdlike movements of her mouth were as soothing as prayer. When I winced at the scene in which one man pulled out another's eyes with his bare hands, she just rocked gently in her seat, as if to steady me and everyone else in our row. At the end, when King Lear ran out onstage, his beautiful dead daughter in his arms, Paul Scofield sobbing in one long braying cry that sounded as if the whole earth were aching, she just nodded, looking more thoughtful than sad, as if she had seen it all before and knew it had to happen again.

Once the play was over, the audience reacted as no other I had ever seen. As the curtain fell, not a single person clapped. When the curtain rose again, the entire cast assembled onstage, flooded in light, and the whole audience stood up, as if on cue, but still in silence. Only then, as if seventeen hundred people had all at once taken a deep breath and then exhaled, did they start to applaud, softly at first, as if they were trying to regain their strength. The applause grew louder and louder, but when the curtain call was over, the audience didn't rush out as it usually did. I could understand why: No one wanted to let go of this memory while it was still fresh; this play was a dream that would dissipate too quickly upon awakening.

I thought of Mom and Joel in Paris. I was glad they were gone, and yet: There was no one else with whom I could talk about the sights and sounds of *King Lear*, no one else who could share with me this never-to-be-repeated experience, no one else who could serve as a corroborating eyewitness to this play, with its fool in sackcloth cradled like a child by the mad king as they huddled together on the very edge of the stage, warding off the storm crashing all around them.

———

I could tell Harry about it, of course, and did, in one of the two-hour tie-line conversations that were mine to instigate at will whenever Joel was abroad. In weeks, Harry and I would be back together at Indian Hill — my third summer, his second. He had skipped the previous summer to go to the Riviera, where his father had filmed a TV series whose title, *Harry's Girls*, had, to Harry's horror, become a running gag on the popular satirical show, *That Was the Week That Was*, that unceremoniously replaced it on NBC. "My name is now a synonym for utter idiocy," he lamented. "Thanks for *everything*, Dad!"

But Joe Stein had already moved on from this latest debacle. He was at work on a Broadway musical called *The Old Country*, based on stories by Sholom Aleichem. It had been on and off again ever since Harry and I had first met. We'd both read the script — the first time I ever saw a Broadway script in its mimeographed form, in a supple red binder like those we used for our school papers. Once, during a visit to New York, Harry's dad let us watch a "backers' audition" for possible investors held in the Steins' living room after dinner one night. Joe Stein told the story and acted out some of the lines while the composer and lyricist, the same team who wrote *Fiorello!* and *She Loves Me*, played and sang the songs that went with each scene. Harry and I just assumed we'd be seeing the show on Broadway in a matter of days.

That had been ages ago, and after a while Harry and I stopped talking about it. Now *The Old Country* had a new producer, the same man who had produced *A Funny Thing Happened on the Way to the Forum*, and Zero Mostel as its star. It also had a new title that Harry and I found as silly as *Hello, Dolly!*—*Fiddler on the Roof*—even if it was, his dad told us, inspired by a painting by Marc Chagall. Harry and I admitted to each other that it sounded like a children's show, not a real Broadway musical. What was wrong with *The Old Country*?

Just like *Hello, Dolly!* the year before, *Fiddler*, as *Variety* referred to it, was going to have a tryout that would start at the Fisher Theatre in Detroit and then move to the National in Washington in late August—just after camp ended. Much as Harry and I would have liked to see the Detroit tryout, we were even more excited to be returning together to Stockbridge.

I was desperate for Harry to meet Sara, my other New York tie-line friend, a pianist who had become my closest confidante at Indian Hill during his absence the summer before. She came from Greenwich Village, always wore black, no matter how sunny the weather, and despised sports as much as I had come to. She loved to go to concerts, and whenever she felt down during the school year, she'd open the paper and spend hours choosing and buying tickets for them "the way other people shop for clothes." She spoke in a smoky murmur, cracked wry jokes, and spent hours practicing her music.

Harry and Sara indeed hit it off, and soon the three of us had become a floating Greek chorus, dissecting at every pass a scandalous summer such as Indian Hill hadn't seen before. One pianist among the seniors was sent home early when a counselor discovered that through a deceit of Houdini-like flair the boy had smuggled two girls into his tepee at night. ("What if he had only been caught with *one* girl?" we wondered.) Another boy, nastily teased by all of us when he was discovered writing his mother six or seven times a day, was diagnosed as having "mental problems" and carted off—it was rumored—to a mental asylum called Austen Riggs that an alarming number of Indian Hill campers and counselors seemed to know about in intimate detail. Most notoriously, five of the cutest girls were docked from the annual night out at the movies—to see the "international sex romp" (so the ads said) *Tom Jones*—because they had avoided the Tanglewood field trip to the premiere of Benjamin Britten's *War Requiem* by drinking soapsuds to induce a disabling afternoon of vomiting.

In drama class, I performed an alcoholic monologue that I memorized from *Who's Afraid of Virginia Woolf?* Rick Hondel, a new playwriting counselor from Johns Hopkins in Baltimore, encouraged Harry and me to write and direct one-act plays, and we both adapted stories from *Goodbye, Columbus*, by a new writer Mom had told me about named Philip Roth. I chose one about a kid studying for his bar mitzvah who calls his obnoxious rabbi "a bastard" and threatens to kill himself unless everybody in the neighborhood says that they believe in Jesus Christ. It was almost too much fun—if only I had thought up this scene in real life in Washington!

When I wasn't rehearsing, I stopped by the barn to watch Sara rehearse in the chorus of a one-act opera by Leonard Bernstein that some of the music campers were doing, complete with jazzy dance steps from Jimmy Waring, a choreographer from Greenwich Village who also dressed in black. The opera was called *Trouble in Tahiti*, and though I'd never heard of it before, many of the other kids had. I was astounded by how familiar its story seemed. "How could you say the things that you did in front of the kid?" an angry husband sang to his wife in the first scene. I couldn't believe it—a *musical* about divorce. It ended on a note of resignation I recognized—it was the sound of Mom capitulating to Joel.

Our camp revels were dampened, however, when *Variety* arrived with bad news from the other Stein family theatrical front: The Detroit legit critic said that *Fiddler* was "ordinary" and condemned it to a brief Broadway run. Harry and I carefully composed a letter of commiseration to his father. Joe Stein scrawled back an answer in pencil from the Belcrest Hotel in Detroit: "We have some things that might be fixed, but we are quite sure that we have a very good show. Zero is marvelous. I was surprised that you were upset."

When what would be our last summer at Indian Hill came to its end, we didn't have time to mourn its passing. *Fiddler* awaited us in Washington, and Harry was going to stay at our house while his father camped out with the show's company at the Willard Hotel downtown.

The desultory Washington that *Fiddler* entered in that late summer of 1964 invited ridicule from Harry, who'd seen the city only during a school trip. With Congress out of session, the city was a landscape as still as death. The monuments seemed to sweat, impervious to the scraggly lines of wilting, melted end-of-season tourists seeking their shade. The downtown department stores, from Lansburgh's to Garfinckel's, stood deserted, waiting for the first back-to-school shoppers to end their months-long evacuation; the traffic signals clicked their changes gratuitously on Reno Road, the leafy, car-free artery linking Cleveland Park to Chevy Chase. Next to the sleek skyscrapers reaching for the sky in Manhattan, the excretions of Washington's latest office-building frenzy looked like corrugated boxes squatting in the swamp. As we went to the National on a Monday afternoon to watch the final rehearsal before that night's first performance, Harry mocked the thinness of the traffic and the empty sidewalks, so different from the nonstop human parade of Times Square: "I bet Dad's gonna be homesick for Detroit!" The only inhabitants of E Street were those we recognized as members of the *Fiddler* company, coming from the direction of the Willard, and the occasional stray Negro in some variety of menial uniform.

In the cool, dark theater, Joe Stein sat us down on the opposite side of the house from the set designer, Boris Aronson, and the director, Jerome Robbins, who had, like Aronson, shadowed my young theatergoing life, from *Peter Pan* to *Bells Are Ringing* to *Gypsy*. The curtain was up, and costumed actors were milling about the stage. An orchestra was in the pit, though the conductor was wearing shorts and a polo shirt, not the usual tuxedo. The rehearsal began, and while Harry and I recognized bits and pieces of the long-ago backers' audition, *Fiddler* was no longer the old *Old Country*. Sometimes it was hard to tell what was going on. A stern woman—the stage manager—kept interrupting scenes with impenetrable commands like "Go to eleven-B." When Zero Mostel appeared dressed as the Jewish milkman, Tevye, he had a cigarette dangling out of his mouth, as Joel might; he sounded like Joel, too, when he growled his lines. Soon he sang a song full of what sounded like either yodeling or gibberish, which he intermingled with epithets and obscene gestures apparently directed at Robbins, Harry's dad, and the other show people watching him across the orchestra floor from us. He was funny, but I worried: Is this how a milkman behaved in turn-of-the-century Russia?

As soon as Harry and I were back outside in the August steam bath, Harry said what I was thinking but didn't have the heart to say: "I can't believe it. I can't believe that my father has another bomb."

I knew he was right, and I knew that if I lied and told him I was sure *Fiddler* would be a hit, he'd see through it. So I settled for a half-truth. "Come on, Harry, it's not *that* bad. I'm sure they can fix it."

"Yeah, sure," he snapped back. "Just like they fixed *Mr. President.*"

———

That night, we had orchestra seats next to Joe Stein and Harry's mother, Sadie. The theater was not full, and our expectations were so low that we almost dreaded the show starting, since that meant it would lumber to its certain doom. Without an overture, *Fiddler* had no means even to create the temporary illusion, however misleading, that something exciting might happen once the curtain went up. When the auditorium darkened and the curtain rose, the audience heard only the thin sound of a single violin, and saw only a darkened stage—on which was illuminated nothing more than Mostel and that childish fiddler on the roof.

What a far cry from those dancing teenagers of *Bye Bye Birdie*, those gamboling waiters of *Hello, Dolly!*

I didn't look at Harry for fear that we might have a laughing fit. A sideways glance confirmed that he was already holding his head in his hands, a gesture that I knew from those afternoons when the Indian Hill baseball team lost (as it always did) to the athletic campers of nearby Mackinac.

The fiddler receded into the background, and bit by bit the rest of the cast came onstage in a number led by Mostel that, strangely, we had not seen while watching the show that afternoon. The idea of the song was to introduce the impoverished Jewish community, Anatevka, where Sholom Aleichem's stories took place. As the stage filled up more and more, with the characters each in turn joining the larger group in what seemed to be a circle dance like the hora, the whole atmosphere in the theater started to change. The band became louder and richer, and with no warning whatsoever the scattered cast suddenly converged into a single mass of people, stampeding forward as much as dancing, everyone's arms raised toward the sky, everyone's fingers snapping as they did so. The pack was led by Mostel—a big, fat man, hardly a dancer, but he seemed the natural leader anyway, dominating the stage with his sheer bulk, with the stern, almost angry, determination of his facial expression, and with his arms, which he waved like the others to the swelling beat of the music but with a violent frenzy unlike theirs, as if he were a revolutionary leading a mob. Then, just as the song crested in that agitated swirl of movement, all but raising the hair on the back of my neck as it did so, it subsided. The music calmed down. The onstage crowd did too, lithely dispersing into its constituent parts, each small group drifting off just as it had entered only minutes earlier, until finally no one was left except Mostel and the mute fiddler on the roof, just as they had been when the curtain rose.

With that, Mostel ended the song alone, and as soon as the band played its last note, I looked at Harry. His face was plastered with a smile, and I saw him share it with his father, who leaned forward to give him a happy I-told-you-so look. Then came a roar of applause. We knew at that moment we had completely misjudged *Fiddler* that afternoon—a fact confirmed only a few minutes later, when Mostel whipped up torrents of laughter with the comic song that had only hours earlier struck us as such an embarrassing display of nonsense that we had pleaded with Harry's dad that it be cut.

The audience seemed to like the show right through to the end, but we were so startled by the discrepancy between our afternoon and evening reactions that we weren't entirely sure which response to trust. Once Joe Stein explained to us that the afternoon's rehearsal had been "a partial technical run-through," in which the show had been truncated to accomplish the sole goal of perfecting the lighting and scenery cues, and not the dress rehearsal we had thought, it began to sink in that we might actually be witnessing the birth of a hit.

Two days later, *Fiddler* received Washington reviews nearly as good as those for *Hello, Dolly!*, and Harry and I, with still a week to go before school, started hanging around the National all day until the evening performance, at which point Joe would "walk" us into the theater without tickets and deposit us in the unoccupied seats in the back rows of the orchestra. By now I preferred to stand in the back, rather than sit; it was fun to watch the audience along with the show, as well as to see the scurrying back and forth of the authors, who came to study their handiwork as the creators of *Mr. President* had during their tryout three years earlier. By week's end, as Joe Stein said, "business caught up with the reviews," and there were no unoccupied seats anyway, and then no unoccupied standing room places either. So we'd gladly stand anywhere we could, hanging behind the standees and sometimes wandering into the lobby for a few minutes in emulation of the men who ran the show.

It was hard to fathom that I was on the inside of a Broadway tryout now, rather than on the outside looking in. I actually knew Joe Stein, the author of a musical's book. The others seemed to glancingly recognize me, at least, as Joe's son's nameless friend. One night our playwriting instructor from the summer, Rick Hondel, turned up from Baltimore to see the show, and we filled him in on what was going on backstage, the songs being cut and added, as well as confiding to him our crush on one cast member, Tanya Everett (only three years older than us, according to the *Playbill*), a dark-haired, dark-eyed girl who played one of Mostel's daughters. Rick asked if he could meet Harry's father, and we secretly savored the advantage in status we enjoyed over our Indian Hill counselor.

———

At the Wednesday matinee the first week — when the houses were still half-empty — Harry and I had been standing in the back when in the middle of the "gibberish" song, "If I Were a Rich Man," Mostel had stopped singing in midphrase and announced, "Ring down the curtain — I'm going to be sick." Since the audience didn't know the song or the show, it thought the line was part of the script and laughed uproariously — until the curtain actually did come down for a few minutes before the performance resumed with an understudy in Mostel's role.

"Paul's only been rehearsed as far as this scene!" Joe Stein whispered to the two of us as he and the others rushed in once the show started again. But to our astonishment, the understudy, Paul Lipson, ad-libbed his way through the rest of the script, even managing to improvise lyrics that by some miracle of miracles actually rhymed. The audience gave him a standing ovation, though his performance was hardly comparable to Zero Mostel's.

"Z always said Washington audiences are morons!" said the star's son, Toby, who seemed more concerned with his dad's replacement than with his health. I didn't dispute him, pointing out that I'd seen his father play to an empty house in A *Funny Thing Happened on the Way to the Forum*, the hit that Washington was too moronic to appreciate.

Harry and I had struck up a friendship with Toby and found him endlessly fascinating—an Indian Hill type of kid who might have been too precocious even for Indian Hill. Toby was as tall and spindly as his father was mountainous, and like his dad, who was a painter as well as a performer, he aspired to be an artist. He often turned up at the theater with odd objects tucked under his long arms: He was collecting plaster figurines and old bricks from demolished buildings in downtown Washington, he said, to further his collection of urban archaeology. Toby hated *Fiddler*'s director, Jerome Robbins—as did his father, who would give Robbins the finger or stoop down to wiggle his considerable backside at him whenever the director's back was turned. Harry told me that the animosity began when Robbins named names during the show-business witch-hunt of the McCarthy period; Mostel, who had refused to be an informer, was blacklisted. But Toby maintained that his father hated Robbins mainly for artistic reasons—his work on *Fiddler*. After one particularly triumphant performance, he turned to Harry and me as the excited audience was filing out, rolled his eyes, and declaimed in a voice loud enough to be heard by anyone within shouting distance: "I can't believe what Jerry is doing. This show will never make it on Broadway—it's *the worst* second act in the history of the American musical!"

Some nights, after the curtain fell, Harry and I would go with Toby and a girl our age who was the daughter of Miltie Greene, the conductor, to the roof restaurant of the Hotel Washington around the corner. I had never been there before, and as a pianist played Broadway songs amid the musical lilt of the chattering customers, I thought that maybe my city had a nightlife after all. On three sides of the dining room were terraces protected by candy-striped awnings that opened up to reveal the alabaster city below; Cokes in hand, we stepped outside to survey the White House and the monuments, as well as the deserted downtown streets. In those brief moments, my hometown was transformed—by the late hour, by the tinkling piano, by the barest hint of an autumn breeze in the sultry August air, and by my new Broadway siblings.

Back inside, Toby and the conductor's daughter regaled us with stories of their childhood adventures around their parents' shows. Their parents themselves were never in evidence, nor were any members of the cast except a young man in the chorus everyone called "Seattle" (a name that reminded me of Tulsa, who sang "All I Need Is the Girl" in *Gypsy*) but who, as the *Playbill* revealed, was actually named John C. Attle. Harry and I had decided, invoking our Indian Hill expertise, that he was the best dancer in the show. With his Beatle haircut, dopey grin, and button eyes, John C. Attle exuded a shaggy friendliness. He always made a point of saying hello to us when we ran into him on E Street, asking us how we were and for our considered opinion of the show's latest changes. His solicitude emboldened us to confess our infatuation with Tanya Everett, and when Harry came up with a plan that we give her flowers, John C. Attle offered to take them to her backstage.

Fiddler was about to enter its final week in Washington, and there was no time to waste: Harry had to get to New York before the show did, to begin school. We spent hours trying to compose a note to our beloved, settling on a single sentence of admiration for her thespian abilities. We figured out how many flowers our pooled finances would allow us to buy, bought them at the Willard Hotel's florist, carefully domesticated Harry's handwriting to a legibility appropriate for the card, then presented the bouquet to John C. Attle so that he could deliver it backstage at the Saturday matinee. He gave us a wink and told us to be at the stage door after the show, when we'd meet Tanya at last.

It was the first time I had dared enter the covered alley alongside the National, which seemed as long and conducive to titillation as the In the Dark ride where we made out with girls at Glen Echo amusement park. There was a tremendous bustle as actors and stagehands popped in and out after the performance, chatting and gesticulating with an urgent sense of purpose. Harry and I were uncharacteristically quiet as we waited nervously for our rendezvous with Tanya. Finally she did appear, carrying our

flowers in their cone of white paper against her chest, and we were introduced by John C. Attle. With downcast eyes she thanked us, as young and
shy as we were. Then she was pulled away by Miltie Greene, the conductor, who emerged from the stage door saying he needed to talk to her
about something in the show—and our audience was over.

Our first meeting with Tanya Everett proved to be our last. Harry and I
knew but didn't admit to each other that our quest to win her love had
failed. This was the last time we would talk with John C. Attle as well,
though Harry and I followed his career beyond *Fiddler* as best we could:
His name turned up in fine print in ads for one show or another, then disappeared, only to surface a final time, not in an ad but in that wave of tiny
obituaries of theater people that washed over Broadway in the 1980s.

But now it was the Saturday before Labor Day 1964, and Washingtonians were flocking back to their awakening city, unaware of the Broadway
hit that had been hatched when no one was in town. On E Street at intermission of the last performance, I noticed that it was dark out—not the last
burnt-red remnants of sunset, as had been the case during intermission
when *Fiddler* first arrived in Washington, but night. The show wasn't getting longer—it had been cut, in fact—but the days were getting shorter.
Summer was almost over.

The next day, Harry returned to New Rochelle. On Tuesday, I'd begin
high school. And by the end of the week, *Fiddler on the Roof*, and everyone who had been a part of it, was gone.

CHAPTER 10

On the day *Fiddler* opened on Broadway, I sat down and wrote my New York friend Sara a letter, telling her that I wanted to kill myself or, failing that, write a short story about a boy who slits his throat—just to shock the Writers' Club I'd joined when I entered tenth grade at Woodrow Wilson High. But I was puzzled: "I can't actually put my finger on one thing that's bothering me so much," I wrote, counting my blessings: friends, an ability to glide through school, my own room at home, the theater. So why, I asked, did I feel "lonely and depressed"? I rewrote the letter before I mailed it, removing the idea of suicide except in its literary incarnation. I knew I wasn't going to kill myself, and if only there was some way to get to New York for the *Fiddler* opening, my woes would be forgotten.

My own family was no substitute for the departed *Fiddler* family. Mom was often distracted and depressed herself. She had given up her ghetto students and traveled almost all the time with Joel. As I began high school, they took two separate trips overseas in two weeks, returning only to change their bags. When Mom was home, I'd sometimes find her dead asleep when I returned from school, lying in bed, the curls of her silver-flecked hair ("I'm not going to be one of those phony women who dye it") flattened against the mattress, whatever new book she was reading splayed beside her on the white bedspread. More and more, Mom was reading about ancient civilizations and archaeology: "I want to find the meaning of it all," she'd say lightly, almost self-mockingly, after stating once more her distrust of "all organized religions." She recorded her anthropological findings on three-by-five cards and, with Joel's approval, mapped out future itineraries that would take them on whirlwind tours of Greece and Egypt and Italy and Israel—the sites of her mental digs. The file cards for future trips, and the supplementary clippings and books, multiplied until they took up half the den she now referred to as her office.

If Mom woke when I entered her bedroom on those late afternoons, she'd focus her watery post-snooze eyes and gladly listen to my vague unhappiness, then tell me she felt the same exact way at times, and not to worry, because she knew from her own experience that it would always pass. I kept waiting for her to mention Joel and their increasingly conspicuous battles, but she never did. Unhappiness was only a phase, she said, speaking of it as if it were as transitory as the measles. "Though I hope," she added, "that you aren't still going through it like I am when you get to be my age."

John's phase didn't pass. He retreated into a deeper and deeper silence that not even Joel's most violent thrashings could rupture. Much as I collected *Playbills*, John had become obsessed with a TV series about gangsters with machine guns, *The Untouchables*, and with his growing piles of *Famous Monsters of Filmland* magazines, which chronicled the past, present, and future of Hollywood horror movies. He squirreled away his allowance to order costly Frankenstein masks, elaborate and tight-fitting rubber contraptions in sickly green, and would try to wear them to dinner, until Joel threatened to punish him if he didn't cut it out. Though John was football-player-size once he entered his teens, Joel would drag him forcibly into the car when he resisted his appointments with his doctor, who we all knew was a psychiatrist. If John didn't respond to his treatment, Joel threatened, he might end up in Shepard Pratt, the hospital where Joel's sister, Selma, was confined. I wondered if I, too, could end up at Shepard Pratt.

In our tie-line conversations in the days after *Fiddler* opened in New York, Harry regaled me with tales of its dreamlike Broadway success, but they didn't lift my mood as I languished two hundred miles away. When the original cast album came out, I found, for the first time with a new show, that I didn't want to listen to it. The songs would only remind me of Harry and our late-summer nights at the National, and of Tanya and John C. Attle and Toby: all out of reach.

To counter my isolation, I tried to throw myself instead into life at Wilson, which was not only next to Deal on Nebraska Avenue but indistinguishable from it. There were some good classes, like Mrs. Perazich's and Mr. Morgan's for English and creative writing, and Mrs. Haynes's for art, but the jolliest period was chemistry, taught by an elderly man who moonlighted as an underwear salesman in the boys' department at Woodies at Wisconsin Circle. His class was largely run by those girls who had figured out that hiking up their skirts to reveal their own underwear could distract him from his academic chores, frequently prompting him to send beakers and test tubes crashing to the floor in midexperiment. Other curricula were abridged as well. Mark Twain's *The Adventures of Huckleberry Finn* was removed from American lit, for fear it might stir up "racial tensions," and in American history, we skipped right from the Louisiana Purchase to the Spanish-American War for the same reason. This did not stop our teacher—whom Mom had also had, during World War II—from good-naturedly asking us to petition Congress to change the National Anthem to "Dixie." Her logic was irrefutable: "When you hear that 'Star Spangled Banner,' " she drawled in her Tennessee accent, "you just can't sing it. But when they play 'Dixie,' you just can't help but join in!" Some of us were relieved that there were no blacks in the class to hear her sentiments; as at Deal, blacks were confined to sports teams and to the lowest, "basic" rung of a citywide "track system" that, we suspected, consigned them to Washington's unfathomably huge Negro junk heap.

Like our chemistry teacher, I was mesmerized by those short skirts. It was possible for most everyone to pair up in dates on weekend nights, our mobility now increased by the spread of learner's permits, the prelude to the driver's licenses most of us would have by the time we turned sixteen over the coming year. We lived for Saturdays, when we would go to a dance party, or a movie, or the Hot Shoppes, before ending up in a car seat or a darkened den unmonitored by sleeping parents. There we'd rub our bodies together in various degrees of undress until we achieved the desired level of friction, all the while exploring each other's bodies as far as the precisely drawn boundary that Chanukah Heights decorum insisted we observe.

On Saturday mornings, I worked in my father's downtown store to make extra money, then broke off to buy standing room or, failing that, the cheapest balcony seat I could for the two-thirty matinee at the National. Rich's Shoes was celebrating its ninety-fifth anniversary in a bright new downtown store: After decades of occupying a narrow four-story sliver carved out of the fortress-like Woodies that took up the entire block at Tenth and F, Dad had prevailed upon Grandpa to allow a move to a larger, single-floor store four blocks farther down F Street, right across from Loew's Capitol. That way Rich's could escape the part of downtown that had been swallowed up by the slums and, some said, was becoming unsafe.

Each Saturday would bring a steady, hectic flow of Negro men to the new Rich's. They were young black men I'd never seen—or noticed—before. Taking out wads of bills—all ones and fives, not the twenties and hundreds that Joel would spill on the floor every time he bought anything—they counted out the amount due on the shoes they bought in installments, the will-calls. I marked their receipts PAID and ran to the stockroom to retrieve their purchases.

Grandpa Herbert was celebrating an anniversary too—his sixtieth at Rich's—and still came to work every day. It was best to stay out of the line of fire; nearly eighty now, Grandpa was crankier than ever, and Dad, coping with a new store and another new baby, my second "new sister," was finding him more and more irritating. At Wednesday-night dinners as well as at work, he would campaign with Grandpa, hoping to persuade him to stop the Sunday-afternoon field trips in which he and Grandma Rose got all dressed up and drove Grandpa's Packard into the ghetto to chase down any customer who had bounced a check. They were considerably less welcome there than in even the restricted suburban neighborhoods where Grandma liked to see the flowers each spring, but Grandpa wouldn't be deterred. Dad confided in me that the only hope for ending these rides was for his father's car to break down permanently. Packard had gone out of business, and Grandpa had already decreed that he would never drive another brand once his current car was kaput.

Dad alluded to his travails with Grandpa on those Saturdays when he invited me to grab lunch with him just before I left my Rich's job for the National. He'd take me for a sandwich at the Old Ebbits Grill, and we'd have our first private conversations in as long as I could remember. He no longer mentioned Joel or Mom. Maybe there was nothing more for him to say. The theater—or sex and girls—didn't make it onto our menu of small talk, which was mostly about school and the business of shoes. I had started to realize that I would always inhabit a different world from my father; perhaps that had been my fate from the moment he moved out of Somerset. I'd never know for sure. But at least Dad was willing to let me seek my own world now, whatever it was. If he didn't love the theater, he understood that I loved it, and he didn't pretend to hold out hope that I would ever enlist in the family business. As I listened to Dad worry about Grandpa and the expense of the new F Street store and the growing amount of theft in the stockroom, I wondered if he wanted freedom from Rich's and his father too.

Much as I treasured my increasingly liberated weekends in Washington, I longed for trips to New York. When I could, I would go up to visit Harry and we'd stay at a new studio apartment his father, with his *Fiddler* wealth, had taken as an "office," right by Columbus Circle, only a few blocks from Broadway's theaters. "It's more like a bachelor pad," Harry told me as we made our plans to pack in as many shows as possible on a Thanksgiving weekend.

Our first stop, of course, was *Fiddler*. Harry beat a path through the Imperial's cramped lobby, with its double-snaked line of ticket-seekers, to walk us into the theater, much as his dad had done at the National. There we stood behind the standees, the ushers acknowledging Harry's right to be there, sans ticket, with any guest of his choosing. But the show didn't seem to belong to us anymore—the whole world had embraced it now, and we, who had been present at its creation, were castoffs in its new promiscuous life.

When the show was over, Harry and I walked up Eighth Avenue. "My parents are in Europe flaunting their loot like bandits," Harry said. "They've become so elevated, they're even pretending to like classical music!" We were savoring our new independence from all adults, and I took in the city around us with fresh eyes: After the shows let out, Broadway belonged to outlaws. Yet the erotic vices I was for the first time recognizing on every corner were inseparable from the theater, whose own outlandish personalities and gypsies and voluptuous women were in some way, I felt, kindred spirits to Times Square's other flamboyant nocturnal denizens. This was as far away as I could get from Washington, where a few decrepit dirty-movie theaters and magic-trick stores on Ninth Street constituted the only visible enclaves of "sin."

As we headed toward Harry's father's apartment, we noticed that almost every show poster was defaced by the Magic Marker letterings of a phantom Broadway scribe named "M.K.," who added his own, neatly written quotes to those of the official drama critics. "Better than 'Fiddler'—M.K." was his serial citation for *Bajour*, a poorly received new show. While Harry was infuriated, I was intrigued: Who was M.K.? He—or she—seemed like someone I wouldn't mind having as a friend. Fellow young theater fans (and who but a teenager would deface posters?) were hard to find.

Harry said that he was going to buy a Magic Marker and start scrawling " 'M.K. is an idiot'—H.S." on any *Bajour* poster he could find (though he never did so). As I returned for further weekends on Joel's shuttle passes, M.K. continued to add alternately enthusiastic and damning new comments on posters throughout the theater district. Only some months later did I realize that the ubiquitous initials had disappeared from Times Square as suddenly as they had first arrived.

—

In Washington, there was none of the inaugural anticipation of four years earlier. Though LBJ had been reelected—incongruously enough, with the assistance of Carol Channing, who turned "Hello, Lyndon!" into the official campaign song—the war that wasn't a war weighed on the town like a low-grade fever, bubbling up at Mom and Joel's dinner parties on Cleveland Avenue. I was surprised to hear Joel say, "Lyndon is fucking up this one."

Instead of watching the Inauguration Day parade downtown, some of the non–Chanukah Heights Wilson kids organized a hunger strike for peace. Jeremy Pikser, the rare boy at school who didn't look askance when I mentioned a play, knew about a peace march scheduled in February — with writers we had read, Philip Roth and Saul Bellow, participating. Harry heard about it too and came down from New York to stay with me for the weekend.

The Saturday of the march, when I would normally be fetching will-calls at Rich's, we took the bus downtown to the White House and joined the small crowd of picketers parading back and forth. It was a far more placid scene than we had anticipated, and so we talked about girls even as we joined in the occasional chant, perused the literature distributed by different factions of protesters, and sampled the new fashion in political buttons.

In mid-protest, Mom picked us up at the appointed time right in front of Lafayette Park, across the street from the White House, to drive us the few blocks down Pennsylvania Avenue to the National for the matinee. Whatever our disdain for the war, Harry and I didn't want to miss the latest tryout, *The Roar of the Greasepaint—The Smell of the Crowd*, and Joel had bought us orchestra seats in honor of Harry's return to D.C. "Peace march and a new Broadway show—the perfect double feature!" Harry declared, laughing, as we slid into Mom's car.

The show, it turned out, was also about politics. The setting was "a rocky place" that was supposed to symbolize the entire Earth; it was oppressed by a despot known as Sir, who not only seemed as villainous as Captain Hook but was played by Cyril Ritchard, whom I knew as Hook from Mary Martin's *Peter Pan*. At one point the Bomb dropped, with a deafening sound effect and lots of smoke, flattening the rocky place. A Negro man playing a character named "The Negro" sang a song that sounded as if it was about civil rights.

Afterward, and in fond memory of our beloved Tanya, we decided to go to the stage door and check out the bosomy blond actress who played "The Girl." ("Miss Jillson, just eighteen, is another new talent to Broadway," said the "Who's Who" in the *Playbill*.) We waited and waited with the few other autograph-seekers in the shabby alley that adjoined the National, and though we saw Cyril Ritchard exit in a rush, The Girl proved elusive. Yet we continued to wait, largely because we had started flirting with a pair of girls about our age who had also lingered after everyone else had fled. One of them didn't say much, but the other—short, compact, with pixieish brown hair and eyes to match—talked volubly about the theater. I quickly realized that she read *Variety* and knew its contents as well as I did. She had opinions about all of it, including her verdict that "Everyone knows *Fiddler* is mediocre." Harry was already losing patience with the minutiae of the theater talk, and this was more than he could take. He announced that he was Joe Stein's son, then launched into a detailed rebuttal of the girl's criticisms. I hung on every word of their argument. What was a girl like this doing in Washington?

Soon it was too dark and cold to keep waiting; an hour had passed. If we didn't get to the bus soon, we'd never make it to that night's Wilson party.

It was only when Harry and I got to the bus stop that I realized I didn't know the girl's name. Given her contrariness about *Fiddler* and Harry's resentful dismissal of her as an "ass," I was too embarrassed to confess my regret at not knowing how to find her again. I wrote Sara instead: "The girl at the stage door hated 'Fiddler.' But she is unquestionably the first girl I've ever met in D.C. who shares my interests. All I know is she lives in the Washington area—that's all. It sounds stupid, I know, but I want to find her and find out who she is. I'm not the type to wait at stage doors, but I'm going to from now on until I find her again."

My first attempt to find what I called "my mystery girl" was fruitless. I figured she'd show up at *The Odd Couple*, yet another new show that opened in Washington to great reviews and then waited for the audience to catch up. As I waited alone in the dank, frosty air of the stage-door alley, I could hardly remember what she looked like. Her opinions—disagreeable, outrageous, sweeping opinions informed by the same hardwon knowledge about the theater that I had gathered—were more memorable to me than her appearance. She was a little like Sara, whose impassioned edicts about mysterious directors like Carl Dreyer and Erich von Stroheim both charmed and intimidated me, as I had no access in Washington to the movies that were hers every day in Greenwich Village.

Only my mystery girl didn't live in New York. She lived here, if I could just find her.

But I couldn't, not at any of the shows that followed. Finally, summer was arriving, and I'd soon be off on a "teen tour" of Europe. The last show at the National before our departure was the touring company of *How to Succeed in Business Without Really Trying*. Though I hadn't heard of any of the actors in it, its presence in Washington amounted to a kind of vicarious infusion of places I'd rather be: I'd seen the show in New York and London with Mom and Joel, and the sets, surely, would be the same, allowing me to summon up the ghosts of the departed companies that had previously occupied them.

How to Succeed was having an unusually long run for Washington — five weeks — and I planned to go to two or three of the matinees, more if I could afford it. At the first of them, the company proved not as good as the others I'd seen, and I found that the show wasn't the balm I had anticipated. My mystery girl was nowhere in sight, and I was overwhelmed by a loneliness that made me feel sorrier for the actors than I was for myself. These performers weren't famous. Their houses weren't full. The audience was pleasant but unenthusiastic, chuckling lightly where there had once been cacophonies of laughter, as if *How to Succeed* had never been a Broadway hit, a favorite of JFK's, a show whose box office I had called on the tie-line to New York just to hear the man at the 46th Street Theatre growl, "Sold out."

But I was not going to stop my search for my mystery girl no matter what, and I returned the following Saturday. It was a sunny day in Washington's late, post–Cherry Blossom spring, and the breeze seemed to whisk me down Fourteenth Street from Rich's to the theater. When I walked through the glass doors into the lobby, I knew from the scarcity of box-office patrons that this would be another so-so house, ensuring that I'd be able to snare a cheap seat in the second balcony.

I was waiting for my turn, straining to hear what tickets were being offered to the customers ahead of me, when the man I recognized as Scott Kirkpatrick, the National's manager, approached me. He was a tall, wide man in a dark suit with a matching vest spread over his ample girth. His shirt was white, his narrow tie black, and he wore a white carnation in his lapel. His thinning, well-greased, silvery-black hair was combed back over his bald pate. I had noticed him countless times before shows, standing in the lobby and staring idly, blankly ahead unless a patron or a member of his staff interrupted his reverie. Once thus engaged, he put his hands behind his back, adopted an expression of mild concern, and acted as subservient as the similarly dressed floorwalkers at department stores.

He looked at me with tiny dark eyes hidden behind big black-framed glasses, then extended his large hand. His grip was soft, and he didn't so much shake my hand as fleetingly graze it before pulling his own away. He didn't say hello or ask my name but murmured, in a deep Southern accent, "Ah, didn't . . . ah . . . you, mm, see this show at last week's matinee?" He spoke so mildly, in such an agonizingly slow drawl, that I had to strain to hear him, despite the lack of competing noise in the deserted lobby. I said yes, I had.

"Young man, I don't think you should buy another ticket this afternoon," he said evenly, almost without expression. Before I could figure out what he was getting at, he signaled that I should follow him out of the line and into the corner of the lobby where he always stood. While I waited expectantly, he reached into his vest pocket and removed a small pad and the thickest black fountain pen I'd ever seen. He readjusted his glasses on the bridge of his nose, nervously licked his top lip with his tongue, and scribbled a few words. Then he ripped the top sheet off the pad and handed it to me.

"Give this to the man at the door," he said. I looked at the piece of paper and saw that it was a coupon on which he had written a seat number I couldn't make out and, in thick black ink, the signature "Scott Kirkpatrick." It was a pass!

"Thank you! *Thank you!*" I said. He looked down and gave me a weak, embarrassed smile in which his thin lips hardly moved, then looked up again, back to the lobby, seeking more business to take care of.

I turned and walked the few steps to the ticket-taker, who ripped the pass in two without looking at me. Once inside, I proudly handed my half to an usher, who glanced at it before declaring: "Star box—follow me." I followed her down the far right aisle of the orchestra and up some stairs to a chair in a box that, I soon discovered, I had to myself. In fact, all the boxes in the theater were empty. I knew that box seats cost the same as orchestra seats and calculated my incredible financial windfall. I recognized that I was sitting in the same place where they had put JFK's rocking chair so that he could see *Mr. President*.

When the overture started, with the orchestra pit shimmering below me in the darkened house, as if I were leaning over a ravine filled with gold, I was almost too happy to concentrate. Then the happiness curdled: For a second I thought of that movie theater in Pennsylvania Dutch country, on that first trip to New York, the night I'd been so frightened by the Incredible Shrinking Man. Then I realized why: The angle at which I was looking down, across the theater, across the gaping rows of seats below, was the same as that from the balcony Mom had led us to in Lancaster that night.

I banished the memory quickly enough. Now I was seeing a Broadway show on a pass. I had been noticed by someone who worked in a theater — noticed because of who I was, not because I knew Harry or his father. A man I'd never met recognized that I belonged there because I loved to be there, and he had taken me in.

And so I didn't mind that my mystery girl wasn't at the stage door again that afternoon, or that when I went home I found my mother in tears once more, no explanation offered and Joel nowhere in sight, as I passed her doorway quietly, hoping to make my way unimpeded to the third floor to dress for that night's Wilson party. I had just turned sixteen and was only days away from leaving for Europe. I knew that when I returned at the end of summer, whatever else happened, I'd be remembered at the National Theatre and be at home there, if nowhere else.

PART

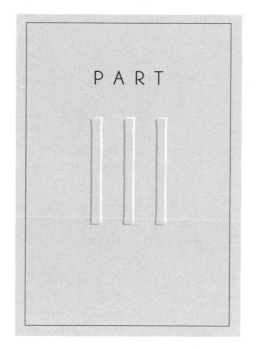

CHAPTER 1

Scott Kirkpatrick had not just remembered me—he had called while I was away to ask if I wanted to work at the National. Mom explained that Joel, who knew the manager from opening nights, had thanked him for giving me a pass, and that's how Mr. Kirkpatrick got my number.

I had not looked forward to returning once more to a deserted late-August Washington. A new world, scary and alluring, was opening up elsewhere. In the forlorn industrial landscape of northern England, the high point of my teen tour of Europe, I'd seen firsthand a brazen young society of Mods and Rockers. "The hair is so long on everybody," I wrote Sara, "that you really have to wait to be introduced to tell the boys from the girls." Over the summer we had also both devoured the stories about Sue Leary, one of the soapsuds-imbibing girls at Indian Hill, who had been arrested with her father, a Harvard professor, for bringing marijuana across the Mexican border.

But the theater still had the power to concentrate my mind, to push all else away.

What work could I possibly do at the National? It took me a couple of hours to find the courage to call Scott Kirkpatrick back. My hands were sweating, and I feared I'd do something wrong. Once I did phone, a man's voice said, "Manager's office," I was put on hold, and then that pallid Southern voice was pouring into my ear as slowly and thickly as molasses.

Mr. Kirkpatrick made a perfunctory greeting, then said: "I was wondering, ah, Mr. Rich, if, ahm, you might be interested in working the second door at Saturday matinees." The second door? As he continued, I figured out that he was actually offering me a job, every Saturday afternoon, taking tickets. I said yes—well, I have to ask my parents, I added—and he said that was fine, and a week later I was in his office to discuss it.

I hadn't realized that the manager at the National had an office: It was upstairs, on the same level as the first balcony and the rest rooms, through an unmarked gray door. I was escorted there by a Negro man in a shiny black suit who materialized after I identified myself at the box office. I ended up in a large room fronted by windows that looked out over the National's marquee to E Street and Pennsylvania Avenue. A man sat with his feet up on a gray metal desk, an extinguished cigar stump dangling from his mouth, reading a newspaper. He didn't look up as we entered. The Negro man told me to wait as he crossed the room to another gray door and knocked. The door opened and out came Scott Kirkpatrick—again dressed in a three-piece suit with a carnation in his lapel. But this time— befitting a strict sartorial observance of the seasons, since Labor Day was still a week off—the suit was white. He walked over and shook my hand in the same elusive manner I recalled from our first meeting.

"Mr. Rich," he said, "thank you, ahm, for coming."

With no further niceties, he explained that the job would require me to show up at one-thirty—an hour before curtain—every Saturday, except when the theater was dark. I was expected to wear a suit and tie. The doors opened to ticket-holders promptly at two—I knew that, of course, but greeted the revelation as if it were the secret initiation ritual of a privileged club. From one-thirty to two, my only duty was to set up the seats in the boxes, on either side of the first balcony. After the curtain went up at two-thirty, I had to help sort the tickets so that the theater could do "the count"—I didn't have to understand too much about that now. Once the count was done, I was free to leave—unless, of course, I wanted to stay for the rest of the show, in which case I could take any unoccupied seat. The pay was four dollars a performance.

I was so animatedly nodding agreement that Mr. Kirkpatrick might have found me strange, except that he looked as distant as he had during our first meeting; I couldn't be sure how much anything I did or said registered. His voice and expression were benign but blank.

When he was satisfied that my answer was yes, he gave me a W-2 form, showing me as an example one that had been filled out, a decade earlier, by a "Warren Beaty." Mr. Kirkpatrick asked if I recognized the name. I didn't know what to answer, because I knew that the movie star didn't spell his name that way. "Yes," he said, without waiting for me to resolve my confusion. "It's Warren Beatty before he added another 't' to his name. He worked the second door, too." Really? Maybe I showed too much awe, because Mr. Kirkpatrick added, "You do not want to end up as he did, with all that scandalous behavior in Hollywood."

And with that, our meeting was over.

Mom took me to Woodies to get a tweed suit—with a vest, just like Mr. Kirkpatrick's—for my new job. On my first day the following week—the Saturday matinee of a new musical tryout, *Pickwick*—I was so exhilarated that I executed my duties at Rich's that morning in a trot, coming to a full halt only to try on the heavy cordovan wing-tips that Dad had picked out to match my ticket-taking outfit.

I skipped lunch and arrived at the National at one; I couldn't wait another half hour. Then I worried that if I was there *too* early, it might reflect ill on me. So I walked down the block and window-shopped at Doubleday's bookstore. Finally, at one-fifteen—early, but not *too* early—I walked under the marquee and through the glass doors of the National. There was a line at the box office—*Pickwick*, produced by David Merrick, was SRO—and I walked past it as if I had graduated from that lowly station forever. I pushed open one of the chrome doors to the inner lobby and slipped inside as if I were an actor walking past autograph-seekers through a stage door. I had always wondered what people meant when they talked about crying out of happiness—it was a non sequitur in my household—but now I understood. I felt as I had at the end of *King Lear*—as if some powerful, nameless spirit were rising within me, raising my whole being to a more elevated place, the sort of heaven people talked about in religious school but that I had never glimpsed before.

The inner lobby was dark, but a dim glow seeped out of the auditorium, whose doors had been left open. I entered softly and stood for a second at the standees' railing. Before me spread the ocean of empty seats, carpeted in shadows thrown by the single bulb of the ghost light standing on the empty stage. Though I knew that *Pickwick* had an ice-skating rink with real ice as part of its set, the light was just too weak to reveal it; I would have to walk all the way to the front row to see the stage floor—and I wasn't sure I was allowed in the house at all yet. I returned to the inner lobby, then skipped up the darkened stairs to the manager's office.

My eyes adjusted to the early-autumn light streaming in the windows from E Street. The door to Mr. Kirkpatrick's inner office was open. I glanced inside from a distance but saw only huge piles of what looked like newspapers; the blinds must have been drawn, since the room was dark. I was startled when, a minute or two later, Mr. Kirkpatrick emerged from deep within this seemingly empty inner sanctum. He and his desk, assuming he had one, had been completely obscured by the hedgerows of papers.

There were towers of papers and boxes along the periphery of the outer office, too. One box was open, revealing neatly stacked rows of tickets, a sight more dazzling to me by far than the bundles of will-call twenty-dollar bills in the safe at Rich's. The tickets looked crisp and new but were, I realized, old—the sides of the boxes were labeled with dates going back to the 1950s. They were unsold seats, and no wonder they were called, as I would be told, "deadwood." They were, in a sense, tombstones—each imprinted with the row and number of a specific empty seat that had gaped at some forgotten, hardworking actors some Washington night long ago.

Mr. Kirkpatrick greeted me in his predictable manner, then officially introduced me to the Negro man I'd encountered the week before, Mr. Johnson, who gave me an opaque smile not unlike that of his boss and a formal, featherweight handshake to match. Then I followed Mr. Kirkpatrick out of the office, across the mezzanine, and into the first balcony. The houselights were on now, and the National's gold curtain had been lowered; the ghost light was gone. Once we had descended into the boxes, reaching the lowest on the right of the house, the star box, Mr. Kirkpatrick began breathing a bit heavily as, with fierce concentration and a careful navigation of his considerable bulk, he leaned down to rearrange each chair to the precise angle that, he said, was best for seeing the show. I decided not to raise the question of what happened when the ticket-holders actually took their seats and inevitably disrupted his meticulous ground plan. Instead, following his instructions, I drew precise geometric maps on a pad so that I could replicate his scheme for each box on subsequent Saturdays.

By the time we were done, it was almost two. I went with Mr. Kirkpatrick to the orchestra level. Mr. Johnson, I learned, worked the first door and was equipped with a wooden box, perched on a stand, with separate compartments for the tickets according to color, which designated price. I had no box and was to keep in my pockets the longer stubs of the tickets I tore. So that the traffic inside would flow evenly, I was instructed to send customers with balcony tickets up the stairway to the left—as Mr. Johnson sent his up the stairway to the right—while all those with orchestra seats were to go simply "straight ahead."

Beyond the heavy chrome doors we could hear the gurgle of a crowd. All the lights inside the theater were at their brightest now. Then Mr. Kirkpatrick gave us a nod—he had been checking his watch for the zero hour—and Mr. Johnson and I, now a few feet away from each other, simultaneously opened our respective doors.

I might as well have been raising a curtain on a show of which I was director, author, designer, and star, so proprietary did I feel about the National Theatre and my position guarding its threshold. As the matinee theatergoers swarmed toward me from the sunny and packed outer lobby, many of them smelling and sounding and looking like my blue-haired grandmothers, I focused on the job at hand, elegantly instructing each comer on where to go next as if I were rattling off verse from Shakespeare. My three-piece suit came in handier than I could have imagined, once I realized that each of its many pockets could serve as a repository for a different class of ticket—the orchestra and boxes, the three different prices in the first balcony, the second balcony, and standing room, if any had been

sold. Sorting as I went—white orchestra in left pants pocket, purple second balcony in right vest—I diligently kept an eye out for two specific seat
locations that Mr. Kirkpatrick had recited to Mr. Johnson and me just before we opened the doors. They were mail-ordered tickets paid for with
checks that had bounced, just like those of the delinquent Rich's customers Grandpa Herbert and Grandma Rose pursued each Sunday. If
these tickets turned up, we were not to tear them but to direct their hold-
ers to Mr. Kirkpatrick at his spot in the outer lobby.

At 2:35, I could hear that the doors a few yards behind me, those separating the inner lobby from the auditorium, were closing. Deep within
were the strains of the orchestra playing the overture. Latecomers kept arriving, and we took tickets for another few minutes. Once the lobby was
empty of all but a couple of customers at the box-office window, Mr. Kirkpatrick came toward us and gave a nod indicating that we were to close the
heavy chrome doors.

Once we had, I followed him and Mr. Johnson to the back of the house.
The curtain was up, and I could see the actors singing and ice-skating onstage, but Mr. Kirkpatrick kept moving behind the standees' rail until we
reached another unmarked door I'd never noticed before. He opened it just
enough for us to scoot behind him into a tiny room with a low ceiling,
where an old man in a suit sat at a small round table on which had been
spilled the contents of Mr. Johnson's ticket box, each color ticket in a separate pile. The old man in the suit grunted when I was introduced. He was,
Mr. Kirkpatrick said, "the company manager of *Pickwick*." I assumed that
he was some kind of business manager who worked for David Merrick.

I was asked to add the tickets I'd taken to the appropriate piles, which I
proudly did, pocket by pocket. Only a few strays, I was pleased to see, had
been misrouted along the way. Then we just sat there in silence, the performance audibly if inarticulately present through the thick walls around
us, as the company manager neatly stacked the sorted colored stubs, then
held each stack right next to his ear and flipped through it rapidly as if he
were shuffling a deck of cards. After each pile was "fanned," as the process
was called, the company manager said a number—which I realized was
the number of stubs in the pile—and Mr. Kirkpatrick compared it to a
number on a form he had before him. If the number was right, he made a
check mark next to it with his big black pen. It was always right.

Then Mr. Kirkpatrick gave a figure in dollars, and the company manager assented to it, and I realized that they were talking about the gross for that matinee. Soon another man entered the small room from another door that I could see opened directly onto the box office. The three men chatted, and more figures were mentioned, and the company manager said that it was looking like "sixty-three on the week"—which, I knew from *Variety*, must be the week's gross. The figure would be finalized after that night's performance, the week's last. Capacity for the National with a musical with the ticket prices of *Pickwick* was $66,500, I knew.

Eventually we emerged from the count-up room, threaded stealthily through the rear of the house, and found ourselves back in the hushed inner lobby. Mr. Kirkpatrick asked me to return with him to his office; there, he reached into one of his vest pockets and handed me a small brown envelope with "Riggs Bank" printed on it, just like the pay envelopes at Rich's. My name was written on the envelope in what I now knew to be his handwriting. Only at home did I dare open it, and count out the $3.72, representing my pay minus withholding taxes.

What would I do with the money now that I could go to the National every Saturday afternoon for free? I answered that question quickly: Taking tickets and doing the count meant missing the first fifteen minutes or so of each play, so naturally I would have to buy a ticket to the National earlier in the week to see each show in its entirety.

———

On the cover of the *Playbill* for every show at the National was its slogan: "America's First Theatre." A back page inside carried a brief history: "The National Theatre was built in 1835 on its present location, and is the oldest stage theatre in the United States that during its entire history has been used for the entertaining arts. It is revered by all American citizens because it is the link to their dramatic past. There is no great actor of the modern era whose name is not inseparably connected with the National. It is historic ground, sacred to Thalia, Terpsichore and Melpomene. . . ." Theatergoers, it was noted, could take a lecture tour, "frequently given after a performance."

Mr. Kirkpatrick, I discovered, gave the tour himself, mostly to schoolchildren, and told of how the theater had been burned down and rebuilt on the same spot five times in the nineteenth century. President Polk had held his inaugural ball in one of those Nationals; every president since 1835, except Ike, had seen a play there, and Lincoln had seen John Wilkes Booth play Hamlet there in 1863. Two years later, he had initially been scheduled to attend a play at the National, not Ford's, on the last night of his life.

The National was thought to house a ghost lingering from Reconstruction, that of an actor named John McCullough, said to have been shot and killed by another actor after fighting over an actress in their touring Shakespearean troupe. But other specters, those of segregation, were never mentioned in the tour or anywhere else around the theater. Not until 1952, four years before I first came to E Street to see *Damn Yankees,* had the National stopped turning away Negroes who wanted to see plays. Mr. Kirkpatrick, who was born in Arkansas but had traveled the country after the war as a road press agent for the American Ballet Theatre, became the National's manager two years later.

Even now there were only a few old Negro ladies scattered among the crowds on Saturday afternoons. The only time I saw more than a few Negroes at any kind of theater in Washington was at the Republic and the Lincoln, the Negro movie theaters on U Street in the ghetto's own "downtown." Almost all the movies that played first-run near the National, at Loew's Capitol or at the nearby Warner and RKO Keith's, opened simultaneously on U Street, though you could discover that only by reading the fine print in the newspaper entertainment section's neighborhood theater listings; the exciting pictorial ads for new movies in *The Washington Post* on Sundays maintained that the films were playing only at a single theater in white downtown. But Mom and Joel often went to see the latest openings on U Street, where the lines were shorter and the prices lower. We never saw any other white people there, just as we almost never saw any Negroes at the movie houses on F Street. Washington was "integrated" now, but as far as I could tell, it remained segregated, though no one ever said so.

Yet if there were almost no Negroes in the audience at the National, many of the people who worked there were Negroes. Mr. Johnson worked weekdays as a teacher in the city and was so highly respected by Mr. Kirkpatrick that he was the only employee allowed into his inner office without knocking. Once each week, Mr. Kirkpatrick sent the jacket and pants of his suit to the Willard Hotel to be pressed, and it was Mr. Johnson who was entrusted to take them away while Mr. Kirkpatrick awaited their return at his desk, wearing only his shirt, tie, vest, underwear, socks, and shoes. The two young men who worked my post, the second door, the rest of the week were Negroes, too—a pair of brothers with the last name Luck. Mr. Kirkpatrick's favorite entertainer was also a Negro, a singer named Josephine Baker, whom I knew to be a legend—the ad said "the legendary Josephine Baker" when she came to the National with her revue—though I didn't know why. The night she opened, Mr. Kirkpatrick overcame his stammering reserve to present her with flowers onstage—a gesture he had never made before and would never repeat—and he was said to have been deeply hurt when her show, despite good reviews, had grosses so low that the National was forced to drop the second week of the engagement.

As far as I could tell, there was no other woman in Mr. Kirkpatrick's life. There was no Mrs. Kirkpatrick. There was no Mrs. Johnson, either—no one who worked at the National Theatre, it seemed, was married or had a family; they were all single men. It was hard to figure out where in Washington any of them lived, since they never referred to their homes or to any specific place other than the National. Every couple of weeks there would be one or two temporary additions to the office whom I'd meet as I arrived for the matinee: the company manager of the new show that had opened, the advance press agent heralding the next booking. These visitors were all from New York, though they lived in a cross-country string of hotels when touring, and most of them, too, were men—short men, either wiry or plump, in dark suits they might have slept in, with voices that sounded as gravelly as Sam Levene's in *Guys and Dolls*.

I no longer went to the stage door at the National: Mr. Kirkpatrick decreed that no employee but him was allowed backstage, and I didn't want to risk being seen in even close proximity. But there was no need to hang out in the alley anyway—I could see much on my regular rounds as a man on the second door. And, as I soon discovered, Mr. Johnson and the Lucks let me walk in without paying on the nights I wasn't taking tickets, permitting me to watch every tryout as avidly as I did *Fiddler* and to mull over its revisions.

One Saturday afternoon before Thanksgiving I arrived for work and discovered that a movie star, Lauren Bacall, who was in the middle of a tryout for a comedy call *Cactus Flower,* was rehearsing a scene right on the mezzanine floor outside the manager's office with another actor and with her director, Abe Burrows, whom I knew to be the author of *Guys and Dolls* and the director of *How to Succeed.* As I stopped in my tracks to watch, the actress flubbed a line and muttered to herself "Oh shit!" Burrows took the pause to explain a point to the actor, who was holding a script; he had not been in this scene when I had stood for the play earlier in the week. In that moment, Bacall's eyes wandered across the foyer and she acknowledged me by flashing a conspiratorial smile and a wink, as if to say, Hey, kid, you can stay and look if you want to, I don't mind. So I sat down on a ledge by the window and watched. When I slipped into the office to report for duty, I learned that the actor in the rehearsal was the new leading man, Barry Nelson, who had flown in the day before after David Merrick had fired his predecessor. When I finished the count and slipped into the theater to watch the performance, Nelson seemed comfortable his first time onstage in the role, even as I could hear a prompter yelling lines from the wings. He was already better in the part than the actor he'd replaced.

I stayed in the back of the house after the curtain call, wondering if I might crash another rehearsal before the evening's performance. But as the crowds departed, I saw a familiar figure coming up the aisle, pushing an old woman in a wheelchair.

It was the "mystery girl" I'd met seven months earlier, wearing the white blouse and black tie of a National usher. She immediately noticed me and gave me a nod and a half-smile, indicating with her eyes that she'd return after her chore was done. I wondered if I had enough money to take her for a Coke at the outdoor café at Bassin's down the street, but once she reappeared we immediately veered into a detailed discussion about *Cactus Flower,* violently disagreeing about its prospects for repeating its Washington success on Broadway. Then we talked about another play, and another, and I realized that there was no point in showing off any of my knowledge, because she knew everything about the theater I did. She'd been working as an usher just as long as I'd been a ticket-taker, but I hadn't seen her because she was only a fill-in girl. She couldn't always come downtown, she told me, because she lived far out in the Maryland suburbs and her parents didn't like her driving so far to work in the theater.

We stood there on E Street, oblivious to the growing dark and the November chill, rarely advancing beyond the subject of Broadway. All I learned was that she was a year older than I was, seventeen and a senior, and that she went to a private girls' school, Madeira, in Virginia. Her name was June—the same, I couldn't help but notice, as the girl in *Gypsy* who eventually runs away with Tulsa after he sings "All I Need Is the Girl."

Before we knew it, two hours had gone by, and we both had to get home. She scrawled her phone number on my *Playbill* and all but ran away.

I now had my driver's license, the key to seeing her again soon; Joel had initiated me into his illegal parking place, in the courtyard of the Commerce Department building, half a block across Pennsylvania Avenue from the National, so I would never have to pay for parking downtown. But though June and I kept seeing each other at matinees, it was several months before I could convince her to go out; when I did, I didn't know what to do with her. There was no point in taking her to a party with my Chanukah Heights crowd. Already I could tell that June, far more than I did, lived a life apart from other teenagers in Washington. She wasn't much interested in going to college, though she had a brother at Princeton, and she didn't care about movies or rock and roll or the war or the news or books either, unless they were about Broadway. Lacking other options, I decided to take her to an affordable French "bistro" Joel recommended on Wisconsin Avenue.

I had to drive an hour to pick June up. She lived far past Rockville and Woodmont, where there were farms and rambling old houses on grounds far too large to be called yards. A lot of her neighbors seemed to have horses grazing on their property.

The drive was so long that we had to rush through dinner so that she and I could both be home by our midnight curfew. We picked up our conversation just where it had left off in front of the National. I couldn't believe that I had met a girl who shared my obsession with the theater—and who, like me, wanted to run away from Washington to New York. She was pretty, too, I decided. But when I reached over to kiss her as we left the restaurant, she froze. When I grazed her lips, she barely responded, as if embarrassed or painfully shy. When I tried to draw her close to me, so that she might nestle in my neck, she didn't seem reluctant but she wasn't at ease, either. I wondered if she liked me "only as a friend," and I felt the faint anxious sweat of being rejected. Or was it just that, going to an all-girls school, she hadn't learned what I had at Deal and Wilson? But if she was pushing me away, then why did she say she hoped she could see me again?

We did go out again, just as Christmas vacation was beginning, and we talked as we had before, and she seemed to kiss back less tentatively at the evening's end. I told her that thanks to Joel's "in" with the airlines, I was traveling on a free ticket to London for ten days and staying with the family of a West End producer whom he had known from the war.

"What are you seeing in London?" June asked.

"Everything," I said. "The producer can get any tickets he wants, and what he can't, my stepfather can."

"How is that?"

"Well, Joel—that's what I call him—is a lawyer, and he had Lyndon Johnson eliminate some tax on theater tickets, so he can get house seats to any show." I couldn't believe it—I was *bragging* about the man I had spent years wanting to escape.

June was transfixed. She looked at me with new respect. I could tell she was a rich girl, but I had something money couldn't buy: Not only did I know Harry, whose father wrote Broadway shows, but I had a stepfather who worked (sort of) in the theater!

"Joel's an interesting guy," I went on, eager to sustain the conversation. "A real character. You'll have to meet him sometime."

"Could I? I don't know anyone in the theater except the ushers at the National," June said. We were parked in the car outside her house. Even now, she spoke in a calm voice that seemed to carry a remote hint of sadness. She rarely mentioned her parents, and I wondered if my home might not, in some oblique way, be less painful than hers.

"I don't know anyone like your stepfather," she continued. "I don't know anyone, really." I wanted to make her feel better any way I could: I promised I would bring her back duplicate programs of every play I saw in London, the way Joel always had for me, and told her I would miss her. She thanked me and let me kiss her one extra time, though when I looked into her eyes they revealed nothing except the vast distance between us. I felt in some way that without meaning to at all, I was violating her. All I wanted was to be Tulsa, to hasten our escape out of the National's stage-door alley and into the bright lights of the theater, where we would be happy together.

As we parted at her door, she told me not to forget to bring her back those programs. I reassured her that I would bring back every one I could find, then drove home wondering if loving the theater as I did, and as June did, meant that it was impossible to love anything or anyone else even half as much.

CHAPTER 2

More and more I spent my free nights at the National. It was my saloon until I reached drinking age—the one place that promised me surefire intoxication. During the more tedious first acts, I hung around the outer office, free, as I wasn't at home, to indulge the cigarette addiction I'd picked up in Europe. I'd smoke and talk with, or just listen to, whatever managers were there. Mr. Kirkpatrick always gave me the same distracted yet sly smile when I arrived, as though he knew that I was destined to end up at the National most nights, and that somehow he understood. He certainly never asked me about school, or whether I should be doing my homework.

His outward behavior was as unvarying as it was opaque. No matter how abusive the National's elderly matinee patrons might be because they couldn't see or hear the play from their seats, only once was Mr. Kirkpatrick ever known to have been outwardly ruffled. The dread day occurred when David Merrick's secretary called from New York to ask how he had liked the producer's Christmas present, sent weeks earlier. The call sent Mr. Kirkpatrick on a panicked search operation through the mountains of paper in his office until the precious blue Tiffany & Co. box could be unearthed.

It was hard to tell if Mr. Kirkpatrick talked with anyone about anything other than the theater, unless it was with Mr. Johnson. When the two were in the office together, you could hear Mr. Kirkpatrick's voice lower to a soft and indecipherable pitch as the door closed behind Mr. Johnson, as if the two men had some secret code, a private tenderness, unbeknownst to the rest of us caught up in the alternately languorous and hectic dailiness of the National.

During spring vacation, I went to visit Harry in New York for the last time in a foreseeable future; he was a senior and had decided to go to college in California in the fall. His father had leaned on David Merrick for seats to a hit play our friend Sara had already seen twice, deeming it "awfully pretentious but still a fascinating production," with the strangest long title yet: *The Persecution and Assassination of Jean-Paul Marat as Performed by the Inmates of the Asylum of Charenton Under the Direction of the Marquis de Sade.* It was directed by Peter Brook, whose *King Lear* still lingered in my memory, as bleak as graphite.

Our friendship was about to be cleaved by three thousand miles. Back in his father's studio after the play, I confessed to Harry that I was still drawn to June, her disdain for *Fiddler* notwithstanding. Apparently she wasn't as indifferent to me as I had previously figured, since she had asked me to be her escort to her debutante party at the Chevy Chase Club a few weeks hence. Harry joked: "A debutante? A country club that doesn't allow Jews? Of *course* she despised *Fiddler*—she's a Nazi!"

Laughing, I had to concede the possibility that I was the first Jew that June had ever met, and I admitted to Harry that she *was* the only person my age I knew who still called Negroes "colored." But there had been a real nastiness to Harry's joke. I didn't know it then, but perhaps he was agitated because he'd guessed that his parents were on their way to splitting up, as mine had. Like so much else, it seemed, divorce was proliferating in New York ahead of Washington: There were whispers at my Rich grandparents' dinners that Aunt Jane had left Uncle Herbert, but I still had no friends at Wilson with divorced parents.

June and I would soon be having a separation of our own. She was departing the National and Madeira for destinations unknown. Though she paid lip service to the idea of going on to college, I knew that her secret plan was to run away and join the theater. She wasn't going to wait for me to finish high school and catch up with her. She just couldn't delay a moment longer.

When I picked her up the night of the Chevy Chase Club party, she was wrapped in a pale gown of unseasonably heavy silk that looked two sizes too big for her and was equipped with a huge tail she wielded awkwardly behind her. (A few hours later, when I stepped on it accidentally as I walked behind June at the club, I learned that this tail was called a "train.") Though I was her date and this was her party, I boiled with anxiety—could everyone tell I went to public school and was Jewish?—and thought the night would never end. I didn't know anyone there besides June, and she hardly seemed to know anyone either; her friends might have been extras hired for the occasion. She withdrew, too, into some private place, I realized—an onlooker at her own celebration, ostracized by her peers. Surely she was as miserable as I was, and yet she was unwilling to pool her loneliness with mine, which only compounded the isolation I and, no doubt, she felt.

I saw her for a last time a week later, at the Memorial Day matinee of the final show of the season, a road company of *Barefoot in the Park.* Despite the old-time movie star in the cast—Myrna Loy—the house was empty.

Though the touring version of a Broadway play was rarely equal to the original, I was curious to watch this one nonetheless. For me, a road company had its own kind of drama. The experience was like visiting a house whose occupants had moved on to bigger and better quarters and left their discarded furniture and clothing behind for the use of poor relations who had a hard time living up to their surroundings. You could see the strain and the frustration of these actors on the road, who valiantly tried anything to win the approval of an audience that was also desperate to sustain the illusion that it was being entertained by the play's founding family, not anonymous impostors. Sometimes both cast and audience would succeed in convincing each other of the performance's authenticity, but even then the event had an etiolated quality, an undertow of grief, for no one on either side of the footlights could quite shake the ghosts of the fabled actors and more excited theatergoers who had come before them, back when the show was young.

June, now back in the usher's uniform she wore more comfortably than her debutante gown, popped down from the first balcony to say hello just before Mr. Johnson and I opened the doors. We agreed to talk once she was off-duty, after intermission; it was her last matinee before going with her parents to Nantucket for the summer. I was leaving Washington, too, to take a five-week journalism course for high school students at Northwestern University, near Chicago. Polly was going off on her own European teen tour, now that she'd been deemed old enough to be given my experience of a year earlier as if it were a hand-me-down, and Mom and Joel had planned a summer itinerary that included, in no particular order, Cape Cod, Bermuda, and Japan.

June hadn't liked *Barefoot in the Park* when it tried out at the National three years earlier, so I assumed we'd skip Act 2 and go to Bassin's for a Coke—a tolerable sacrifice for me in order to be with her, even if very little now remained of my romantic idealization of the former "mystery girl."

As it happened, though, I never made it to Act 1. When I went into the count-up room to sort tickets after Mr. Johnson and I had closed our doors, there was a discernible, if not instantly definable, change in the usual atmosphere. For one thing, there was literally a potent scent in the windowless cell's normally stuffy air—that of a man's aftershave. And then I noticed its source: a company manager unlike any other I'd seen occupy that same chair.

In place of the usual rumpled road veteran was a tall young man with amused eyes and long blond hair, almost Beatles length, though neatly combed, slicked-down, and parted. He was wearing some sort of sport jacket that looked like a Navy officer's tunic, and the moneyed glint of its many gold buttons matched the gold coins that were his cuff links. He held a cigarette in the side of his mouth, though it was thrust upward by a black-and-gold cigarette holder, like FDR's in *Sunrise at Campobello*.

As I started unloading my pockets of tickets, Mr. Kirkpatrick introduced me.

"Mr. Coots," my boss said, "this is Mr. Rich, the man on the second door."

Mr. Coots put down his cigarette holder and shook my hand with the firmness that seemed to elude everyone else at the National. Then he took in the meager piles of tickets I was placing on the table and looked at me again, a joke tugging at the corners of his eyes.

"Something tells me the second door isn't going to bail us out," he said, laughing.

It was clear that business had been poor all week: The men started talking numbers, and I detected a gross that was less than half of capacity.

"I reminded New York yesterday," Mr. Coots said, "that they should have listened to me before they made this booking: Just because you can sit down for fifty weeks in Chicago doesn't mean you can do five in Washington. This isn't a five-week town."

Mr. Kirkpatrick gave one of his noncommittal smiles, and he and Mr. Coots started the usual checking of numbers. When they finished, Mr. Coots turned to me again and asked, "Shouldn't you be in school, kid?" I stammered at first a reply about its being Saturday—until I realized he was joking—and then elaborated that I was almost out of school for the year but was going to a summer school at the end of June. To study what?, he asked. I explained about Northwestern, and he said, "I'll be in Chicago, too. If they give you a day off and you and your schoolmates want to see a play, look me up and I'll take care of you." He explained that he was being transferred in a couple of weeks from the *Barefoot* company, which had played the Blackstone Theatre in Chicago for a year before coming to Washington, to the *Odd Couple* road company, which was just now opening at the Blackstone. The two Neil Simon hits both had the same producer.

As we all left the count-up room to walk to the manager's office, Mr. Coots continued his conversation with me as if we'd known each other from previous encounters at the theater. "They think they can get a year out of Chicago again," he said. "They've got a good company—you and your pals would enjoy it." I told him that I had seen the original cast when it had tried out at the National. Was I working at the theater then?, he asked. No, I replied, I had started only a season ago.

Once we were in the office and I had collected my pay envelope, I started out, as I always did, to go downstairs and watch the show. But as I reached the door, Mr. Coots called out to me. "Mr. Rich," he said, his voice as resonant as an actor's, "I meant that offer seriously, so if you can wait a second, I'll give you my phone number at the Blackstone. There's always someone on the switchboard who can find me." Though I had serious doubts that I'd ever be allowed away from Northwestern on my own, or that I'd have the nerve to call him, I sat down beside the desk where he had placed himself. He pulled out a black-and-gold fountain pen that matched his cigarette holder and wrote a phone number on the front of a National ticket envelope. Then he barraged me with more questions about myself: Where did I go to school and who were my parents and how did Scott hire me and what plays did I like and had I been to Chicago before?

I'd seen Chicago only once, in the middle of a cold and rainy December night, I told him, when my stepfather, juggling two different airlines' passes on a trip to California, hired a cabdriver to take us on a midnight tour of the city during the wait to change planes at Midway Airport. I told Mr. Coots that my stepfather worked for the theater sometimes as a lawyer and had insisted the driver include the theaters around the Loop on his tour—all of whose names I knew from *Variety*. The cab's windows were so cloudy and the city so dark that, even wiping the glass beside me with my mittened hand, it was hard to see much. And yet I must have seen more than I'd thought, for even now I could picture those shadowy façades distinctly—the Shubert, the Studebaker, the Blackstone. What I hadn't admitted to anyone was that my memory of those houses was propelling me toward Northwestern as much as my growing interest in newspapers, which had burgeoned while working on the school monthly at Wilson.

Mr. Coots and I kept talking and smoking, with Mr. Fox and Mr. Kidwell, the assistant managers, occasionally joining in as they did their business around the outer office; they seemed more jovial and at ease with this company manager than they did with the usual occupants of his desk. Soon it was intermission and time for me to meet June, who was already, in her mind, far away from Washington. She said goodbye with only the vaguest indication of where she'd be next fall.

At the next Saturday matinee, and the one after that, Mr. Coots was still around, and as the *Barefoot* business got worse and worse, he became funnier and funnier once the count was done, cracking up the entire office (the grave Mr. Johnson always excepted) with his mordant wisecracks about how he'd soon have to go door-to-door to sell tickets "to the good theatergoing women of our nation's capital." I lingered on the fringe of the room after collecting my pay, just to hear him talk about the theater. No matter who else was in the office, he always made sure I was included in all the chatter; it didn't faze him that I was the lowest-ranking employee there.

When I said goodbye to him on his last Saturday in Washington, he had become such a fixture that I found it hard to imagine the office without him. "Don't forget—I'll be at the Blackstone beginning Monday," he said as we shook hands. "So tell your folks that you'll have a friend in Chicago you can call if you need to make bail during the summer."

Our conversations were so unexpected, and he was so unlike any company manager I'd met at the National, that I didn't know what to make of him. Was he sincere when he expressed an interest in me, or just patronizing a stagestruck teenager out of boredom in a strange town? I would be too shy to ever call him in Chicago, so it didn't matter, anyway.

"Thank you, Mr. Coots," I said.

"When you see me in Chicago," he said, his deep, theatrical voice pitched to earn the laughter of everyone in earshot, "you're going to have to call me Clayton, because I can't have that company thinking I'm as geriatric as I look."

Clayton Coots—could there ever be a name more outlandishly redolent of the theater? I doubted I'd ever see him again, but I kept the small envelope with his number on it in my wallet just in case.

———

Arriving at Northwestern three weeks later, I didn't have time to think of Clayton Coots, the Blackstone Theatre, my insomnia fears, or much else. The summer program the university's journalism school had created for seventeen-year-old high school students was run on a boot-camp schedule: We did more work in a day than I had in a month at Wilson. The other hundred students, though from better schools than mine, found the regimen no less severe. Yet the nickname Northwestern gave its summer kids was "cherubs," and for all the work, there was a heavenly camaraderie to the place.

Chicago was in the grip of a record heat wave, as if to guarantee that a new single called "Summer in the City" would become the campus's unofficial theme song. The hundred-degree-plus temperatures were high even by Washington standards. Air-conditioning could be found only at the Huddle, an ice cream parlor in a hotel in Evanston that became our hangout in the late afternoons, between the end of the class and the long nights of homework back in the sticky dead air of our dorms.

Though I had to make friends from scratch, I felt no homesickness, just as I hadn't in my summers at camp. Sheer exhaustion ensured a sound sleep each night; my panic was forgotten. Joel's secretary sent the usual brown office envelopes stuffed with *Variety*s and *New York Times* drama sections and *Village Voices*, also throwing in weekly tear sheets sent to the office by a tabloid Broadway columnist named Leonard Lyons, who Joel claimed introduced him to Picasso and Gertrude Stein and Alice B. Toklas in Paris when it was liberated at the end of World War II. But I had so much work to do, I barely had time to study the *Variety* grosses.

I wasn't so busy that I failed to notice one beautiful girl in the enormous lecture hall where we sat at long tables each morning, a typewriter in front of each of us, banging out news stories assembled from the scrambled facts barked at us by instructors from the stage. Within a day I had figured out the girl's name—Emily Kaufman—and learned from the student directory that she was the only student in the whole program who was from Chicago itself. She had long brown hair that ran straight down her back and, it seemed from my furtive glances, a constant smile that wasn't exactly open but was nonetheless as wide as her face. I could also tell that she was at least as shy as I was; she talked only to girls and was frequently alone, absorbed in her reading or just looking distracted, as if she was trying to sort through a complicated thought. I set out to meet her, and it turned out to be easier than I'd feared. Emily, I learned, spoke to anyone who spoke to her as if she was both amazed by and grateful for their slightest interest. She greeted everyone with the same guileless and warm, if reserved, welcome.

When I first struck up a conversation with her at the Huddle, I realized that she would talk to me for as long as I wanted, not necessarily because she liked me but because to break off a conversation prematurely would strike her as being impolite. As we walked back toward the dorms in the orange late-afternoon sun, I learned that she lived on Chicago's North Side, in an apartment building near Lake Michigan, and that she went to a private school, that she was in its drama club, and that her favorite subject was art history. "It's so wonderful that you have a job at the theater and that it makes you happy," she told me. "I can think of nothing more thrilling than going to the theater." Except going to museums: What plays were to me and concerts were to my friend Sara, art was to Emily. She wasn't particularly interested in journalism, but her mother believed it was a valuable skill to have. Her mother had gone to Northwestern and sometimes regretted that she had gone into insurance instead of becoming a reporter.

There was a luminosity to Emily that was more than beauty, I decided, though surely she was striking—nearly as tall as I was (I had finally started to grow), with olive skin, hazel eyes, and long legs whose dark coloring was set off by the white shorts she almost invariably wore. She radiated sweetness. She was smart and a reader and had a sense of humor, and yet she spoke kindly even of the obvious dullards and jerks who had found their way into the generally likable ranks of our course. She had infinite patience for the most onerous of our teachers.

In a matter of days, we became inseparable, but not in the formal manner I was used to from the rigid social rituals of Deal and Wilson. It just seemed inevitable that we be together. Occasionally we stole an earnest, extended kiss after dinner, but there were times in the very shank of the afternoon, just as the heat broke, when we would wander as slowly as we could between the Huddle and the dorms, talking all the way. Only with difficulty, however, could I induce Emily to describe her own life in the city just an "L" ride away.

Her parents were divorced, I knew that. She lived with her mother, her grandmother, and a younger sister. She loved them all, she said blandly, and I told her that I wished I felt the same way about my whole family— though sometimes I did. I was as vague as possible.

I couldn't tell her—any more than I had ever told any friend, girl or boy, Harry and Sara included—about what went on in my house some nights; I didn't even think of telling her, so successfully did I suppress even the freshest memories—of Mom's sobbing, and Joel's rage, and the slammed doors, and the smashed furniture and china—as soon as I could get away from Cleveland Avenue. Perhaps Emily had done the same. Her past was buried and I could extract it only in the tiniest nuggets. Her father, I learned, was a rabbi who had moved away to Phoenix. Like my dad, he had a new wife and new children; but Emily, unlike me, had not so much as met her new stepfamily. It was unclear to me whether she had seen or even spoken to her dad in a very long time, and no matter how persistently I questioned her about him, she avoided answering.

Within a matter of days, we had decided we were in love, and I believed it. Unlike any other girl I had been involved with, Emily was always available; she wanted nothing more than to be with me, and I felt the same about her. Just seeing her made me happy, and our frustratingly minimal opportunities for making out only made those that we could find all the more passionate. We basked in each other's company no matter what we were doing, whether eating at the cafeteria or reading together in the library or talking with the other kids we had grown fond of during the summer. The thought that we might be separated when the five weeks at Northwestern ended was intolerable. If we could have set up house at that moment in Evanston, we might just have done so—our senior years at the Latin School of Chicago and Woodrow Wilson High could wait. When Mom called me long-distance one evening, I told her about Emily, and how important it was that I be with her, and that I had never been happier in my life.

"I'm so glad for you," Mom said, without even an ounce of adult cynicism. She almost seemed relieved when someone else shared the burden of my emotions, and always had, right from my first steadies at Deal. But she added with a chuckle: "You are aware, I assume, that you are not going to drop out of high school, and I'm sure that Emily's mother feels the same way."

We laughed about it, and I advanced an idea that Emily and I had already been concocting: When the Northwestern program ended, I would stay on in Chicago at the Kaufmans' apartment for a three-day weekend, after which I would return for my trip with Dad to look at potential colleges in New England. Mom listened and, as always, said, "I'll have to discuss it with Joel"—code for not wanting to inadvertently anger him, however unlikely the provocation.

Approval, though, was forthcoming right away. Mom asked for Mrs. Kaufman's number, to make sure she had actually agreed to the scheme, and Emily and I started making our plans, even as we reached the breathless rewards of Northwestern's final week: a Rolling Stones concert at McCormick Place and a "Chicago Night Out" to see the comedian Corbett Monica at the nightclub in the Palmer House hotel. On our own extended weekend, Emily wanted to take me to the Art Institute, and on Saturday night there would be a party with some of her closest friends from Latin, all of whom were dying to meet me, she said.

I wondered what I could contribute. Mom said she'd send money so that I could take Emily and her family to lunch at a nice restaurant. Then I told Emily about this guy I'd met at my job, Clayton Coots, and that I felt awkward about calling him, but I just might, because he'd make it possible for us to see a play. I knew from *Variety* that *The Odd Couple* was SRO in Chicago, so we couldn't see it without his help. Finally I summoned up my nerve, calling the Blackstone and leaving a message that I would be in Chicago with my girlfriend for four days beginning that Saturday.

I was disappointed when he didn't call back the next day; I decided I had been too presumptuous to call him after all. Why would he want to pass us into a hit? Instead, we heard from Mrs. Kaufman—or Emily did— that it was no longer possible for me to stay in her Chicago apartment. It turned out, Emily explained, that another relative was coming to town at the last minute and there was simply no room: Emily and her mom shared one bedroom, her sister and grandmother another, and the relative was going to use the couch in the living room. Maybe a cousin of Emily's could put me up instead; failing that, there was a teacher at Northwestern who might, though that would mean an arduous commute back and forth from Evanston.

That Wednesday night, when I met Emily on the bus for Chicago Night Out, I found her upset for the first time since I'd known her, though it was hard to tell at first. Her disappointment showed hesitantly through her usual smile. Her cousin was going out of town, she told me, so I couldn't stay there. She had begged her mother to ask their visiting relative to stay elsewhere, and her mother had yelled at her for being selfish and threatened to punish her by restricting her activities the weekend I'd be in Chicago. Why? What had Emily done wrong? "Mom just gets cross sometimes," she said, not so much angry as resigned. "That's how she can be." I reconciled myself to staying with our teacher in Evanston, but now he was starting to renege too.

It was when I picked up my mail the next morning that our fortunes abruptly changed. In my mailbox at Elder Hall was a special-delivery letter from Clayton Coots. His name was engraved in thin capital letters on the flap of the sky-blue envelope. Underneath his name, in rubber-stamped black letters, was:

ODD COUPLE CO.

BLACKSTONE THEATRE

CHICAGO, ILL.

My heart raced. The typed letter inside said that he had tried to phone me but that no one had answered the phone in my dorm. He said that he could not see Emily and me Saturday or Sunday, but was free Monday and Tuesday. "Let me know where you are staying. As a matter of fact, if you need to, you can stay at my place, for I do have an extra bed. I could give you the key and you can come and go as you please." He noted his phone number at the theater again, as well as that for his apartment.

I showed the letter to Emily, and she was as excited as I was. She read out the address of his apartment, 14 West Elm: "That's only four blocks from where I live!"

I couldn't believe my—our—good fortune. Our weekend would go as planned after all, and what's more we'd see this man, Clayton Coots, who promised to be the first real friend I'd made on my own in the theater.

I phoned Mom in Washington and told her what was going on. She set down the phone to tell Joel, who then picked up the extension.

"Frank," he said, "tell me again who this Clayton Coots is." I reminded him of *Barefoot, Odd Couple,* and the rest of it. There was a pause, then he asked, "Do you know if he's a homosexual?"

Not only had it not occurred to me, but I'd never heard an adult use the word before. At Indian Hill everyone had known that Jimmy Waring, the modern-dance teacher who choreographed *Trouble in Tahiti*, was a fairy, and I'd seen lesbians onstage in a play in London, *The Killing of Sister George*. But I didn't know much about what these people did—except that it was so disgusting that people talked about it even less than they did about divorce. Joel never had explained what "that poor son of a bitch," Lyndon Johnson's assistant Walter Jenkins, was caught doing when he had scandalized Washington by being arrested in a men's room at the YMCA downtown.

Now my hopes of being with Emily were held hostage to the possibility that Clayton, of all people, might be a homosexual. How could he be? He was a good guy. My heart sank.

"I'm sure it's fine," Joel continued, good-naturedly, sounding as if he wanted to grant me permission. "But we don't know him, and we have to be certain."

Well, sure, I said. He had a point, for once.

Joel continued: "I'll call Scott Kirkpatrick today and ask him. Your mother and I need to have a reference."

I couldn't disagree.

Joel promised I'd hear from him or Mom one way or the other the next day. I decided not to tell Emily about this part of the conversation, and just prayed that the worst wouldn't happen, capsizing our weekend once again. Every ounce of my being, it seemed, was invested in spending these four days with the girl I loved, and I didn't know what I'd do if I couldn't.

For once, my worst fears were not realized. At lunchtime the next day, a yellow Western Union envelope was stuck into my mailbox. The telegram read:

YOUR MOTHER ASKED ME TELEGRAPH SHE AGREEABLE YOU STAY WITH CLAYTON COOTS—PLEASE WRITE ME ADDRESS AND PHONE CONTACT NUMBERS LOVE JOEL

CHAPTER 3

The farewell day of the Northwestern session, Emily's mother picked us up in Evanston in an old but meticulously cared for black Cadillac. She was a formal woman, attractive but buttoned-up, in a business suit as funereal as her car. She gave me a firm handshake, an assessing stare, and, finally, a guarded half-smile before driving Emily and me back to her apartment for lunch. We made stilted small talk as we headed into the city.

The Kaufmans' home was small but elegant, in an old apartment house off Lake Shore Drive, just down the street from a grand pile of a hotel called the Drake; from the living room's third-floor windows you could see the beach stretching in a sensuous curve north toward Evanston and the crystalline, seemingly infinite blue lake that had imbued the entire summer with an air of romance and ceaseless possibility. Emily's grandmother, a squat, bustling woman with a warm manner in pointed opposition to her daughter's regality, served us lunch. As we ate, Emily's mom made no mention of her rescinded invitation, though she did mention that she had enjoyed talking with my mother on the phone a week earlier. Emily and I finished the meal as hastily as we could without being rude and were soon outside, holding hands and feeling as tall and dynamic as the towers that surrounded us. Once I dropped off my bag and picked up the key at the reception desk in Clayton's apartment hotel, we were off on a tour of those sights that had eluded our earlier excursions into the city: the Mies van der Rohe apartment buildings nearby that looked just like New York's Seagram Building; and Old Town, which was Chicago's Greenwich Village and London's Carnaby Street combined; and the Art Institute.

At the museum, Emily led me immediately to the Impressionist galleries, where picture after picture looked like a familiar face that I couldn't quite place: I realized I was unconsciously filling in the blanks of the art history Mom had taught me at the Phillips in Washington and the Museum of Modern Art in New York and then the Tate and the Jeu de Paume abroad. I knew Mom had never been to the Art Institute, though, and I couldn't wait to tell her what she was missing. I knew she'd love the pictures, and I knew she'd love Emily. I fantasized that I would come back someday with both of them—Mom sharing in the happiness I'd found in life with Emily and art. The three of us would stand together in front of Seurat's *Island of La Grande Jatte*, drinking in its light together, Joel nowhere in sight.

Nightfall brought Emily's friends—as smart and funny as she had told me they would be. They treated me not as a stranger but as a friend of long standing. They talked about politics and even plays. They were more like Indian Hill kids than Wilson kids; only the black turtlenecks and ostentatious invocations of psychotherapy were absent. Everyone at Latin wore clothes from Brooks Brothers, a New York store that did not exist in Washington. Emily told me she would take me to the branch on Michigan Avenue and buy me a blue button-down shirt like her friends' as a present.

When I brought Emily home after dinner with her friends on Wells Street, we stood in the shadows outside her apartment house kissing each other over and over, hoping, perhaps, that we might in some way be permanently bonded by the congress of our hungry lips. Then, after she had carefully refreshed my memory about how to make the brief walk to Clayton's, we declared our love to each other and said good night.

That walk took only ten minutes, and I savored it. The breeze from the lake caressed my back. The city was warm, and as embracing as Emily's arms. I passed town houses and shuttered shops reminiscent of New York, and then, as I walked the two blocks up Rush Street to Elm, one crowded bar and club after another, in a continuous urban blaze of neon and boisterous camaraderie unknown in Washington. Though the hour was late, I felt safe and free—much as I had when I took that first solo walk down Broadway when Dad let me stray from Capezio. Only this time I wasn't heading toward a play, and I didn't know the neighborhood. It didn't matter. My map was defined on one border by the girl with whom I wanted to spend every minute of my life and on the other by a new friend who was literally inviting me into the only family I had ever aspired to be a part of, the family of the theater.

I didn't know what to expect, though, at 14 West Elm. I had hardly met Clayton, and knew almost nothing about him. A quick look in the Northwestern library's theater section had yielded his name in a single context; he was listed as a performer in the credits of a flop 1957 Broadway musical called *Rumple* that had never been recorded. His small role was "Chief of Oblivia"; he was also listed as the production's assistant stage manager.

The man at the desk called Clayton to let him know that I was on my way up. Clayton had told me that he would be home early that night, since he always left the theater after doing the count on Saturdays. The week's books would be closed, he said, and "all the hopheads and idiots and farmers are out in Chicago on Saturday and I cannot abide them, so I retreat."

He greeted me at his door with an enthusiastic handshake and ushered me in to "Oscar's other pad"—a joking reference to the lead character in *The Odd Couple*, a slob New York sportswriter named Oscar Madison. The apartment wasn't as messy as he had billed it, though. The only signs of clutter were a makeshift bar of liquor bottles and dirty glasses on a counter leading into a tiny kitchen, and a couple of bowls on the floor for his dog, Decker, a mutt who greeted me nearly as warmly as Clayton did.

Clayton was dressed in an opulent silk bathrobe and leather slippers; his cigarette holder was perched in his mouth at its usual jaunty angle. He wore glasses and chatted while putting away some business papers— "boring payroll stuff"—that he had been working on when I arrived. The room smelled of cigarettes and his now familiar aftershave; I pulled out my own cigarettes and lit up. He offered me a drink, and I asked for a Coke;

Clayton was sipping a golden liqueur from a brandy snifter. I was welcome to try some if I wanted to, he said, as long as that was okay with "your folks." I wasn't entirely surprised to learn that he had been called by Joel—twice—in the forty-eight hours since I'd given my stepfather my Chicago contact numbers.

"He sounds like a marvelous guy," Clayton said, sounding as if he really meant it.

The television set was on at a low volume. "There's one channel here with the best old movies," Clayton said. "A week of Mae West, and then a week of Ronald Colman, and then a week of some of the worst stinkers Hollywood ever made—you never know what they'll come up with, but it's always fun. Even Decker likes them." I mentioned that Washington, unlike Chicago and New York, didn't have good late movies on its four channels and, some nights, had no late movies at all.

"Well," said Clayton, "you are missing an essential part of your education. You must watch them every night while you're here."

I laughed with him, and then he asked about my day with Emily, taking enormous interest in every detail and constantly interjecting how much he looked forward to meeting her. That would happen Monday night, when he was taking us to *The Odd Couple* at the Blackstone and dinner after. On Tuesday night—if we were free, and if we were interested—he would get us passes to *Hello, Dolly!*, whose road company was at the Shubert, the musical house a few blocks north of the Blackstone. The company manager was a pal of his.

"Let me ask Emily," I said, "but I'm sure that she'll want to."

Clayton got up and clicked off the television. "No old movies tonight," he said. "You need your beauty sleep for Emily tomorrow, and I need mine for Louis and Christel." They were, he explained, a European couple with whom he had dinner most Sunday nights. They lived in a modern tower overlooking the lake, and had "the finest grand piano in Chicago this side of Orchestra Hall." After dinner with his friends each Sunday, Clayton said, he'd sit down and play until "everyone conks out or the brandy runs out, whichever comes first."

I laughed, but I could tell it was the rare wisecrack he didn't mean entirely as a joke.

Clayton disappeared into his bedroom, then reemerged with a pile of linens.

"Welcome to Fourteen West Elm boot camp!" he said as we started making up the couch in the living room.

When we had finished, he turned off the lamps and flipped the TV back on. "Listen, kid, I was just joking about the TV. It's your holiday and you can watch all goddamn night if you want. Just be sure to keep it down in the morning. I don't have to get up until four tomorrow. And if I'm awakened too early, you don't want to see it, trust me. I molt."

He said good night, added that of course I could wake him at any time if I needed anything, and then disappeared into his bedroom, closing the door behind him. I stretched out on the couch, allowing myself for the first time to feel the exhaustion of my packed day with Emily.

I tried to watch TV and found that I couldn't concentrate. For once, just the fact that I had a TV in the room to keep me company was reassurance enough; I got up and turned it off. Then I closed my eyes. I could hear no sound now except the purr of an air conditioner. Clayton, I imagined, was already asleep in the next room.

It was the kind of moment that on other nights would have been tainted by my usual fear of insomnia, but this night I was possessed by a new sensation—I was overtaken by, of all things, peace. My makeshift bed on a couch felt more comfortable than any bed I'd ever slept in. Was this what people meant when they talked about contentment? Why did I feel more at home in a near-stranger's apartment in a strange city than I ever had in all my actual homes? The question was no sooner posed than forgotten as I drifted luxuriously into deep sleep.

—

It would have been hard to imagine how my stay in Chicago could have been any more joyous than it already was, but Monday night, when Emily and I went out with Clayton, we seemed to leap beyond the ecstatic reality we had been inhabiting to ascend to a higher plateau where all sights and sounds and emotions were transposed into a different key previously unknown to us or, we decided, to anyone else.

When we arrived at the Blackstone, I spotted Clayton in the mobbed lobby; he was dressed in a glittering, regal jacket and monitoring the entering crowds. The Blackstone was a revelation to me, now that I could see it fully lighted, rather than just through that scrim of rain and fog that shrouded its façade in my memory. With its dark wood paneling and ancient box-office cage, the theater looked more like a Broadway house than the expansive and sunnier National.

Clayton greeted us as if he owned the place and we were royalty who had ordered a command performance. Emily's usual smile widened into a huge grin when Clayton took her hand and said how much he looked forward to getting to know her over our dinner after the show; he handed me two punched tickets—the free passes known as "Annie Oakleys" because of their "bullet holes"—patted me on the back to propel me in the direction of the ticket-taker, and told us to find him in the manager's office during intermission.

I could hardly pay attention to the play. Emily hadn't seen *The Odd Couple* before, as I had, and I was keenly focused on her, not the stage, hoping that she would find the same jokes funny that I did. We held hands tightly, and she soon relaxed into the comic rhythms of the performance and its story about two recently single men, Oscar the slob and Felix the fussbudget, who are forced by financial and psychological necessity to room together in an apartment on Riverside Drive in New York. Seeing the show for the first time since its tryout in Washington a couple of years earlier, I was struck by how funny it made divorce seem—why couldn't my parents have had one with so many jokes? In *The Odd Couple*, we never saw the divorced men's children, wherever or whoever they were.

At intermission we found Clayton in an office off the rear of the orchestra floor—just where the count-up room was at the National. I knowingly asked him if the count was done and he said yes, "It always goes fast when you go clean," invoking Broadway's vernacular for a sold-out house. He asked us how we were enjoying ourselves, introduced us to the house manager, and offered us soft drinks. Then, with a solicitousness that adults, in my experience, rarely bestowed on teenagers, he showered Emily with detailed questions about her school, her family, her interests in theater and art. They were still talking animatedly, as if they'd known each other forever, when the lights started blinking for the second act.

"I love Clayton," Emily said, her eyes gleaming in the reflected glow of the curtain, as we took our seats just as the houselights were going down. I squeezed her hand even harder. For all the time I'd spent in theaters, I'd never had this experience before—holding on for dear life to someone I loved at the very second the auditorium fell into darkness, someone who felt as excited about the theater as I did, someone who'd be with me after the curtain went down, when I had to make that rude climb back into real life.

And there was not just Emily, but Clayton. After the play, he whisked us away by cab to his favorite restaurant, the Italian Village, on Monroe Street, a block from the Shubert. It was dimly lighted and almost a stage set in itself, with a mural, just like a backdrop, of a village whose picturesque houses and markets were sheltered by a star-sprayed cobalt-blue sky that extended up the walls to cover the entire ceiling.

It was the first time I had eaten after a play rather than before; in Washington, where no restaurant downtown was open that late, it would have been impossible; in New York, Joel couldn't wait so late to eat. The festiveness of an after-theater dinner was obvious: It was just the thing to prolong the night, easing the descent from the adrenaline of a show into the necessity of bed.

Clayton ordered a red Italian wine with a gold label that he said was "the only wine to have with this food" and spoke to all the waiters and captains by name as he guided us through the menu. Though he knew as much about foreign food as Joel did, and had Joel's familiarity with the restaurant's staff, the mood was merry, not foreboding. Everyone in the place seemed to know and dote on "Signor Coots": The ashtray was emptied repeatedly without his asking, and a second bottle of wine materialized as soon as we finished the first.

Emily and I worked our way through dishes we had never heard of before, veal with exotic words like "scallopini" and "saltimbocca" after it, each as delicious as Clayton had promised. Along the way, we learned more and more about our unexpected benefactor, who kept protesting that his life wasn't all that interesting and glamorous. It was the only thing he said we didn't believe.

Clayton was the son of J. Fred Coots, a songwriter who had started out as a pianist in vaudeville when he was a teenager, then had gravitated toward Tin Pan Alley and Broadway, where he wrote revues for the Shuberts in the 1920s. Clayton called his dad "the little oil well" because the old man continued to collect large royalties on the hit songs he'd written decades before: "Santa Claus Is Coming to Town," "You Go to My Head," and one that had had a whole new vogue in the recent rock-and-roll past, "Love Letters in the Sand."

"It must be wonderful to have a father like that," Emily said, but Clayton would have none of it.

"He sent me to the best boarding school in Germany," he said, "and I haven't taken and wouldn't take a dime from him since. He's mean and he spends all his afternoons drinking in his club in New York, and I'm not going to give him another reason to be angry at me or my mother." It seemed that his father had not approved of Clayton's decision to stay in Europe, forgo college, play piano in bars, and take the modeling offers that came his way after his success on a school gymnastics team. Clayton had spent several years in Berlin before deciding, somewhat reluctantly, to return to America and go into the theater. He felt more warmly about his mom, from whom, he said, he had inherited his temperamental Hungarian sensibility.

But surely his father must be happy that Clayton had followed him into show business.

"Not especially," said Clayton. "He doesn't approve of it."

It was the only sour note during a meal in which our sentences kept tripping over one another as we talked about the Art Institute and Broadway and even Washington, which Clayton regarded more fondly than I did. He always took a suite at the Jefferson Hotel on Sixteenth Street when he was in town, he said, and knew everyone there. He admired the National, too, and Scott Kirkpatrick. "He is a true gentleman, a fine person," he said, "and he runs a first-class theater. Everyone wants to play the National, and that's why it's never dark."

I wondered if Joel had really asked Mr. Kirkpatrick if Clayton was a homosexual. It was impossible to picture Mr. Kirkpatrick in such a conversation, and harder still to imagine him recounting it to Clayton or anyone else without dying of mortification. I prayed that Joel had for once kept his mouth shut, though I feared he hadn't.

Emily asked Clayton if he enjoyed playing Chicago, and Clayton said that it was easy when the company was as good as *The Odd Couple*. He told us how much he liked Dan Dailey, the old movie star playing Oscar, and Dick Benjamin, the young comic actor who played Felix.

"They're pros," he said of his cast, "and that makes life much easier for a manager." There were times, though, when he missed his New York apartment in the East Sixties, a few blocks from his parents'. He told us how he had been on the road for the producer Leland Hayward with the tour of *A Shot in the Dark* a few years earlier, during the Cuban Missile Crisis, and how he'd despised the married couple who starred in it and had fought with him, house managers, and newspaper interviewers at every stop along the way. "I thought, Jesus, I'm going to be with this horrible company in Pittsburgh, hundreds of miles from my family and friends, when the world ends in thermonuclear war."

The conversation flowed as extravagantly as the wine did, and we might have stayed there forever if the restaurant didn't have to close for the night. The maître d' told Clayton, "Mr. Coots, you stay as long as you wish," but eventually we were back on Monroe Street, the night-shrouded Shubert looming up the block, its marquee now dark, much as I remembered it from that rainy nocturnal tour with Joel.

Clayton hailed a taxi and directed it first to Emily's address. He waited while I walked her to the door and gave her a good-night kiss.

When he returned to 14 West Elm, I stayed in the apartment while he walked Decker. Then we caught the end of a hilarious movie with Peter Lorre, Clayton adding his own wisecracks after almost every line. During the commercials, as he fixed himself a brandy at his makeshift bar, he told me how lucky I was to have met someone as bright and lovely as Emily. He talked about some of the women he was closest to—including an actress who had until a month before been in *Hello, Dolly!* at the Shubert, and another whose name I remembered from the company of *How to Succeed* that had played Washington a year earlier. The trouble with being on the road, Clayton said, was that everyone's conflicting touring schedules often made it difficult for friends to see one another; he had to settle for talking to Pat, his *How to Succeed* pal, on the phone every day, though she was hoping to spend a Sunday in Chicago when her show hit Cleveland in a few weeks. Despite Clayton's caveats, it all sounded very romantic to me—the proof of my conviction that a theatrical company was an extended family, a happy family, with enough love to go around for all who were in it.

As if to add further evidence, Clayton took us the next night, after *Hello, Dolly!*, to a bar on Rush Street called Punchinello's, which he called "the Chicago Sardi's"—a hangout for show people when they were in town. Sure enough, Dan Dailey was there, waiting for the arrival of Eve Arden, the Chicago Dolly we'd just seen, and Clayton introduced Emily and me to them as if we were the most fascinating people who'd ever attended a play at the Blackstone Theatre. In the convivial, rowdy Punchinello's, everyone was welcome at the party.

The only problem was that the next morning I was flying back to Washington, first to go on my New England trip with Dad, then to simmer in the city's sweltering August, waiting for senior year and pining for Emily. Clayton extended my last night as long as possible, but Emily began to get nervous that she would try her mom's patience. I walked her back toward Lake Shore Drive while Clayton returned to Elm Street.

With the lake as our reliable backdrop, Emily and I hugged each other as hard as we could in front of her apartment house. I pulled back a second so that I could see her face, and found that her eyes were brimming over with tears.

"I love you," I said, wiping away her tears with my fingers.

She pulled back as if embarrassed.

"Are you sure?" she whispered.

"Yes," I said, kissing the tears off her cheeks now. "I never want to leave you."

"I don't want you to leave, but I know you can't stay."

Then we hugged some more. Torn between frustration and sadness, I fantasized about that elusive moment when we might someday be alone together indoors to neck at will and hold each other forever. But when? We pulled ourselves apart with one final kiss, then I walked back toward Clayton's apartment with little of the propulsion of my first night in Chicago just seventy-two hours before.

Clayton was in his bathrobe when I returned; he read my mood immediately. I tried to pull myself together. I didn't want to seem like a sulking teenager. I wanted to be like he was, grown-up and sophisticated and able to play any hand life dealt me.

But I couldn't fool him.

"Look, kid," he said—Emily loved how he called me "kid" and referred to me as "The Kid"—"I know how you feel. I'm older, I know—*God*, am I older—but I know how you feel, trust me." Then he gave me a pep talk and reminded me that I was only seventeen and just beginning with Emily, and that we had our whole lives ahead of us.

I smiled and agreed, suppressing the gloom that had started to wash over me. Clayton turned on the late movie, and it was some funny old Hollywood antique again, and we started to watch, with him providing his impudent supplementary soundtrack to the movie's actual dialogue. He kept pouring himself more brandy, and then the movie was over and he looked over at me as he got up to go to bed and said, "You look miserable, and I'm telling you again, you shouldn't be."

Then he told me that one thing that sometimes made him feel better at times like this was a back rub. He asked if I'd ever had one, and I said no, I hadn't.

Would I like to try one? If I didn't like it, he'd stop, but it might make me relax. I thought nothing of it, except that I already trusted him more than any man I'd ever met, and I thought he knew more about life than any friend I had yet found, and if he said a back rub would make me feel better, then I was sure it would.

He told me to move over to one side of the couch, then he got up from his easy chair and disappeared into his bedroom. When he returned, he had shed his bathrobe and was dressed only in a white undershirt and briefs that were nothing like those Mom bought me at Woodies: They were black, not white, and they were tiny. In his hand was an ornate bottle of his German cologne, which bore the cryptic name "4711" ("*Not* an aftershave," he'd pointed out)—the one he had worn since he'd been in school in Europe. Clayton believed that European brands were better than American and had instructed me in the merits of products I had never heard of bearing the names Dunhill, Cardin, Patek Philippe, and Mont Blanc. He was also a devotee of Bally shoes, a brand that was familiar to me from the will-calls on Saturdays at Rich's.

Clayton sat down behind me on the couch and told me to take off my undershirt. Then I felt him smacking some of the cologne on to my shoulders, after which he put down the bottle and started massaging me, kneading my flesh until his thumbs felt as if they were right against my bones.

"Does that hurt?" he asked.

"No," I said, lying a little. It didn't hurt, but his hands did feel sharp.

"It should feel relaxing. Does it?" he asked, his tone uncharacteristically businesslike, as if this was a professional chore akin to doing the box-office count.

"No—well, yes, I guess it does," I said. I didn't want him to think I was unappreciative of the attention he was giving me, and I was—for the moment, anyway—diverted from the cold fact of my departure from Chicago the next day.

He continued for a few minutes more, then stopped. Before I knew it, he was standing up.

"I know you can hold your liquor, you're so damn young," Clayton said, "but I've got to go to bed."

I thanked him and put my T-shirt back on; I was again feeling the frost of the air-conditioning.

"What time is Emily picking you up to drive to the airport?" he continued.

I told him.

"Well, I'm not going to tell you what to do, but my advice is that you not watch the late movie but go to sleep. That back rub should make it easier—I think I got rid of some of your tension."

I wondered if that was true; I'd never had a back rub before and couldn't tell what it did. For a nervous second I wondered if there was some sexual undercurrent to Clayton's touching me—I didn't detect any, and besides, how could anyone with so many girlfriends be a homosexual? The moment passed, and I blurted out to Clayton that I was very grateful for everything he had done for me and Emily in Chicago. I hoped I hadn't inconvenienced him by keeping him out late and monopolizing the past two nights and contributing to the dirty ashtrays and Oscar Madison mess of his apartment.

"Not at all," he said. "I'm going to miss you, kid." And with that he went into his bedroom, calling behind him that I had to be sure to wake him in the morning to say goodbye, especially since he should be getting up at that inhuman hour anyway, since it was, after all, Wednesday, a matinee day.

—

Back in Washington, there was only my job to keep me company: The National was booked for August with a revival of *Annie Get Your Gun* starring Ethel Merman, who had originated the show on Broadway before I was born and who to me was inextricably identified with the unhappy divorced mother she had later played in *Gypsy*. The National's houses bordered on full, and Mr. Kirkpatrick was in his white summer regalia to greet the mostly tourist audiences who found their way into his domain. My house on Cleveland Avenue, though, was empty. Mom and Joel were still away, as were most of my friends. June was gone, and Harry was no longer a tie-line phone call away.

I went to the theater every night; the National stood almost alone as a fount of teeming life in the deserted pre–Labor Day downtown. But even there, I couldn't suppress the intensity with which I missed both Emily and Clayton. A classmate of Emily's had given me a black-and-white photo of the two of us sitting on a couch in profile, my arm around Emily's shoulders, both of us looking expectantly, almost spellbound, past the frame of the snapshot, as if we were being given a glimpse into a wondrous future we might have together. I mounted the photo on the bulletin board where I used to put my Broadway clippings; next to it I put the professional head shot of Clayton that Emily and I had each begged him to give us a copy of—a souvenir of his modeling days.

While waiting for school to start, I poured my energy into my correspondence with both of them and lived for the morning mail, hoping that it would bring their replies. Often it did. Clayton typed his letters on *Odd Couple* stationery imprinted with the show's festive logo—the black and red diamonds and hearts of playing cards, an important prop in a comedy that revolved around poker games. Emily wrote hers in a tiny, neat hand on thick wads of small paper. We frequently exchanged our letters by special delivery, and some nights, when I wrote her upon returning home from the National, I'd leave my air-conditioned third-floor aerie at two or three in the morning to walk to the nearest mailbox, on Cathedral Avenue, to make sure my letter would be on its way to her at the morning's first pickup. The neighborhood was so still on these sultry August nights, when the humidity was thick enough to blur the outlines of the streetlamps that illuminated it, that life itself seemed to have slowed to a halt.

In our correspondence, Emily and I said over and over how much we missed each other and how much we loved each other, as if no one had ever felt the way we did. But the letters didn't seem to make either of us happy. Emily described vacant days in which she waited, often in vain, for her mother's permission to carry out almost any activity that took her out of the house, except for her two days a week working as a volunteer at a hospital. When the Beatles gave a concert in Chicago a couple of weeks after I left, Emily and her Latin School friends were lucky enough to get tickets, yet at the last minute Emily's mom refused to let her go, without giving a reason. That Emily accepted her mother's decision—"that's just the way she is"—rather than getting angry was beyond me.

Not wanting to dishearten Emily with my own gloominess, I wrote Clayton instead about the dark thoughts I just couldn't shake. It was not something I had ever confided to anyone outside my family—not even to my closest friends, except tentatively to Sara—and yet somehow I felt he would listen to me, that I could talk to him without feeling humiliated by my admission of what I figured to be a childish weakness. I was quickly proved right, for Clayton wrote me back in a way no adult had ever addressed me before, giving me advice, distracting me with humor, trying to help as best he could from a thousand miles away.

"All those colleges you visited sound great," he wrote,

so make up your mind slowly and choose the best for what you want. I don't mean to sound "preachy" but you know what you are doing now is far more important than just having fun and being with any- one. There will be a time for that later on when you are somewhat established. I think Emily is a wonderful girl but until you have met plenty of girls you have no basis for comparison and until you have that basis it's possible to make a mistake. God knows, I've made them. End of "Big Brother Lecture"!

He continued as though I were back in Chicago and he was just sipping his brandy and talking:

At the moment it's intermission here and the audience seems in good spirits. I thought of you the other night because I saw the absolutely WORST late movie ever made. The beautiful moll of the gang leader looked to me like a female impersonator and not a very good one.

Hey! I just reread my lecture and I don't mean that the feeling you have for Emily isn't a true and valid one, what I meant was, you don't help the feeling or yourself by allowing the loneliness to take control and affect your life or your studies to a large degree.

At the company costume party, Billy Pierson came dressed up as me as a boy. He had short pants on, a dinner coat, a formal shirt with gum-drop studs, large gum-drops for cufflinks, and he and Diana got a blond wig and cut it to look like my hair and he carried a black cigarette holder with a chocolate cigarette and a brandy snifter. Last weekend we went to the Governors Ball at some Polo Club out of town. All outdoor marquees and candles and society and I was a success because of my long hair. All the older women wanted to dance with me but they don't Frug too well. It was fun and then we went out and closed a Discotheque around 5 a.m.

Can't wait til Pat arrives so I better start saving my dough. God can that girl put away a steak—it's fascinating.

I think Decker missed you cause after you left for the following four nights she would walk to your bed and turn and look at me, and, really, if dogs like you, you can't be all bad.

For reasons I couldn't explain, just reading the letter from Clayton cheered me up. I couldn't figure out how this man I hardly knew, and had met by chance, could understand what I was feeling. From afar it seemed that he could touch and soothe the part of my mind where that anxious sinking sensation had started to tear at me again, so strongly now that it was as if I were still back in Somerset and couldn't see beyond whatever day I was trapped in.

The theater must have had something to do with his powers, for who was Clayton Coots if not the incarnation of those characters who I'd for so long hoped would rescue me? He was Peter Pan and the unseen advance man with the traveling show in *Carousel* and the Music Man and Tulsa. I pictured that somehow Clayton would help me and Emily escape—to where I didn't know, from what I wasn't sure anymore. But if the details were fuzzy, I felt protected by him—as if he were the magical parent that I had always hoped would materialize like a hero in a play, the kind of parent I had wished for, a parent who had stepped off the stage and led me by the hand to safety.

I wrote back, telling him how much his letters meant to me, and that I felt better, and sharing my news that a recruiter had unexpectedly contacted me to see if I wanted to apply to Yale. Though I had no nocturnal adventures to match his nightlife in Chicago, I scraped together what few modest anecdotes I could from life on the National's second door during *Annie Get Your Gun.*

He replied in a style reminiscent of those Leonard Lyons columns Joel had sent me at Northwestern:

Dear pal Frank:

Well I'm here at work and just finished reading your letter which I enjoyed tremendously and was glad to get. Life is dull here and sometimes the days pass slowly and it's great to have a letter to answer!

Yes I can read your letters and they are interesting and well written but the hell with that because I'm so excited about YALE and what they told you and really it's wonderful news. I'm very happy and very proud but even though I'm all for Yale I'll not urge you to rush, for you are smart enough to go where it's best for you. Well, now I've said that, so I'll start in by making comments about your letter's items and then write the fast one sentence that will fill you in on the details of my fascinating life.

I know too well, that feeling of just "yetch" and being alone and it is funny how a small thing like a letter can pick you right up. Funny and kind of wonderful too! . . .

Hope you patch up that quarrel with your mother. Maybe she is difficult but try to understand that being a parent isn't the easiest job in the world and try and roll with it a little. She may have problems you know nothing about.

Glad you enjoy talking to me and yes, I like listening, it's easy if you care. I think I make a fine older brother.

Now for the EXCITING, TREMENDOUS & SENSATIONAL report from the Windy City concerning the reports in the life of the HANDSOME, RICH AND LEGENDARY Manager . . . HERE GOES:::::it is dull!

Splurged on a copy of the Gala FLEDERMAUS at Vienna Opera last year. I played the aria that Rosalinda sings called Strains of the Homeland and cried.

Oh how bad can Saturday nights be when you are alone on the road?

As for me, personally, I sort of don't know how I feel. I guess mainly all right, but in a way, unquiet and sort of sad and I don't know why. Chicago is fine and the money that comes in is wonderful but I know in my heart this is not what I'll end up doing. Frank, it's funny, I tell you things that I've told no one, but maybe you understand. It's as if I know that I will spend the greatest part of my life back in Europe and I'm just marking time until I finish up life here and leave, never to return. Happily, I am well adjusted to life enough to keep cheerful and "up" but there are times I'm not and I get terribly lonely as I am today. The theatre is dark, it's cold and empty and I come here for there is no where else to go. Then I come here and thoughts of the past come back and although they don't get to me as they used to do, they still can cause a "twinge" or two. Like a scar that is perfectly healed but nonetheless acts up when the weather changes. Perhaps I long for Paris, Berlin and Florence for I was so happy there. It is as the aria I loved went: Oh Land, where I was so happy.

You know what I mean. That hotel is great if there's someone around, but that room can be depressing alone. What a strange business. So many people every day, so much to do, and so many lonely moments and it isn't just me, it's that way for everybody in it. Please don't get mad because I'm writing of trouble to you, but these are things you don't tell just anyone. Also I'm sort of a legend around here and I'm always Happy and with it and this is a side you don't show to just anyone. When you are a manager, your troubles come last and it's the company that needs you and you owe them that. Anyway, these moments don't last and there is no truth to the rumor that I intend to leap from the balcony some night. I am grateful and cognizant of the good things in life and my work.

I feel better for having put on paper what I feel, many thanks for listening.

> All the best to you, really, your pal—
> Clayton

It was hard to believe that Clayton, on the road with a play, could feel some of the loneliness that I did and understood how I felt. If I had no place to go but a cold, empty, and dark theater, would I still feel depressed? It didn't seem possible. Better an empty theater—let alone one in Chicago, with Emily and Clayton nearby—than my room on Cleveland Avenue. Even when Mom and Joel were home, our house felt deserted. They were always running out to a movie, or dinner, as if they feared that spending a night alone would lead to a fight, which it almost invariably did, driving Mom into the den, where she'd hide behind the closed door and sob herself to sleep, thinking Polly and I couldn't hear her.

Maybe Polly didn't hear her; I could never tell. We had stopped comparing notes about what went on between Mom and Joel, or about much else. Polly was, in Sue's words, "the lucky one" of the four children: Though subjected to Joel's temper no less than the rest of us, she was the only one he never hit. Neither she nor the rest of us ever found out why, but that didn't stop us from resenting her for it. Even so, she took no pleasure in her status and made no secret of her contempt for Joel and her fear of him; she simply retreated into silence about him, much as Mom usually did. In that sense, Polly wasn't "the lucky one" after all, for the blows she absorbed, surely no less deep than any of ours, were also out of reach.

On one of those stormy nights of late summer, I tried to break through

Mom's silence. I had found her in the kitchen drinking white wine and smoking when I came downstairs in search of a midnight snack. I sat down at the table across from her and started talking about my almost unbearable longing for Emily. She listened with her usual sympathy, offering the same encouragement in love she had given me with so much else, but when I tried to turn the subject to Joel, she steered it away as she always did, her will reinforced by alcohol. As I enumerated his recent sins—against all of us, starting with John—she cut me off: "Joel has given me and all of you exciting lives we never would have had without him. You'll be grateful for it one day, and so will John." She reminded me that Joel had volunteered to pay for the summer at Northwestern, had facilitated my stay in Chicago afterward, and would expedite a future rendezvous between me and Emily. "Tell me about the theaters in Chicago," she said. She guessed correctly that I would warm to the topic and forget all about Joel.

School seemed as much on edge as my household once Labor Day brought senior year, as if Wilson's atmosphere were being roiled by unseen forces. In a game of Murder Ball—Wilson's name for the dodgeball we played in the gym in lousy weather—a tall and quiet Negro boy who led most of the school's hapless white varsity teams was hit so hard in the chest by a basketball that he retreated to the locker room—where he collapsed and died. It was an accident, but Washington's tabloid, the *Daily News*, screamed MURDER BALL KILLING, implying that white boys might have been aiming for the Negro.

The school was riddled with other disruptions too—about the length of boys' hair and girls' skirts and the antiwar meetings my friend Jeremy and I and a few others attended. But my parallel existence with Emily and Clayton in Chicago had, without my realizing it, separated me from the Wilson crowd even more effectively than my anomalous broken home had. For all the tumult at school and the hours spent putting out the newspaper there and the pressure of applying to college, I often carried out my senior year at Wilson as if I were an actor walking diligently through a role. My real life took place in Chicago, I decided, even if I could carry it out only in letters and the occasional rushed long-distance phone call.

Emily's birthday was in October, on the same weekend that I was visiting a cousin at Harvard, the first kid in my family to go to an Ivy League

school. Emily and I planned to meet in Boston that weekend; she had per-
suaded her mother that it would be a good time to tour the colleges there
that interested her. But a week before we were to meet, Emily's mom ve-
toed the trip—again, without explanation. Emily took the bad news better
than I did; she was used to her mom's sudden changes of heart. I told my
mother that I wanted to cancel my own trip to Cambridge and go to
Chicago for Emily's birthday instead.

Clayton wouldn't hear of me canceling my college visit. "This year is
the big one and you won't get a chance to do it over again," he wrote. "Responsibility can be very tiring and wearying. But it's also good for one to
develop a sense of it—some never know what the word means. I'll bet
you're accepted at Harvard—just make sure that you work harder this year
THAN EVER. God I don't want to be ashamed of you."

As always, his admonitions were accompanied by theater stories that
had the effect of making his "Big Brother Lectures" seem all the more serious in contrast. His friend Dick Benjamin was leaving *The Odd Couple*
to be in a new Neil Simon play on Broadway, and as a surprise on his last
night, Clayton and Dan Dailey had hired a stripper from the nearby Rialto
Theatre to stand in the wings and hand him a suitcase he had to fetch offstage when Felix leaves in the play's final scene:

> Inedea Mann and her husband came at 10:45 and she undressed
> in Peter Boyle's dressing room. As Dick came off to pick up that gar-
> ment bag, she handed it to him as she opened the robe and WOW is
> she built. No pasties and no G-string—completely nude. Well, Dick
> took the bag and said thank-you. He is very near-sighted and she said
> hello and then he REALLY LOOKED. He said hello and then
> screamed OH MY GOD and went white in the face and had to have
> help finding his way back on stage. It was so funny.
>
> Later at my party we gave him his going away gift—a silk dressing
> gown with F.U. (Felix Ungar) as the initials in black. Dick saw it and
> then saw the initials and screamed. He said he bet the clerk in
> Brooks Brothers was a fag and after being requested to put F.U. as the
> initials on the pocket the clerk said, "Fine, in that case we should
> also embroider SHIT across the back."

Having made me laugh, Clayton ended the letter with one more set of instructions, ordering me not to cram in my classes—" 'Beowulf' is great and very enjoyable"—before adding, "If you feel low or anything, call me collect cause I'll cheat the show out of the cost."

Once I had reconciled myself to going to Cambridge, I corralled Sara into taking the train up from New York and meeting me. We faked some interest in the Harvard-Cornell game on Saturday afternoon, then ducked out of the after-game parties at my cousin's dorm, figured our way by subway into Boston, and found its Shubert Theatre downtown, where we bought tickets for a new tryout, about which we knew nothing, called *Cabaret*. The show's cast included Lotte Lenya—the widow of one of any Indian Hill camper's pet composers, Kurt Weill—and had opened so recently that no review had yet appeared in *Variety*.

We were energized by the show, which was confusing at first, then terrifying. Though racing to South Street Station to make sure Sara made the last train back to New York, we pulled out the *Playbill* to reconstruct what we'd seen. The ominous mood of *Cabaret* somehow reflected the unsettled atmosphere of that fall; it was set in Germany before World War II, and in one scene Nazis threw rocks through the window of a fruit store owned by a Jewish man. The sound of the broken glass was a shocking Act 1 climax for a Broadway musical. Instantly, Sara and I adopted a fatalistic line as our own catchphrase: "So life is disappointing—forget it!"

Once Sara had boarded her train, I reverted to dwelling on how much I missed Emily. It was impossible for me to call her late at night, and I was praying that she had received the special-delivery birthday card I'd sent on Friday. Folded into it as a present was a round-trip Chicago-Washington airline ticket that Joel had helped me purchase at a discount—I hoped it would ensure that she would visit me over Thanksgiving or Christmas.

Back in Washington the next morning, I ran up to the third floor to dial Emily's number in Chicago to make sure she'd received my card. Her mother picked up the phone, gave me what I thought was a frosty greeting, then called for Emily.

When she picked up the extension, she seemed to be crying. Or was she just whispering? I couldn't tell. The upshot was clear enough. She told me that my birthday present was the best she'd ever had—a miracle, she said.

Still, her mother might not give her permission to use it; she didn't say why.

I tried to find out more details, but Emily said that we should wait and see, things could change, and she had some good news to tell me about too. Her tone was not enthusiastic. Was her mother eavesdropping, or in the room? I couldn't tell, and I felt the fever of anxiety rising within me, making it almost impossible for me to listen.

My reaction to Emily's good news, as a result, was dulled; I was having trouble breathing. For the first time, she started telling me, she had felt confident in a school drama-club audition and had overcome her shy-ness—because, she said, of my faith in her. Now, to her astonishment, she had actually won the lead role in a school play. The part was that of Catherine Sloper in *The Heiress*, a Broadway hit of the 1940s. What Emily didn't say—and maybe she just didn't know it yet, as I didn't either, never having seen *The Heiress*—was that the play's story told of a refined young woman whose sole parent, a father, would rather destroy her than let her be with the ardent suitor she loved.

CHAPTER 4

Y ou do have a knack for vitriolic description," Clayton wrote after I
sent him a lengthy account of the battles of Wilson High School.
He was being generous, however, for I didn't have the wit to convey
the full fury of the civil war that had erupted during senior year. Whether
it was the insistent lapping of the flames of the civil rights movement, or
the fact that our new automotive mobility widened our circumference beyond the confines of upper Northwest, a growing number of us were awakening to the black Washington we'd seen mainly through car windows.
Jeremy and I infuriated our journalism teacher, Dr. Boyle, by proposing
that *The Beacon* run an editorial in favor of the District's having its own
elected government rather than continue being ruled by a committee of
racist white Southern congressmen. Dr. Boyle was firm: We'd run such an
editorial over her "dead body"—and it was her body that I described in
coarse detail in my letter to Clayton.

Some of our incentive for the editorial was selfish: Congress meted out
so little money to a public school system with a ninety-percent Negro student population that extracurricular activities, including a drama club,
were curtailed even in our otherwise privileged ninety-percent white Wilson, for fear of driving up after-school heating costs.

Maybe it was the music, too, that fired us up. Our dance music remained soul: Martha and the Vandellas, the Supremes, Smokey Robinson, the Four Tops, the Temptations, Percy Sledge, James Brown. And not just our dance music; Motown's rhythm, we instinctively knew, set the beat for our Saturday-night couplings, in backseats, in dens with all the lights turned off, in bedrooms when our parents were out.

Once we began to notice the rest of the city, we belatedly discovered that these musicians, unlike their British counterparts, were passing through Washington in person almost weekly. They played at the Howard Theatre at Seventh and T, right around the corner from the U Street Negro movie theaters I'd been to with Mom and Joel.

Could white teenagers just buy tickets and go to these concerts? There were rumors that some Wilson kids did, and there were also rumors of scuffles and switchblades when they did so. I was determined to go one night—in my case, not just because I wanted to see "When a Man Loves a Woman" sung in person but because the Howard was a theater of a type I'd never been to, a vaudeville house like those Mom had told me about, like those the mom in *Gypsy* barnstormed with her kids.

When James Brown was in town, we finally forged ahead—four boys and two girls piled into one car. We worried about looking conspicuous, which of course we did. We guarded our wallets zealously as we entered the lobby.

The crowd at the Howard was as black as Wilson was white. I recognized the sharp look of the young Negro men from Saturdays at Rich's: They were the will-call customers, out in force. But no one seemed to notice or care about us, and the atmosphere in the theater was too thick for anyone to upstage it: smoky and raucous. From our seats in the rear of the house we could enjoy a panoramic view of the whole scene: the tight, ritualistic choreography of the singing groups bathed in shifting, kaleidoscopic lights, the hard-driving horn players deployed like military platoons behind them, the screams of the crowd, who sometimes danced to the hit songs right at their seats. It was a euphoric Washington nightlife that had been here the whole time I had been starving for it, I realized, but which had been invisible in my Washington orbit. Not even the Man Who Owned Midnight on my radio ever talked about the Howard.

Mom and Joel, unlike most of my friends' parents, weren't afraid of the Unsafe Neighborhoods, as Negro Washington was called; they hadn't thought twice about moving into the city from Maryland almost a decade earlier, when middle-class white families were stampeding in the opposite direction. Though Mom had long ago stopped tutoring at Cardozo High, and Grandpa Herbert and Grandma Rose had curtailed their Sunday bill-collection outings, no one in my family was fearful of the other city. Joel regarded the ghetto at the very least as a fount of discounts on products from liquor to gas to first-run movie tickets. Still, we knew little about life in this Washington. Though virtually every one of our households had a Negro maid, we never saw our servants' homes as they saw ours. They came and went as we pleased, disappearing on their days off to who-knew-where.

On just one night was this unspoken etiquette breached. It was a Wednesday, and I was with Dad and Anadel and their kids at Grandma and Grandpa's. At the end of dinner this rainy night, Dad decided to drive Irene home, so she wouldn't have to wait for her usual D.C. Transit bus.

Irene had come to work for Grandma and Grandpa back when Dad was still a child. She was old and cranky now, a tiny woman with thick glasses, balding, with tufts of snow-white hair. When the dishes were done and it was time to leave, she wrapped herself in a torn old raincoat, placed one of those twenty-five-cent clear plastic pocket rain hats on her head, and stuffed the *Evening Star* sports section into her purse. For the first time, as we waited with Polly in the lobby for Dad to bring the station wagon to the front of the apartment house, I noticed that she seemed frail.

Irene rode in the front seat with Dad and gabbed on about the weather as we drove down unfamiliar streets into a neighborhood I wouldn't have been able to name. Her house was at the end of a quiet block and looked as tiny and bony as she was; it was dwarfed by its scruffy lot. To my surprise, she asked if Polly and I wanted to come see where she lived. "You'll be runnin' to college soon, Mr. Frank Junior," she said to me in her loud, sand-papery voice, still turned up to the volume she blasted toward Grandma Rose, "so this here could be your last chance."

We walked up the path to her door and waited while she struggled with her key. Once inside, Irene turned on a switch to reveal a square living room smaller than my compact bedroom on Cleveland Avenue. The light-ing was poor, casting the room into shadows.

Immediately I gravitated to the only wall that wasn't bare. It was deco-rated with framed artifacts, like a religious shrine. On one side was a framed portrait of President Kennedy, on the other, one of Martin Luther King, and a florid color painting of Jesus held the middle to complete the holy trinity. Given that Irene had always seconded my grandparents' vague Republicanism on those rare nights when politics surfaced while she was dishing out dinner, I was startled by the sacred Democratic images. But if Irene didn't entirely echo Rose and Herbert's views after all, her house was a letter-perfect embodiment of their taste. Everywhere around me, I real-ized, were the furnishings, from easy chairs to side tables to the tchotchkes of mass-produced chinoiserie, that had graced the Riches' apartment years earlier—all of them now as decrepit as their present and former owners. Seeing these relics in such an unlikely and unfamiliar setting didn't arouse fond memories so much as queasiness. What kind of existence had Irene lived each night, alone among these dim and soiled castoffs from Grandma and Grandpa? What did it say about me that I had never both-ered to find out?

———

Mrs. Kaufman changed her mind almost weekly as to whether Emily and I could see each other in either Chicago or Washington over either Thanksgiving or Christmas. Through Emily's eyes, my mother and Joel seemed like ideal parents, especially with her limited knowledge of them, all of it benign. Sometimes I found myself sharing her perspective. Maybe I had it lucky after all, as Mom always told me. Each barometric downturn of Mrs. Kaufman's unpredictable emotional weather left us distraught— for Emily and I had invested all our hopes for happiness in seeing each other, much as I had once put all my hope in visits to the theater. Emily tried to avoid the subject of her mother's whims in her letters whenever she could. Her expectations from life were, if anything, lower than mine. She wrote that she felt good only on rainy days, because only in contrast to an overcast sky could she think of herself as relatively sunny.

I tried to keep myself busy with the new David Merrick musical tryout at the National, *I Do! I Do!*—a two-character show uniting two of my favorite surrogate parents from childhood: Mary Martin, of *Peter Pan*, and Robert Preston, who had played the Music Man. Yet the ache of missing Emily, the desire to nuzzle her, to walk down a street holding her hand, was so intense that following the show's progress from the back of the house didn't offer its usual distraction. Or was the problem that the stars seemed older, no longer as lithe as I remembered now that they were clearly middle-aged? Or was it that a show with only two people in it exuded loneliness, or that its story, of a happy marriage spanning decades, bore so little resemblance to marriage as I had observed it? If Mary Martin's voice in *South Pacific* had once been inseparable in my mind from Mom and the records we first listened to together in Somerset, now they diverged. The woman onstage still radiated the exhilaration of "I'm in Love with a Wonderful Guy." Mom's exuberance had clouded over, reemerging only in odd moments when she still got caught up in our shared enthusiasm for a play or a museum or a book, or when she doted on what I could tell her of my romantic adventures in Chicago.

As for Mom's own marriage, I knew there was nothing I could do but stay out of its way; her and Joel's union was a runaway train that mowed down anything in its path, from the immediate family to innocent bystanders like waiters and Joel's constantly changing law partners. Not even a temporary uncoupling could diminish the wreckage. When Joel went away alone on business trips to Stockholm or London or Frankfurt for a couple of days, he would call every half hour, it often seemed, to bark orders concerning his return. And Mom would either resist, slamming down the phone in tears, or comply maniacally—helping Willie Mae cook his first-night-home dinner a day in advance, just in case he walked through the front door earlier than expected (as he often did). She was never at peace.

In Joel's absence, Mom also had to contend with John. He was spending more time than ever at our house in lieu of his mother's, but he was more specter than presence. He seemed to have no friends. The phone never rang for him. When the rest of us tried to engage him in conversation, he was aloof, replying to any question with monosyllables, vacant pauses, and enigmatic smiles. I'd watch Mom try to engage him as she always tried to engage me and Polly—turning the subject to books or movies he might be interested in or could be interested in, trying to mask her concern about him with a patina of empathic banter and light laughter—but to no avail. Though he was polite to Mom, humoring her as vaguely as he could, all the while he was steadily inching away until he could make his escape. Where he escaped to was unknown. When Joel returned from his travels, he'd lash out at John on general principle, but even a sharp slamming against the wall failed to rouse a response.

In the end, Mrs. Kaufman lacked Joel's ability to punish: She decided to allow Emily and me our Thanksgiving rendezvous in Chicago, though once again she didn't invite me to stay in her apartment. I was more than happy to stay with Clayton, and it felt as if I'd never been away. His digs at 14 West Elm were my home away from home, and he was glad to entertain Emily and me at dinner at the Italian Village or Punchinello's any night we cared to, after his chores were done at the Blackstone. He showed us photographs of him that had run in the *Chicago Daily News*, and they looked impossibly glamorous: The paper had paid him to model the Cardin suits he had made to order in New York. "They are a little *much* for Chicago," he observed, "but these hicks can go to hell as far as I'm concerned." Clayton added the modeling money to the savings he was using to buy Christmas presents for the entire *Odd Couple* company, for his friends stretching from Chicago to Berlin, for his mother, and even for his distant father. It seemed that people loved him wherever he went, and Emily and I wanted more than anything to be counted among his prime acolytes.

Though it was hard to say good night to Emily after our kisses outside her apartment house each night, the walk back to Elm Street wasn't dispiriting. For the first time in my life I was certain that someone who cared for me would be waiting up for me when I came home. Clayton lived the life I had long aspired to live, and he was teaching me, I thought, how to live it. He stayed up watching TV or listening to records or just talking as late as he wanted; if he didn't or couldn't get to sleep until dawn, it didn't matter, as long as he was at the theater for that night's performance. Though we always kept an eye on the late movie, we just as often ignored it as we talked on; we never ran out of subjects to discuss, from the theater to parents to Emily.

The conversation never let up. Once I was back home in Washington, and depressed again, Clayton communicated with me as no one ever had, not even Mom. He would rescue me from halfway across the country:

Dear Pal Frank:

It rains. It's about noon at the theatre. The rain comes down in big fat drops and makes lots of noise. It's sort of nice to sit here and listen to it. After I finish this I think I shall practice the piano for awhile.

Your letter, as all of them, was very welcome. You know that your "big brother" will be glad to listen to whatever you want to talk over.

Don't worry too much about feeling confused about things. It's a rotten way to feel but that's what happens in this life. What's happening? Frank, until we next sit down and really talk, let it ride. Things do work themselves out and give the problem a chance to be looked at in the perspective it deserves. Its all perfectly normal and the first of probably many problems of similar nature. Just hang on to YOU. The rest will take care of itself.

Frank, being seventeen is just about the toughest thing in the world. Compound that with brains and sensitivity and it's absolute hell at times. I DO know how you feel and I DO understand. But after you talk it out it doesn't seem so difficult anymore. Now I shall go play for awhile, and try and forget where, who and what I am.

Stay well, and for God's sake, keep studying. There is plenty of time for settling down and going steady. But you won't be good for anyone until you are good for yourself. That means a degree and a life ahead of you. (END OF SPEECH. . . . SLOW CURTAIN.)

Emily was able to overcome another set of her mother's objections and visited me in Washington only weeks later, at Christmas. But as soon as she was back home, I received a letter from Clayton about his Christmas in Chicago, and it was as if I had contaminated him with my sour mood. He had lost his temper with his friend Pat when she told him over the phone about her careless delay in filing for unemployment once her *How to Succeed* acting job had ended, and she had become very upset. "There is no fighting a woman's tears," he wrote. "Man is useless against them. I'm sending her 20 bucks a week to help her out." Though he was happy that all his holiday gifts to his friends in Europe had arrived on time, he had no one to open his own presents with. On Christmas morning, he took them over to a Chicago friend's so that he wouldn't have to unwrap them alone. Later in the afternoon, he "reflected much on the blessings that I have" before throwing a company dinner in the Pump Room, "with goose, string beans, red cabbage, stuffing, sweet potatoes and flaming plum pudding with good Bordeaux, and Champagne with dessert." It was both "very, very elegant and a drunken brawl—that's my company, God love 'em." Later still he ended up playing the grand piano in his friends' twenty-ninth-floor apartment with the magical view of Lake Michigan.

For all that was on Clayton's mind, he still took the time to respond to a school paper I'd reluctantly sent him at his urging, about *Cabaret*. He encouraged me to keep up my writing: "Please send that carbon back if it's an extra copy," he wrote, and "be sure and buy S. J. Perelman's new book—he is a master of the English language."

It upset me when Clayton wrote that he was down. I wanted to make him feel better just as he made me feel better, and I didn't know how. Emily's letters, meanwhile, became less frequent. I was sure she was seeing someone else—a millionaire boy at Latin, no doubt.

Clayton told me to stop moping:

> You have the good fortune to possess a healthy body and an extraordinary mind. Have you any idea where these two things can take you in life? You aren't even ready to begin yet, so cool it. Wait till you think about our exchange of letters when you are 25 or so. As far as Emily goes, maybe you aren't the only one with problems. Many times in the future Frank you are going to have to take loved ones only on faith and you may as well start learning now. Don't sell her short. Wait for reasons.

He was right about Emily, I came to realize soon enough. "The reason I'm very slow to write," she wrote at last, "is because I've been very depressed within myself and I really was afraid to put that self down on paper. I don't realize sometimes that by shutting myself and all my problems and worries off from the people (the one person!) I love the most, I hurt them."

When I asked her why she felt this way, she sounded like me—she didn't really know how she could be so sad even though she was in love, school was going fine, and her play was a success.

> I don't know exactly what is troubling me. Really, the whole thing is undefinable and that's another reason why I couldn't put my thoughts down in a letter.
>
> I want to discuss everything with you. The only thing that stopped me was a feeling that my thoughts were unintelligible and therefore better kept inside.
>
> I love you so much that I'm afraid of what will happen—I'm afraid to face it if it comes and so I'm facing it now, which is wrong. We've just spent two months in English on the Romantic poets. Well, you might call me a wayward Romantic because I always feel beauty not only dies but becomes grotesque. The trouble with me is that I forget that you should enjoy and preserve what beauty there is. I don't even forget, I just feel unable to. As far as dating goes, I just never expected to meet anyone like you, I guess.
>
> Mom has the best intentions but I have become positively withdrawn from her, and everyone in this house. And unwillingly now I find that it's happening with you too. There's a real irony because you're the person I want to share EVERYTHING with now.
>
> I have a lot of worries that probably are unfounded and exaggerated but that I feel I have to bear myself. Heavens, it's awfully lonely.

Clayton had told Emily to call or to visit him at the theater if she needed him in my absence, but she didn't believe him; she couldn't imagine that any adult could ever really care about her. Finally, she went to see him at my urging, but when she showed up at the Blackstone, it turned out to be a night he wasn't working. "Anyway it was exciting just to see the house filling up, with anxious customers in line for cancellations," she wrote in another disconsolate letter. If only I could leave school and run to her in Chicago—but I knew that Clayton would object to my dereliction of responsibility as much as my parents would.

My sole distraction was the growing ruckus at Wilson, where we trig-
gered the confrontation we'd been gunning for: Our editorial in favor of
D.C. Home Rule, and an accompanying interview with a young civil
rights worker from the South who was "organizing" the ghetto near the
Howard Theater, had both been banned by the principal, prompting us to
publish our two forbidden articles in an "underground" newspaper that
was really just a two-sided mimeographed sheet. With relish, Joel turned
over his K Street office to the Wilson renegades, letting us stay there until
four A.M. to use his electric typewriters, copiers, and postal meters to further our cause. Within twenty-four hours, a *Washington Post* reporter was
enticing us to sneak out of school for a lunch-hour interview. Her account,
complete with picture, on the front page of the City Life section got radio
and TV into the act, which in turn motivated the principal to call us into
his office one by one to ask if we had been smoking marijuana. When the
Inquisition failed, he went into full retreat. We at last were able to print in
The Beacon the editorial and our interview with the storefront organizer,
Marion Barry, ending the Wilson civil wars just in time for us to receive
our college admission letters and begin our final lap to graduation and the
prom.

The victory seemed hollow without Emily to share it with. Her letters
were few and remote. She had decided that rather than risk stirring up her
mother, she'd withhold until the last moment the news that I was flying to
Chicago for the first weekend of spring vacation; I'd stay with Clayton anyway, so what could her mother do about it? When Emily belatedly did reveal our plans, Mrs. Kaufman was furious.

Emily wrote special-delivery: "Sometimes I wonder why, when I am so
successful at predicting my mother's reactions, I am such a failure when it
comes to preventing their disastrous effects. It's sort of like a tornado in a
way—they know it's coming but can't stop it." She told me that I should
not call her, because her mother might forbid her to talk to me or eavesdrop, but that she would take a purseful of coins to the library and call me
from there to make clandestine plans for my visit. She was afraid her
mother wouldn't let me see her at all now.

Clayton told me not to worry: He'd help us find a way to see each other;
he'd meet me at the airport if Emily couldn't. "I am so sorry to hear about

Emily and the hell she is being put through," he wrote. "I cannot pretend to understand what causes her mother to act like this. I only hope that she gets over it soon and leaves Emily alone."

But in Clayton's letters, I detected the same inconsolable note I found in Emily's. "I sort of feel that if there is more than 10 weeks left here for this company it would surprise me," he wrote, and he wasn't sure what he wanted to do next. "Life goes on here and I save my dough. I should finish here with five thou, which isn't too bad. This summer I hope for Europe for a brief vacation. Why not come along? Ask your folks for a thou for graduation. We could go to Paris, Florence, Rome, Berlin and London. Give it some thought. It's permissible to dream. Boy, would you flip over those cities."

I didn't have the heart to tell Clayton that my parents wouldn't let me go away; I was expected to earn money for college over the summer, not spend it. But I didn't want to disappoint him—he had given Emily and me so much.

He wrote of his own loneliness now, for the first time in a letter written with his fountain pen and not banged out on the typewriter.

My wonderful Diana left the show last nite. I took her to the airport for the one a.m. plane to New York. I miss her very, very much and it is so hard to say goodbye to those one loves—I guess what I am doing is sitting here feeling alone, unloved and sorry for myself. EQUALS STUPID! I'm afraid I have too much the Hungarian in me but only at times, Thank God. Have Prokofiev ALEXANDER NEVSKY on the phonograph.

Oh, what a shitty day! I think much lately of Berlin—I wonder how the people I know and love are. It is not good to think too much. Also this stupid "alone and unnecessary and unloved" feeling is for the birds. There are times I am angry at me for allowing such thoughts.

From Washington, I wrote Clayton how much I missed him, and that I would be in Chicago soon, and that Emily and I would insist on taking *him* to dinner. It was, I knew, an inadequate response.

When spring vacation arrived at long last, Mrs. Kaufman once again reversed herself: I could see her daughter as much as I wanted, within reason, though of course I would stay at 14 West Elm.

Emily's friends at Latin, like mine at Wilson, were nervous about college admissions; the arrival of letters of acceptance or rejection was only a week or so away. In the end, though, Mrs. Kaufman had limited Emily's applications to schools in the Midwest, and Emily had applied so late she didn't know when she'd hear.

She didn't seem to care that much. Her usual personality, a delicate interplay of poise and playful warmth and shyness, threatened to evaporate into catatonia when we were alone together; I'd never seen her so distracted, with worry lines cracking the planes of her Modigliani madonna's face.

One night we decided to take a chance on a sneak preview at the Esquire Theatre on Oak Street, and were rewarded with a movie by Mike Nichols, who had directed the film version of *Who's Afraid of Virginia Woolf?* a year earlier. Knowing nothing about the movie from its title or unknown cast—it wasn't opening for months—we soon discovered that it was the story of an alienated college student who, over the summer after his graduation, is forbidden by her parents to see the girl he loves. The movie was funny, with a soundtrack of our favorite Simon and Garfunkel songs, but as we left the theater to meet Clayton for dinner, the warm spring air and our enthusiasm for what we'd seen propelling us toward Michigan Avenue, Emily was distracted and gloomy. Her mother could wreck things at any moment; we could love each other only on borrowed or stolen time. In my mind, Emily blurred with the heroine of *The Graduate*, who looked not unlike her, and I wondered how I could fill the role of the boyfriend who loves her so much he kidnaps her from her parents rather than let her be suffocated by them.

We met Clayton at the Blackstone Hotel, right near the theater. He knew the pianist in its lounge and, as a surprise for us, had brought him the sheet music of "Hurry! It's Lovely Up Here!," a Broadway song of a couple of years earlier that had become, for the three of us, a private touchstone of hope. In the show it came from, *On a Clear Day You Can See Forever*, the heroine, a sexy but lost young woman, sang it to a flowerpot, trying to make the seed she had planted grow by the miracle of extrasensory perception:

> *Come up and see the hoot we're giving*
> *Come on and see the grounds for living . . .*
> *Hurry, it's lovely up here!*

"It's such a good number and ends so *up* and so strong," Clayton had told me when he first discovered it. "It's virtually impossible to hear it and not just feel wonderful no matter how low you may be." He put it on his record player every day when he dressed to go to work, he said, and left his apartment singing and high.

Now Emily and I were serenaded by its infectious melody as we entered the bar. We immediately spotted Clayton, crowned by a ceiling light, his golden brow wreathed by cigarette smoke, toasting us with a glass of Champagne. Emily was, for the moment, back to what I hoped was her normal self, our magical chaperon's radiance rubbing off on her as it always did on me. After we drank our own glasses of Champagne, we headed to the Italian Village for a late supper. Clayton and I talked at a galloping pace; Emily smiled all the way; our romantic universe was restored.

The next night was my last in town. Discreetly bowing out so that his lovesick young charges could be alone, Clayton had secured us passes to the road company of *Fiddler*, which had just opened at the McVickers, a few blocks from the Shubert. He had friends in the cast and also knew the wardrobe mistress, who had made for him a couple of the cossack shirts he admired among its costumes.

Variety had reported two weeks earlier that, in its 130th week, the Broadway production of *Fiddler* had ceased to be SRO, with empty box seats at some matinees. I pictured the Majestic Theatre—to which *Fiddler* had moved from the Imperial—and couldn't help thinking of the same theater's empty seats at that Christmas-week matinee when I saw Mary Martin in *Jennie*. I had foolishly imagined that *Fiddler* would never play to empty seats, and it struck me as a blow that it did now. Empty houses of any kind, I was beginning to see, held a terror for me. I wondered if Tanya Everett and John C. Attle were still in the cast in New York, and I wondered what it felt like for them to be on the stage for the first time when seats went begging on beautiful spring afternoons.

In Chicago, the turnout was much worse than in my mental picture of *Fiddler* on Broadway. The McVickers was a dreary old barn of a vaudeville palace that had been converted to movies and now, in a hasty and undignified rehabilitation, into a makeshift legitimate theater. There was no air of expectation in the audience, which at most filled up half the orchestra floor around Emily and me. I imagined the night's count, with all its stacks of deadwood.

Emily didn't seem to notice, but I could think of nothing else, and the listlessness of the cast only deepened my mood. Involuntarily, I was hit with that pang, that sense of loss, that had first washed over me at *Damn Yankees* a lifetime ago at the National. Nothing beautiful that happens onstage can last. Every show must close. There can be no love, not even in the theater, without grief.

—

The day that college acceptances were expected to arrive in the mail, Joel drove me down to the Cleveland Park post office on Connecticut Avenue and, flashing every I.D. at his disposal, browbeat an intimidated clerk into giving us our mail before it went out for delivery by the postman—a feat I had never imagined possible. I tore through the thick white envelope from Harvard as soon as it was handed to me, and my own excitement was almost overwhelmed by Joel's. Big and leaden of foot as he was, he seemed to break into a jig right there, and though we were only a five-minute drive from home, he convinced the same put-upon clerk to let him use the post-office phone to call Mom with the news—after which he went ahead and tied up the phone with a call to his secretary to check for messages.

"Your mother is very proud of you, and so am I!" he shouted as we headed back to his double-parked car. "And you must call your father as soon as you get home," he added with uncharacteristic magnanimity.

I was happy not because I knew much about Harvard beyond the romantic notions an Indian Hill creative-writing teacher had instilled in me—the very notion of a "good school" was an oxymoron in my experience—but because of my dawning realization that I might, in fact, be leaving Washington for the foreseeable future. I called my father and Anadel with the news, and then Emily, and then Clayton, who, to my amazement, told me that he had already heard—for Joel had phoned New York theater friends on the other line, who'd immediately phoned Clayton.

Joel's enthusiasm, which seemed even greater than Mom's, was puzzling. He hated the Establishment and had no respect for the Ivy League–educated lawyers he did battle with. There was some part of his thinking, clearly, that was invisible to me. Was his happiness about my admission to Harvard some manifestation of this love Mom always insisted he had for me and Polly, but just didn't show "in the same way that other people do"? The power of Harvard as an elixir was apparently so potent that it intoxicated Mrs. Kaufman too. Her objections to our plans to attend each other's proms evaporated overnight. Emily could come to Washington for my prom, and I would not only be welcome in Chicago for Emily's but could stay—amazingly enough, after all our previous travails—at the Kaufmans' apartment.

That was a relief, for though *The Odd Couple* was still eking out its existence in Chicago, Clayton thought it unlikely he'd stay through the spring. The actors he loved in the company were all gone, and he described a loneliness that I couldn't imagine befalling anyone in the theater, least of all him:

Today is beautiful, warm and sunny and I haven't got any summer clothes. It is about 1 PM Friday and after I write to you I shall go to the pit and practice a little Bach for a while. It hasn't been the greatest week ever and between low grosses and boredom I've been really down. But I bought a new KLH stereo—so long 300 bucks—and I play Chopin nocturnes before I sleep.

Remember the Blackstone bar, where they played HURRY for you and Emily? I went back, and Joe the player there played Chopin, Mike (the player from the Royal Hunt Room) played Liszt, his wife and I played and we stayed until 2 a.m. playing all this great music. All the waiters came out in their civilian clothes to listen. All the guests had gone and the bar was closed.

He insisted that we celebrate my graduation face-to-face, and we set a date for mid-May, when I'd fly up on a pass as soon as I had finished the count at the National's Saturday matinee and spend the night in New York before returning to Washington on Sunday in time for graduation week.

When the big day arrived, I took the bus from La Guardia into the East Side terminal, then caught the bus up First Avenue to Clayton's much-talked-about home at 405 East Sixty-third Street, a modern apartment building taking up much of a quiet block by the East River. Clayton's apartment had a bedroom and a living room, much like 14 West Elm, though it had a grand piano and was far neater and more brightly decorated, in pastel shades of chintz.

As soon as I arrived, we went out again. Clayton hailed a cab to take us to another modern apartment building, at Sixty-ninth Street and Lexington Avenue, where his parents lived. His mother greeted us there—a tiny fist of a woman, elegantly dressed, with a tight, fastidious hairdo. She looked nothing like Clayton, I thought. The apartment, decorated with antiques, wasn't large, but Mrs. Coots fit my idea of a New York woman of wealth. She spoke to Clayton and me alike in a formal, even stiff, manner, revealing little of her own life and referring to Clayton's father in the past tense as if he were dead—when in fact, I soon discovered, he was merely "at the club."

Within minutes, Clayton and I were on our way again, in another cab, to his neighborhood place, Eduardo's, an Italian restaurant nestled by the Fifty-ninth Street Bridge. The waiters greeted him as jocularly as those in the Italian Village in Chicago did, and the usual Chianti appeared at once, along with the food that Clayton always chose, impeccably, on my behalf.

If I bored him with my lengthy monologue about Emily, her troubles with her mother, and our divided fate come fall, when I'd be in Boston and she'd be at college in Madison, Wisconsin, he didn't let on. He was sympathetic but kept reiterating: "Kid—just remember you're only seventeen—I know, almost eighteen—and it will take care of itself." He was the same ebullient Clayton I knew from Chicago, except when the subject turned to the war. In his last week on *The Odd Couple*, fifty Vietnam vets had come to see the show as guests of the management, and Clayton and the company had gone out with them afterward. He spoke of how much he admired these men, and since he knew I was skeptical, he said that as my "big brother" he felt I should support those who were fighting in the war through no fault of their own. "I don't know about other teenagers— you're the only one I'm concerned with—but I don't want you to forget about these guys. You know that if you were in their place, I'd go for any- one's throat who forgot you."

Soon we were on our way back to his apartment, talking about happier things all the way; he told me of his European travel plans, no longer men- tioning his invitation that I join him. At home, he flipped on a late movie just as he used to do in Chicago, cracking jokes at every juncture, until we both started to yawn.

Clayton stood up from the couch, arching his long back like a cat, and said, "You know, we're not at Fourteen West Elm anymore, thank God, and I have my own big bed here. If you want to take half of it, you don't have to sleep on the couch, and I'm such a sound sleeper that you'll never know I'm there."

I felt a tiny, distant alarm. My mind flashed back to the question Joel had initially raised about Clayton, never to mention it again. I hadn't pic- tured what homosexuals did—I didn't know any, as far as I knew—but I figured that whatever it was they did, they did it in bed. Clayton had all these girlfriends; surely they wouldn't be his girlfriends if he was queer. And yet Clayton loved me, and I loved him, and if he was a homosexual, did he mean something different by "big brother" than I thought? Did ho- mosexuals have another language that I didn't understand?

I didn't know, and I didn't want to know—not if it meant that I would have to think less of Clayton or of myself. I was less afraid of his trying to be homosexual with me than I was afraid of learning he had been keeping a secret from me. And if he was homosexual, I would hate having to say no and hurting him. I would rather die, I felt, than reject the man who had taken me into the theater and given me shelter. Did that mean I should *not* reject him? Would it hurt me so much to do something he wanted and that I couldn't understand?

Maybe his offer of his bed was entirely innocent; I was uncertain and didn't want to risk finding out otherwise. As my questions tumbled on top of one another in my mind during the pause after his invitation, I marshalled the most casual tone I could affect and said, No, the couch is fine, I'll be comfortable there, and anyway he deserved to have his bed to himself. Whether Clayton read anything more into my answer, whether he saw it as a rejection anyway, I couldn't tell. I could only hope he didn't. His tone, at least, remained unchanged as we made up the couch, just like we used to do back at 14 West Elm.

———

School ended in a haze: of beer and punch bowls full of purple sangria and *Sgt. Pepper's Lonely Hearts Club Band*, which came out that June week, just as I turned eighteen. The senior class floated from house to house, in Chanukah Heights and beyond, drinking all the while, Lucy in the Sky with Diamonds no matter where we were, for no other song could usurp her. Our last—some might say most demanding—intellectual activity at Woodrow Wilson High was decoding the *Sgt. Pepper* album cover, the dense collage of faces on the front, the elliptical poetry of the lyrics on the back. For once, there was no Cliffs Notes.

"Now they know how many holes it takes to fill the Albert Hall," sang the Beatles. What did it mean?, I wondered. Had Lennon and McCartney known empty houses of their own?

When Emily made her trip east for the Wilson prom, my friends all thought she lived up to my starry-eyed and no doubt tiresome descriptions of her. They joked that our regal appearance in tux and gown was just a prelude to a wedding, but we didn't think that was a joke at all; such was the future we saw before us.

The Chicago Latin prom followed soon after. I wanted to give Emily a graduation present, but she wrote asking me not to: "My father used to send us presents from Phoenix on important occasions, and for me— because he was my father—they really became a substitute (and a happy one, because I was little) for him and his love. When the gifts stopped, I thought his love did too but actually there wasn't much to begin with." She was more uncertain than I was about the future but had trouble explaining why: "Please forgive me for this letter. I know it doesn't make too much sense, but I'm trying not to close up yet." She thought it might be best if she didn't write at all, "because nobody can really comprehend my fragmented means of communications."

Yet her mood had lightened considerably by the time I arrived in Chicago, and her prom was a nightlong party that flowed from dinner in the nautical setting of the Cape Cod Room at the Drake Hotel to the ballroom at the Chicago Hilton in the Loop, not far from the Blackstone, where *The Odd Couple* had now entered its "final weeks" minus most of the original company and Clayton.

At the Cape Cod Room, we toasted our friend and guardian. It was strange to be at a restaurant in Chicago without him, and we missed him. But many hours later, he was forgotten as we stood with other senior-class couples and awaited sunrise on the Oak Street beach, a few blocks from the Kaufmans' apartment. Emily and I kissed and then kissed again, telling each other in every pause that nothing could get in the way of our love, until finally the sun was high and the bustle of daybreak in the city towering behind us grew too insistent to be denied.

———

Washington seemed even emptier in summer than usual. With my graduating class scattered, Emily out of reach at a summer term in Wisconsin, Mom and Joel and Clayton all in Europe, I shuttled mechanically between home and the National and Rich's, where I worked longer hours to augment my savings for school. The National had a shopworn bus-and-truck company of the musical that had given Emily, Clayton, and me our favorite song, but "Hurry! It's Lovely Up Here!" was at the top of the show, and I heard at most muffled snippets of it in the count-up room. It only made me miss Chicago more than I already did.

One night during the next booking—a dance troupe called Les Ballets Africains that played to houses as sparse as the one in which I'd first seen *A Funny Thing Happened on the Way to the Forum*—Mr. Kirkpatrick asked me if I was free on Sunday evening, his one night off; he wanted to have a drink to congratulate me on my admission to Harvard and to mark my parting from the National.

I was taken aback; he was such a distant and unapproachable figure about anything except ticket-taking matters that it surprised me he even knew what college I was going to. I'd never had so much as a cup of coffee in the office with him.

The following Sunday at five-thirty, I drove to the address he gave me, an apartment building on Thomas Circle, an anonymous part of the city midway between Cleveland Park and downtown. When I rang his door-bell, he greeted me in his usual white summer suit, minus only the jacket with its boutonniere. Speaking in his slow, stuttering drawl, he offered me a Coke and then a seat on the couch.

I hadn't known where Mr. Kirkpatrick lived; I hadn't imagined him liv-ing anywhere. Now, as he poured our soft drinks, I looked around as in-conspicuously as I could. There wasn't much to see. The walls were spotlessly white, the uncarpeted blond-wood floor shiny with varnish, the few pictures as generic as framed prints in a motel room. The furniture was also glossy, for each piece was upholstered in clear vinyl, just as in my Rich grandparents' apartment. The room was bright and transient, as if no one lived there and, perhaps, no one ever would; it looked like a freshly built theatrical set still awaiting its first use by a cast. Mr. Kirkpatrick's home was the antithesis of his office at the National, which was dark and freighted with history—a cave that seemed to hold the locked secrets of a lost civilization.

Once he lowered himself into the chair beside the couch, we had a conversation as stilted as always, though he made a halting effort to inquire about Harvard and my plans. I noticed that the standing lamp next to his elbow still had a price tag hanging from its vinyl-wrapped shade and, as I glanced across the living room, found that the same was true of the lamp's twin.

When our conversation flickered out, I stood up to thank him and say goodbye, and stammered myself as I tried to say, in words that he would not find mortifying, what it had meant for me to work at his theater.

"There will, ahm, always be a spot for you at the second door," Mr. Kirkpatrick said once I'd finished, and I realized that this was his way of saying he was sorry to see me go. Then he gave me the same phantom handshake, more a graze than a shake, that he had on the first day he pulled me out of the ticket line in the lobby and, I thought, changed my life forever.

—

Joel pulled out all the stops in orchestrating my arrival at Harvard. He arranged free shipping for my trunk on one of his airlines so that Mom and I could fly directly to Boston rather than make the long drive from Washington. Once I was in Cambridge and had found my room, Mom took me to the Coop in Harvard Square to stock up on school supplies, notebooks and pens and pads, just as we had always done in Somerset and Rosemary Hills and Cleveland Park—and at Grandpa Nat's old paper-goods warehouse before I had ever gone to school. She was as gay as I'd ever seen her, as hungry for the education that lay ahead of me as I was, if not more so. "I wish I could just stay here and take all these courses myself," she said, her eyes misting with enthusiasm. "You have to send me every reading list the professors give you so I can do all the reading too." I said that of course I would, and hugged her.

When we were done, and the afternoon was waning, and I could feel the pull of a new life actually beginning, I walked her to a cab in the Square. She checked to make sure that she had her shuttle pass in her purse, which was almost as crowded with miscellany as Joel's jacket pockets. Next to the cabstand was the Harvard Square newsstand, which I had already determined was open twenty-four hours—an unheard-of phenomenon in Washington and, to me, a sign that I was at last living in a place where there were others who couldn't fall asleep, who feared the night, who needed every weapon they could find to fight the terror of being truly alone.

Bubbling with excitement for me, talking in a rush of how she couldn't wait to tell Joel everything she had seen on my first day at college, Mom got into the cab to return to the airport. She was on her way to being a stout middle-aged woman, I noticed; she was going gray.

I leaned down and kissed her and thanked her. As the cab pulled away, I waved goodbye.

I watched the cab drive down the street and out of view, heading for Storrow Drive. I knew that Mom missed me, and I knew I would miss her, but not now, not just yet. I gave the man at the newsstand a coin for *The Boston Globe*, opened up to the theater page, and checked my watch. The

Shubert, where Sara and I had seen *Cabaret* a year earlier, had an eight-thirty curtain, and it didn't matter what the current show was, that I had seen it before and hadn't particularly liked it, because I knew I would be at home there, even or perhaps especially if I was alone. Mom understood this; maybe she had from the beginning, from the time she had let me into her own solitary haunt, the Phillips. I knew she'd delight in all the details when I phoned her tomorrow. This shared passion was her gift to me. When, a couple of hours later, I got off the MTA at Tremont Street, I seemed to float down the hill to the theater on sheer anticipation, possessed by all the possibilities of the world that were mine at last.

'd succeeded in avoiding Washington during my first college Christmas
break, choosing instead to fly to Miami Beach in the tow of a freshman
roommate from Coral Gables. I was hungry to luxuriate in the laughter
of Grandma Lil and the deadpan sarcasm of Grandpa Nat, now that they
had retired to the chlorine and condos of Collins Avenue. At my insistence, Nat drove us past the movie palace where once upon a time I'd seen
Around the World in 80 Days. Its buzzing and blinking marquee had
lapsed into silence, for "the nice part of the beach," as Lil put it, had long
since migrated uptown, much as Washington's downtown was trickling
piece by piece into Maryland and Virginia.

From Miami it was on to Chicago, and New Year's Eve with Emily. We
were slipping away from each other now, as inexorably as Chicago itself
had cast off its romantic spring and summer for the deep freeze of winter.
No matter how hard I tried, I couldn't leap across the gulf that separated
us—a distance no longer of geography. Away from her mother on the large
Wisconsin campus full of strangers, Emily had become reclusive. Her letters had trailed off into a vague inertia, as if she were seeing her own experience at college through a fog that blurred its edges, draining it of color

and feeling. My letters had threatened to trail off altogether. I now lived in
a town where half my contemporaries seemed to stay up all night and were
glad to have me join them. The closer we got to dawn, the more of our past
we left behind.

As Emily and I had first met in one of the hottest Chicago summers on
record, so we would part in one of its coldest winters. The punishing
weather wouldn't allow us to kiss in front of her apartment house or retrace
our path to Punchinello's on Rush Street. The Drake no longer seemed
the airy prom-week beach pavilion of June but a bleak fortress presiding
over boulevards emptied of cars and pedestrians by the angry winds whip-
ping off the lake.

It would be another two decades before I'd see Emily again—and only
once, and only by chance. By then, she had escaped her mother by a difficult path that had taken her out of college and far from Chicago's North
Side. Her beauty and her wide, expectant smile were as I remembered
them. She was like an exquisite, fragile figurine preserved intact from another era, and whatever bruises she might have suffered in the intervening
years had been ingeniously masked by delicate repairs that might be visible only if you held them up to the light.

When my first spring break arrived, I still didn't want to go home, but
my college friends had scattered from Cambridge and some of the old
Wilson crowd had threatened a reunion. There might be opportunities to
snuggle up to a girl from Chanukah Heights late at night and, adrift in beer
or grass, pick up the melody we had left off at graduation. True, there were
already new girls for me in Boston, one of whom I thought in some wistful
moments I might marry, though the idea of fidelity struck me as a non sequitur. Girls in brassieres and black mesh stockings, women who would
come to me in the flesh as well as in my dreams, had to be stockpiled,
should I ever be left alone at night once more.

As soon as I returned to Washington on that late afternoon in April, the
old pall fell upon me. National Airport seemed as tomblike as it was on that
day when Mom had first taken Polly and me there for our flight to Miami.

Joel picked me up as usual, a pipe hanging from his bearded mouth, his
car parked defiantly adjacent to the gate in a loading dock with a sign that
read FOR AUTHORIZED PERSONNEL ONLY.

At home, Willie Mae was at her post in the kitchen, cooking dinner. Mom was out just then, but had set an elegant table in the dining room, with candlesticks and the good china and crystal wine goblets and cloth napkins in silver rings. This was not a job she delegated to Willie Mae. My homecoming, I recognized, was being treated as an adult dinner party, and I could see Mom's optimism in the shimmering place settings, bravely set out on the premise that no plan this lovely could be disrupted by Joel.

There was a vacant spot where John usually sat. He had been removed as yearbook editor at Wilson a few weeks earlier, after he took to sabotaging official photos by injecting himself into them in strange costumes and insolent facial expressions. He had an illness now, and it would take him to Shepard Pratt in Baltimore, where Joel's sister, Selma, had lived and died. It was an open question whether he would be out in time or in any condition to enter Pomona, the California college that had accepted him for the fall.

I climbed up to my bedroom on the third floor. Mom had "neatened it up," she had warned me, though, she'd quickly added, "I haven't thrown anything out." She knew I had inherited her habit of holding on to old magazines and newspapers and letters. My yellowing *Variety*s were still in stacks on my bookshelves, and so were the mounds of *Playbills*. The bulletin board that once served as my personal Broadway marquee now leaned in a corner, stripped naked of its memorabilia, which Mom had tucked away in manila folders as tenderly as she had her own scrapbook of her childhood visit to New York. Books—the books I had cradled and slept with and held on to like life preservers—were everywhere. They didn't hold the meaning they once had. They were childhood friends I'd left behind for a newer, faster crowd.

I called around, looking to corral some Wilson cronies. Then I phoned Mr. Kirkpatrick. I was embarrassed to impose myself on him so soon after our formal goodbye of only months earlier, but the road company of *Cabaret* was at the National. An hour in Washington, and already the urge had returned to be at the theater, alone and unencumbered, to take tickets, to stand in the back of the house and be part of the anonymous audience. Was there a vacant place on the second door this week?

Mr. Kirkpatrick acted as if I had never left. After a couple of obligatory questions—"How do you like college, Mr. Rich?"; "How are your parents?"—he rattled off several performances I could work over the week ahead.

The first, an evening performance, came just a couple of nights later. As if sleepwalking, I followed the ritual of my high school ticket-taking days and nights, though with some detachment now, as if I were watching my younger self from a historical remove.

In Mom's car, I followed the undulations of the Rock Creek Park drive downtown, made my way to Constitution Avenue, then turned up Fourteenth Street to park in Joel's most reliable illegal space in the Commerce Department courtyard. I locked the car up tight and walked toward the National. The Washington streets, as usual, seemed deserted. I never did learn just how crowds could suddenly materialize at curtain time to fill a theater that I knew for a fact—*Variety* vouched for it—was SRO.

It was an hour to curtain, a half hour before the doors opened. A couple of people were in line at the box office. I was half-looking for June, even though I knew it was futile to do so. Her parents had sent her to a finishing school, not college. She soon dropped out—"It is really, really lonely going to theater alone," she had written me from Boston—and would never return to Washington. She wanted a life on the road, perhaps like that of her namesake in *Gypsy*, and had found an entry-level job at David Merrick's office high above the St. James Theatre in New York. She offered to secure a position for me there, too; another clerk was leaving. As a further incentive, she promised me free dinners at the Princeton Club— it was the one privilege she hadn't tossed out with her debutante past. But I couldn't imagine making that bold a leap anymore. Maybe I was just a part-timer in the theater after all.

I strode through the National's lobby as purposefully as I had on that very first Saturday of my employment, pushing through the thick chrome doors that admitted me into the darkened house. I skipped up the stairs to the mezzanine, then strolled into the office, where Mr. Kirkpatrick was puttering about in his undertaker's dark suit as if time had stood still. The inscrutable Mr. Johnson still shadowed him from a few steps behind.

Mr. Kirkpatrick greeted me with his non-handshake, his bloodshot bunny rabbit's eyes blinking nervously behind his thick black-rimmed glasses. I asked him about business.

He spoke, as he always had, about the next show that was on the way, and whether it was selling enough tickets to justify a third week "off subscription."

"Have you seen Clayton Coots?" I asked, trying to sustain the conversation. It was as awkward to talk to Mr. Kirkpatrick as ever.

Not this season, he replied pleasantly.

I told him that I had just seen Clayton in Boston the previous weekend, and that he seemed well.

The truth was more complicated. Clayton's letters had become infrequent in the aftermath of his return from Europe in the fall—as had mine, in the frenzy of starting college. Once the season started, he decided to stay in New York and manage one of his favorite late-night movie stars, the now aged Marlene Dietrich, during a six-week concert engagement on Broadway. His expectations had been high—Dietrich epitomized the Berlin he missed—but the reality was miserable. "She's a brilliant artist but an impossible woman," he had written me toward the end of the run. "She is like water breaking against stone and I really am worn down. She likes me oddly enough but that does not stop her from treating me as a dog. I work 12 hours a day and it doesn't seem to be enough. She is truly horrible. She doesn't talk to anyone and I am stuck with the thousand complaints every day. She is a tyrant and can be so rotten you don't believe it."

The experience had been so debilitating that he had turned down the road company of *Cabaret*, now parked at the National. Instead, he had taken a hefty salary cut to tour a small play, a road company of *The Killing of Sister George*—"nothing but six nervous broads"—led by another semi-retired star from our late-night movies, Claire Trevor. But the play's lesbian love triangle offended the theatergoers at many of the show's bookings, and business had been bleak. On my last New Year's Eve with Emily in Chicago, Clayton had been in Wilmington, where there had been only a few dozen people in a nearly two-thousand-seat house—and, he said, "By the time the show was over, there wasn't a bar still open in town." He relished telling how he and Trevor had broken into the hotel's lounge to liberate some booze.

Sister George had reached Boston a week before my return to Washington for spring break. On Saturday night, Clayton came by for a drink at my dorm, and it hadn't turned out as festively as I had fantasized. His grand manner, formal wardrobe, and cigarette holder puzzled my roommates, despite the ample buildup I'd given them. For his part, Clayton seemed put off by the strange surroundings of a shabby collegiate living room festooned with rock records, antiwar posters, and the paraphernalia of marijuana; he talked very fast, gossiping about the theater, oblivious to his uncomprehending audience, or perhaps disappointed by it and, by extension, me. Once we went into Boston for theater and dinner, we never had a moment to talk alone; after the play we joined the company manager of another play in town for a boisterous group dinner at a joint near Copley Square.

That was the last time I saw Clayton. Our correspondence eventually sputtered out in mechanical holiday notes, the last of mine going unanswered. During and after college, I'd pick up rumors: He was bumming around Europe, he was managing a road company of *Hair*, he was taking care of the dying Dietrich in Germany, he had forsaken Broadway altogether and was giving piano lessons in his apartment by the East River, he was engaged to be married to a prominent woman but his fiancée had called the wedding off at the last moment.

I didn't learn of his death in 1984—cause unspecified, at a time of unspeakable wholesale casualties in the theater—until years after the fact. There was no obituary. His last Broadway jobs, I later learned, were as house manager at the Martin Beck and the St. James about a decade before he died. The few who still remembered him told me how, when the Beck was empty in the summer, Clayton would ride his bike across town from East Sixty-third Street to the theater at three or four in the morning. He'd use his key to enter the dark house and, in the solitude of the ghost light, play piano until dawn.

Clayton never knew of Joel's inquiry about him. Perhaps Joel's question couldn't have been clearly answered then, even by Clayton. The answer doesn't matter now, and it didn't then. He was the man who more than any other set me on the path to manhood, who tried to teach me what counted in the world and what did not. He showed me more of the theater than anyone had, even as he tried to tell me, though I barely listened, that the theater could not be a substitute for life. The sordid secret of my love affair with Clayton was that I didn't have anything half so valuable to give him in exchange, even had I known what it was he wanted.

—

It was almost time to open the National's doors for *Cabaret*. I left the office to set up the seats in the boxes. Soon the outer lobby was full, the expectant theatergoers' buzz penetrating the inner lobby as it always did, and when Mr. Kirkpatrick gave us the nod, Mr. Johnson and I once again opened our doors for business in tandem, ripping tickets and giving directions as the wave of voices from the incoming crowd washed over us.

I could hear the raucous *Cabaret* band through the door of the tiny room while I did the count with the company manager. Once we were done, I caught the end of the opening number and, when it was over, ran up to the office to collect my pay, the applause nipping at my heels, so I could rush downstairs again and join the standees for the rest of the act; any further catching up with Mr. Kirkpatrick could wait until intermission.

In the office, though, the manager was agitated—a state I'd never seen him in before. He handed me my brown pay envelope, then raised his voice a jarring note above its whispery drawl. "Mr. Rich," he said, almost quivering, as if he was fighting to keep himself in control, "I'm afraid I have to ask you to stay until the final curtain tonight."

I was about to say "Sure" in response—I was staying anyway—but he uncharacteristically, almost rudely, cut me off. "Dr. King has been shot, ahm, in Memphis," he said. "The police say there may be riots around Fourteenth Street. You're going to have to help some of the audience to the parking lot, Mr. Rich, ahm, particularly the older people."

I asked for details, but not many were known.

The fact that King had been shot was beyond belief—or would have been, had President Kennedy's funeral procession not passed just outside the National less than five years earlier. The idea of "riots," by contrast, was an abstraction, and without a TV to provide pictures, I couldn't quite imagine what Mr. Kirkpatrick was talking about. I sat down on one of the metal chairs in the outer office, nauseated by the mental image I summoned of a bloodied, fallen King. Then I felt fear. Riots?

I thought of calling Mom and Joel, but I knew they were at the movies. Mr. Kirkpatrick had retreated to his inner office. There was nothing to do, really, but go back and watch the show. If I believed anything then, it was only this: As long as I was in the theater, I was safe.

Once I had returned to the back of the house, it seemed unreal that an audience would be laughing and clapping. Soon the first act concluded with its own ominous "riot": the Nazis smashing the window of a Jewish fruit peddler in Berlin.

Intermission jolted me back to the present, but the unaware crowd chatted and bought orange drink as usual. I followed the smokers onto the street, and saw no signs there of anything other than another stultifying night downtown. I went back to the office, but Mr. Kirkpatrick, sweat now beading his brow, knew little except that the president had addressed the nation. Back with the standees for Act 2, I decided that the actors had by now heard the news; they seemed subdued. But maybe I was imagining it; I hadn't seen this company before. The audience didn't notice any difference and applauded mightily at the end of the show.

There had been one full curtain call when, with the entire company flanking her, the actress playing the heroine stepped forward and raised her hands to stop the clapping. The audience expected a pitch for a charity, perhaps—or maybe a thank-you for its ovation, not an unknown gesture from stars on the road. But when the actress announced hesitantly, in her civilian voice, what had happened, some people in the theater, white people almost all of them, started shrieking. Surveying the scene from my vantage point in the back, I realized that this was one sensation I had never had in any theater: bloodcurdling screams emanating from every corner of the house.

The actress took a pause so that the audience could calm itself, then said: "We are also told that there is unrest in the city tonight. Please go to your cars quietly and quickly, and drive safely home."

The curtain fell with a rude slam, bunching up as it hit the stage. The houselights leapt to full wattage in a shocking instant. The band in the pit, which might have otherwise played exit music, was silent. So was the audience, which filed out for once at a Broadway pace and with none of its usual languorous Southern chatter. You could tell who was crying only by looking at the streaks of tears on faces as they passed by.

I stood on the sidewalk in front of the theater so that Mr. Kirkpatrick could direct me toward anyone who wanted an escort to the parking garage down the block. I needed to make only a couple of round-trips with elderly theatergoers. There was no panic, no sense of a city on fire, just an unsettling quiet. E Street was as sleepy after the show as it always was, its pavement dampened by an earlier splash of spring rain.

In minutes, Mr. Kirkpatrick signaled to me that I was free to leave. I waved goodbye and started down the block. Almost everyone was gone now except Mr. Kirkpatrick, Mr. Johnson, and a few stragglers from the second balcony.

I walked toward my car, but for the first time in all the nights I'd been at the National, I was afraid. It was only two blocks to the Commerce Department lot, but the darkness, the desolation of downtown, seemed malevolent. Where were these rioters? Who were they? Might some of them pop out of the many shadows hugging my path and harm me?

By the time I got to the car, my anxiety was at full pitch. I fumbled with the keys, then opened the door, slid in, and locked the door tight again. As I backed out onto Fourteenth Street with much relief and headed past E Street, I looked up above the now darkened marquee of the National, to the office windows on the mezzanine. The lights were still on. It wouldn't surprise me if Mr. Kirkpatrick was staying the night, stretched out on the floor in his black suit, his glasses neatly folded and resting on the mountainous black canvas of his vest, a mute Mr. Johnson standing guard beside him.

Reaching Fifteenth Street, I drove past the Hotel Washington with its rooftop bar, and RKO Keith's movie palace, and the Treasury Department, and started to turn left onto Pennsylvania Avenue toward the White House, only to find that I was in a stalled line of a half-dozen cars. It was soon clear what the holdup was: The street had been blocked off by a small platoon of policemen in helmets and gas masks, an apparition out of a Vietnam story on the network news, now set incongruously against the backdrop of the stately Federal-style Riggs bank.

As I rolled down the window for an officer to tell me the detour that would take me home, I could smell smoke.

It wasn't until the next night that I would learn that my father's F Street store had been looted. It was one moment in a long, delayed, but unstoppable historical chain reaction that five years later would lead Congress to grant a Home Rule charter to the District, and to Dad's new career as a civic leader in the aftermath of the death of Rich's Shoes more than a century after our ancestors founded it.

Though I didn't know it yet, I had taken my last ticket at the National. Nor did I know that the National itself and its neighborhood, like so many road houses and so many American downtowns, were doomed. The theater that had been my second home since Mom and Dad first took me there to see *Damn Yankees* would soon be dark many more weeks than not, eventually to be upstaged and supplanted by a new "cultural center," named after the other assassinated hero of my childhood. The Kennedy Center would be geographically far removed from the now fearsome "inner city" I had revered for my entire lifetime. Suburbanites would reach it via a new kind of road called "the Beltway."

There was much else I didn't know that night. Mom hadn't yet given me the uncensored explanation for what she called my stepfather's "moodiness." Joel's father had not accidentally fallen down an elevator shaft—a cover story that had made Sue elevator-phobic through childhood—but was in fact a suicide. The nine-year-old Joel had discovered his father's body hanging from the ceiling of his first home in Baltimore, the straps of his Orthodox prayer *tefillin* serving as his noose. Not long after that, his mother had remarried, bringing home a new stepfather he despised.

Nor had Mom told me of Joel's heroics—of how, at General Eisenhower's instigation, he had led seventy-five men in a successful mission to find and retrieve Nazi loot stolen from Jews as Europe was being liberated in 1945. Nor had she told me the full extent of his recklessness—of his encounters with the police for binges of kleptomania, and his serial car crashes. His Washington license periodically suspended, he simply used his out-of-state permits instead. Mom looked the other way and was loyal to the end, resisting her family's entreaties that she not drive with him right up until the day of the crash in which he finally killed her.

Mom left behind dozens of journals, each in a different kind of note-book—plain black-covered composition books like we used to buy to-gether at Murphy's, rice-paper diaries from her trips to the East, old pads from her father's warehouse. The diary-keeping habit that never took with me had, I realized, become an obsession for her after Polly and I were gone. Late in Mom's truncated life she also created visual diaries of a sort: huge collages she constructed from a homely patchwork of "found" fab-rics. Some of them reminded me of a Paul Klee picture painted on a burlap bag, *Arab Song,* that she had first showed me at the Phillips.

"I believe that much of life consists of some terrible downs but much of life includes as well some absolutely wonderful renewals," Mom had writ-ten me on my birthday not long before the life had been smashed out of her. She had made me believe that if only I had curiosity, a fresh pad of paper and a pencil, I potentially had a whole new world in my hands. I didn't have to be perfect to be happy; I just had to exercise my mind. The works she left behind testified to her tormented search for peace and happiness—her own private life of the imagination, which I would never fully know.

Joel survived the accident. His theatergoing became more compulsive than ever. He'd fly to London to see a single show in the West End, then return on the Concorde to catch the next performance at the Kennedy Center, across the street from the modern apartment house he and Mom had moved into after they sold the house on Cleveland Avenue. Some-times he'd try to hector Polly to come with him, for she was the only one of us still within striking distance; she had moved back to our old neigh-borhood to live alone there after law school. Polly would deflect him, but undaunted, Joel would type out brief reviews of the plays he saw, streaked with cross-outs, pencil annotations, and grease, and mail them to me at my home in New York.

Our final meeting was in the dayroom of the nursing home where he was succumbing to terminal dementia. With a sudden broad smile, he asked how my job was going at the National, almost thirty years after I'd left it. I told him it was fine, and described the shows that were coming to Broadway next season. His enthusiasm for the theater was intact, even though his once powerful body had crumbled into a sack that was carted about in a wheelchair and his once ferocious brain had short-circuited into babble. I wondered: Had the theater saved him, at least for a while, when he was young and unhappy and alone? Had he taken me to the theater because he hoped it might save me, too—even if what I had to be saved from was, in part, him? Was that his way of loving me? There are times, even now, when I think of Joel as the houselights are going down—when I see him lean past Mom to wink at me in joyous anticipation of the show, when I see him conducting a Broadway overture from his seat with the huge hand that also beat us—and feel despite everything that he loved me as best he could. I can't say that some part of me didn't love him.

With time, perhaps I began to understand why Mom loved Joel. It wasn't only that he had rescued her when she was alone in a world that shunned a young woman with no husband, young children, and a wandering spirit. No, there was more than that: He had given her Adventures, exotic Adventures beyond most people's means, and surely Mom, who gave me so many Adventures, deserved some of her own, no matter how cruel the ending.

When Joel died a few weeks after I last saw him, his daughter, Sue, found drawers full of the worthless items, the towels and ballpoint pens and cheap cigars, he had stolen from hotel rooms and drugstores. From an old file, she retrieved a cache of letters Joel had saved from before he married Mom, a number of them in the dense minuscule hand of Alice B. Toklas, written from the rue Christine in Paris, many of them showering Joel with encouragement as he embarked on his new adventure as the young father of baby twins.

What was truth in Joel's life, what was bluster? We'd never know for sure. Mom had told me when I went to college that the sleeping pills she and Joel had given me were actually saccharine tablets—but were they? Their own medicine cabinets reeked from prescription sedatives and tranquilizers obtained in bulk from suspect doctors who by night ran the restaurants Joel frequented in Washington's Chinatown.

But on this spring night in 1968, I knew very little of this, and even had I known more, would it have made a difference? Knowledge means little without wisdom, and I was a long way from wisdom. The theater had showered me with love, but I had yet to learn how to love anything but it.

—

Hearing the faint cry of sirens somewhere in the distance as I turned off Connecticut Avenue onto Calvert by the Shoreham Hotel, I was satisfied for now just to get home safely. I drove up the hill, parked the car on Cleveland Avenue, and looked up from the sidewalk, as I always did, to the second-floor windows. They were dark except for the barely discernible flicker of the television—a relief, for that meant Mom and Joel were settling in to sleep, the disputes of the day at last retired for the night.

I hurried up the steps. As I pulled out my keys, I could see through the front door's window that the whole house was dark except for the few rays cast by the tiny night-light Mom always left on in the kitchen.

Entering the front hall, I shut and locked the door behind me on the smoldering city. Then I climbed the stairs, heading toward my old aerie on the third floor. As I approached the closed door to Mom and Joel's bedroom, I no longer felt my old dread. The theater had taken me far from home already, and I was sure that it would take me farther. I moved quickly past their door now—very quietly, lest I stir them from their rest— and mounted the final flight of stairs to my room. By the end of the week I'd be gone, and with all the confidence of youth, I was certain I would never again have to look back.

AUTHOR'S NOTE

AND ACKNOWLEDGMENTS

This is the story as I remember it, but I am grateful to those who helped sharpen my recollections with memories of their own. They include Alan Brinkley, the lifelong friend I met as a child in Somerset; Irma Bauman, who let me see her owner's journal of summers I spent at Indian Hill in Stockbridge, Massachusetts; Richard Kidwell, who generously helped me reconstruct the experiences we shared in our overlapping employment at the National Theatre; Theo Wilner, Howard Lesser, and other fellow alumni of Woodrow Wilson High '67; and Walter Alford, Patt Dale, Harry Davies, Terry Erkkila, Gino Gitlio, Richard Homer, Sol Jacobson, Richard Seader, and Edward Weston, who, in response to an ad I placed in the bulletin of ATPAM, the theatrical managers' union, regaled me with their own warm reminiscences of Clayton Coots and Scott Kirkpatrick. Filling in the sporadic blanks in the narrative of *Playbills* and ticket stubs from my childhood, I received invaluable assistance from the staff and materials at the Billy Rose Theatre Collection at the New York Public Library for the Performing Arts as well as from Richard Stoddard and the theater memorabilia community of eBay. Reagan Fletcher, of the Shubert Archives in New York, helped me track down the genesis of the term "ghost light."

I am especially grateful to Sara Fishko, who shared with me letters I had written to her in our teenage years, and to my stepsister, Susan Fisher Sullam, who not only helped me unearth documentary materials about my mother and her father but who was an essential sounding board, providing cheerful moral support as I struggled to sort through the dynamics of our family life in Cleveland Park.

Most books about Washington slight the non-Federal aspects of the District. The following books are exceptions and were useful in enhancing my understanding of the vanished D.C. of my childhood: *Washington Goes to War*, by David Brinkley; *The Secret City: A History of Race Relations in the Nation's Capital*, by Constance McLaughlin Green; *Washington: Capital City, 1879–1950*, by Constance McLaughlin Green; *Washington Confidential*, by Jack Lait and Lee Mortimer, and the revised *Washington Confidential Today*, by Mortimer; *Alley Life in Washington: Family, Community, Religion, and Folklife in the City, 1850–1970*, by James Borchert; *Personal History*, by Katharine Graham; *Bethesda: A Social History*, by William Offutt; *Living In, Living Out: African-American Domestics in Washington, D.C., 1910–1940*, by Elizabeth Clark-Lewis; *Capital Losses: A Cultural History of Washington's Destroyed Buildings*, by James M. Goode; *A Great Curtain Falls*, by George Atkinson and Victor Kiraly; *Power at Play*, by Betty Beale; *On This Spot: Pinpointing the Past in Washington, D.C.*, by Douglas E. Evelyn and Paul Dickson; *Ten Blocks from the White House: Anatomy of the Washington Riots of 1968*, by Ben W. Gilbert and the staff of *The Washington Post*; *The Washington Historical Atlas*, by Laura Bergheim; and *Motion Picture Exhibition in Washington, D.C.*, by Robert K. Headley.

Equally helpful were *Washington History*, the superb magazine of the Historical Society of Washington, D.C., and the exhibitions, tours, and publications of the Jewish Historical Society of Greater Washington and its Lillian & Albert Small Jewish Museum.

Needless to say, I am responsible for any errors that appear in these pages. Some characters bear pseudonyms: June, Mr. Johnson, Emily and Sarah Kaufman, Rick Hondel, and some of the briefly glimpsed kids at Deal (Pauline, David, Linda, Earl). In a few of these instances, some identifying details have been changed.

At Random House, I would like to thank Benjamin Dreyer, whose devotion to this project and brilliant editing skill have given me priceless moral and professional support, and Mary Bahr, Robbin Schiff, Tom Perry, Kate Niedzwiecki, J. K. Lambert, Stacy Rockwood, Laura Moreland, Suzanne Wickham-Beaird, Evan Stone, Kenneth Russell, and Sarah D'Imperio. At *The New York Times*, Arthur Sulzberger, Jr., and Howell Raines kindly granted me the sabbaticals that were essential for my concentration on this project. Also at the *Times*, Carlos Briceno helped hold down the fort above and beyond the call of duty. Bill Evans, Jeffrey Scales, Franklin Foer, Paul Libin, and Rocco Landesman also volunteered to perform invaluable favors.

This book could not have been written without the wise counsel of Darel M. Benaim; the persistent encouragement of Michiko Kakutani; the unflagging support of my agent, Kathy Robbins; the enthusiasm, unerring guidance, and vision of my editor, Ann Godoff; and the love of Alex Witchel, the sharpest and most patient in-house editor any writer could hope to have as well as my perfect partner in life.

New York City
June 2000

ABOUT THE AUTHOR

FRANK RICH served from 1980 to 1993 as the
chief drama critic for *The New York Times*, and is
now an op-ed columnist at the paper as well as senior
writer for *The New York Times Magazine*. He
lives in New York City with his wife,
the writer Alex Witchel.

ABOUT THE TYPE

This book was set in Electra, a typeface
designed for Linotype by W. A. Dwiggins, the
renowned type designer (1880–1956). Electra is a
fluid typeface, avoiding the contrasts of thick
and thin strokes that are prevalent
in most modern typefaces.